B. McDonald.

THE QUEEN MOTHER

BY THE SAME AUTHOR

Queen Elizabeth II: The British Monarchy Today
Prince Charles: Monarch in the Making
Prince Philip: First Gentleman of the Realm

Douglas Liversidge

THE QUEEN MOTHER

Elizabeth R

ARTHUR BARKER LIMITED
A subsidiary of Weidenfeld (Publishers) Limited

Published in Great Britain by Arthur Barker Limited
91 Clapham High Street London sw4 7TA

ISBN 0 213 16655 0

Printed in Great Britain by
Butler & Tanner Ltd, Frome and London

ACKNOWLEDGEMENTS

Illustrations in this book are reproduced by kind permission of the following: Associated Press, 125; The Bowes Museum, County Durham, 9 *above*; Camera Press, 127 *above*, 153, 161, 171 *above*, 173, 179; Central Press, 39, 79, 113, 127 *below*, 129, 155, 175, 181; Daily Express, 23; Fox Photos, 65 *below*; Illustrated London News, 69, 75; Mansell Collection, 17 *above*; National Portrait Gallery, 13; Photographic News Agencies, 147; Popperfoto, 3 *below*, 45 *above*, 61, 65 *above*, 85, 89, 93, 101, 105, 107, 111, 117, 141 *above*, 185; Press Association, 17 *below*, 49, 57 *above*, 135 *below*, 171 *below*; Radio Times Hulton Picture Library, 9 *below*, 97; Scotsman Features, 139 *above*; Syndication International, 29, 45 *below*, 57 *below*, 135 *above*, 145, 165; Thomson Regional Newspapers, *frontispiece*, 121, 141 *below*; The Times, 3 *above*, 139 *below*.

Contents

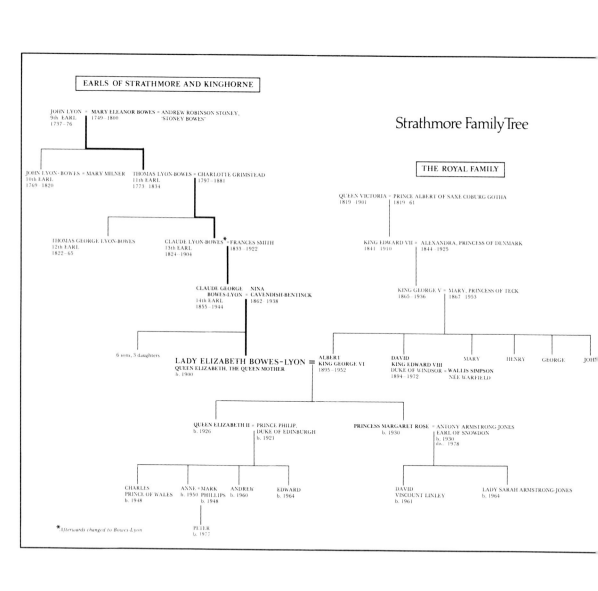

EARLS OF STRATHMORE AND KINGHORNE

Strathmore Family Tree

THE ROYAL FAMILY

JOHN LYON = MARY ELEANOR BOWES = ANDREW ROBINSON STONEY,
9th EARL   1749 1800   'STONEY BOWES'
1737 76

JOHN LYON-BOWES = MARY MILNER   THOMAS LYON-BOWES = CHARLOTTE GRIMSTEAD
10th EARL   11th EARL   1797 1881
1769 1820   1773 1834

QUEEN VICTORIA = PRINCE ALBERT OF SAXE-COBURG GOTHA
1819 1901   1819 61

THOMAS GEORGE LYON-BOWES   CLAUDE LYON-BOWES* = FRANCES SMITH
12th EARL   13th EARL   1833 1922
1822 65   1824 1904

KING EDWARD VII = ALEXANDRA, PRINCESS OF DENMARK
1841 1910   1844 1925

CLAUDE GEORGE   NINA
BOWES-LYON = CAVENDISH-BENTINCK
14th EARL   1862 1938
1855 1944

KING GEORGE V = MARY, PRINCESS OF TECK
1865 1936   1867 1953

6 sons, 3 daughters

LADY ELIZABETH BOWES-LYON = ALBERT   DAVID   MARY   HENRY   GEORGE   JOHN
QUEEN ELIZABETH, THE QUEEN MOTHER KING GEORGE VI   KING EDWARD VIII
b. 1900   1895 1952   DUKE OF WINDSOR = WALLIS SIMPSON
                                                    1894 1972   NÉE WARFIELD

QUEEN ELIZABETH II = PRINCE PHILIP,   PRINCESS MARGARET ROSE = ANTONY ARMSTRONG JONES
b. 1926   DUKE OF EDINBURGH   b. 1930   EARL OF SNOWDON
                     b. 1921   b. 1930
                                                                        div. 1978

CHARLES   ANNE = MARK   ANDREW   EDWARD   DAVID   LADY SARAH ARMSTRONG-JONES
PRINCE OF WALES b. 1950 PHILLIPS b. 1960   b. 1964   VISCOUNT LINLEY   b. 1964
b. 1948   b. 1948   b. 1961

*Afterwards changed to Bowes-Lyon   PETER
                                               b. 1977

1

At St Paul's Walden Bury

'You enjoy yourself to see her.' This succinct remark, attributed to a Frenchman, was not so much the effervescent outpouring of Gallic chivalry as a heartfelt sentiment which has been exuberantly expressed in different words and tongues the world over. The person who has been the recipient of these frank and liberal encomiums is, as many might readily conjecture, Her Majesty Queen Elizabeth the Queen Mother. Few people – if any – this century have been so consistently eulogized since childhood. This universal regard cannot be casually or sneeringly dismissed as servile sychophancy. Neither is it the illusion created by the ersatz image-making of the publicity men. Indeed, in view of the pronounced trends of our brash and cynical age, the Queen Mother's sweeping popularity should scarcely exist. Somewhat incongruously, in a disenchanted world harassed by its own obsession with materialism, in which religious belief and Christian ethics are often the target of derision, this supreme mother-figure unashamedly stands for the four-square, old-fashioned values of God and prayer.

Part of the secret of her unqualified success, as one writer has accurately crystallized, is the 'unerring instinct for the right behaviour, the correct gesture and the apt remark, her rare gift for putting people instantly at ease, her insatiable curiosity about everything she sees, and her gracious, infectious smile which seems to radiate happiness'. Pervading all this, her sense of humour is strong, her wit spontaneous. Noticing, for instance, that someone was wearing a hat identical with her own, she promptly remarked: 'Snap!' And on asking a Londoner where she lived, Her Majesty was told: 'Back o' 'arrods, Mum. And where do you live?' Without hesitation, the Queen Mother replied: 'Oh, I live just at the back of Gorringes' (the store near Buckingham Palace).

Maybe both stories are apocryphal yet they adequately illustrate her quick retort, irrespective of the situation. At the same time, she is noted for her diplomacy and constant discretion. During an official visit to the London Press Club, she first calmly exhibited her dexterity at snooker then addressed the members with an assured, tantalizing skill that disclosed nothing. Her mastery of the non-committal reply is complete. Indeed, in a long, eventful career, it is singular that not once has she uttered the ill-chosen word or allowed her own quite pointed thoughts to penetrate the screen that surrounds royalty. Rather she has concealed her feelings behind the serenity of the impartial smile.

During the war a woman councillor posed the question: 'Don't you think it terrible, Your Majesty, to see all these little children left here in the danger areas?' Parliament was then debating the problem. In private, Elizabeth advocated compulsory evacuation if persuasion failed. Yet, declining to be embroiled, she said: 'I think it is terrible that children anywhere should be in danger.'

Yet whether it is participating in the hula-hula dance or, at forty thousand feet, seated at the dual controls of a Comet aircraft, it is merely the reflection of her uncurbed zest for life.

The Queen Mother – the tranquil, benevolent, smiling personification of stable motherhood – prefers to express it in her own particular way: 'I just simply happen to love people.' But there is appreciably more to her character than that. In terms of age, she is today the senior member of an establishment which, more than anyone, she has attempted to humanize and endear to the people. Much of the erstwhile stiff formality has gone, largely due to the intrinsic qualities of her personality. In May 1960, for instance, when she travelled to the Federation of Rhodesia and Nyasaland, the Earl of Dalhousie, the Governor-General, was puzzled as to the reason she sweetly refused to be accompanied on long car drives. Later he learnt that on leaving the crowds, she slipped off her shoes, put her feet on the occasional seat in front, then produced a bag of butterscotch from her handbag.

In a sense, the personality of the Queen Mother is a mixture of the standards of the earlier eras in her life. The firm basis of Victorian society and belief is undoubtedly the very foundation of her own social and religious principles. But she also possesses the aura of the gay Edwardians. Though she may have come to terms with modern life, she does not necessarily condone its extremes and absurdities.

Neither will she submit to the frenetic tempo of contemporary times, and in personality and fashion still expresses individuality and conveys the composure and leisurely pace of life dating from earlier this century. Indeed, the Queen Mother sets an example to those who never experienced the benefits of that vanished era, and offers a richer and more contented lifestyle, which could be the cure for many current neuroses.

There is one thing with which she declines to compromise and that is time. Notoriously unpunctual, she possesses an innate dislike of being compelled to hurry, and makes it abundantly clear that people and not the rigidity of timetables have precedence (sometimes a problem for those who have to sort out the intricacies of her programme as far as two years ahead). Life, she feels, should not be governed by the tyranny of the clock. In such circumstances, schedules might easily go awry. ('Almost the later we are, the more she still stop and talk if she sees somebody who might need her,' revealed a member of her retinue.)

The little Lady Elizabeth
Bowes-Lyon at St Paul's, a
setting which had bitter
memories for her great-
great-grandmother. Yet for
Elizabeth, in this rural
pleasance the sun always
seemed to be shining.

Lady Elizabeth standing
beside her mother (behind
whom stands the Earl of
Strathmore), with her six
brothers and two sisters
(another sister had died in
childhood). On the
Countess's lap sits David,
Elizabeth's favourite
brother until his death in
manhood.

Her character has been imprinted on her family. Her complexion has flowered afresh in her daughters and granddaughter, Princess Anne, but her traits have bloomed more vigorously in Prince Charles, her grandson – in a love of music, kindly instincts, a sense of merriment and, for a person in the often irksome situation of heir apparent, a relatively unruffled and sanguine nature.

It is not, however, by these slight vignettes that the Queen Mother will probably be remembered by posterity. The lengthy reign of Queen Victoria had almost petered out when the Queen Mother was born. Since childhood she has maintained the practice of keeping diaries. Her entries over the years (combined with her own pertinent comments) are said to mirror contemporary history and vividly reflect her times. Assuming that the diaries are ever published, it is believed that they will outmatch even the personal journals written by the great Queen-Empress herself.

The Queen Mother has contributed handsomely to these times, for her life spans the period which has witnessed the growth of modern British monarchy on which she has deeply etched her character and personality. During her life-time most other European monarchies have vanished in the chaos of strident revolution or in the holocaust of war. In contrast, the British royal institution has not only survived, but it has been revitalized, its present pattern taking shape throughout three generations – the continuing creation of monarch and consort in each reign.

King George v and Queen Mary decided on the initial motif which was temporarily disfigured by Edward viii and the disruptive Abdication. It was at this time that the steeliness which reinforces the resolute character of the Queen Mother was firmly applied. When George vi ascended the throne, a royal aide was credited with the remark: 'Without her he would be only half a king.' Doubtless, to his lasting credit, King George vi would have willingly endorsed this assessment, certainly in the earlier years of his reign. For behind her captivating smile and charm, and the serene and reassuring temperament, there is a toughness which comes to the surface on occasions of principle and conscience. In a complementary partnership, she fostered qualities in the highly-sensitive, sometimes embarrassingly nervous King that were perhaps hidden from others, and from that emerged the essentially ideal monarch for his times. During his demanding reign, the throne grew into a symbol of stability and continuity of national life in a revolutionary age. And with the unwavering assistance of his consort, King George vi left the throne a great deal more secure than he found it.

This new type of monarchy, with its emphasis on modesty and humility, has entrenched itself in the life of Britain and the Commonwealth, imparting to national affairs feelings of unity and confidence. To this the Queen Mother has made a substantial contribution – partly by helping to rid the monarchy of its once rather austere facade. Today it is far more intimate and natural, far more good-natured and less rigid than it was in the previous generation.

Once the consort of a King, she is now the mother of the Queen, 'who', as *The Times* has expressed, 'has shown that steady and modest mastery of difficult times which is both a British quality and a quality the British most admire.'

The Queen Mother's stature as a world figure is the more remarkable because originally the notion of losing personal privacy was repugnant to her. Indeed, in her earlier years, to even contemplate entering within the Court's orbit was quite contrary to parental influence. Somewhat ironically, it appears that her father had instilled into his children the advisability to shun any form of position in the royal household. No one could question his loyalty to Crown and country, yet in 1880 Lord Glamis, then aged twenty-five, was repelled by the Court. As an officer in the Life Guards at Windsor Castle, the sniggers and intimate accounts in barracks of the licentious habits of the Prince of Wales revolted him. Loose morals were totally alien to the deeply religious Claude George Bowes-Lyon and were therefore to be deplored even more strongly in a future king.

His experience as a subaltern in the household troops was equally distasteful, enough to deter him from seeking closer intimacy with the Court. Dissolute drunkenness and gambling in the mess appalled him. Perhaps this triggered off impressionable memories of childhood: the dinner parties at ancestral Glamis when a page boy, secreted beneath the table, loosened the collars of guests who fell into intoxicated stupors. There had been even more raucous nights and his father, the thirteenth Earl of Strathmore, had always been the host.

Such scenes, indelibly engraved on the juvenile memory, might have bred in Lord Glamis a similar vice in later life but in fact they created a strong reaction. Of a kindly and, it is said, a rather ingenuous disposition, happiness for him meant a simple and orderly existence without life's excesses, set preferably against a rural background. The prospect, therefore, of serving for years in his father's erstwhile regiment did not commend itself. To him service in the Guards was aimless, and he yearned for the familiar, domestic and more attractive world at Glamis.

Fortunately in his leisure hours he had an outlet to ameliorate the tediousness and regimentation of barrack life. Often he frequented Forbes House on the fringe of Ham Common near Richmond, the home of Mr and Mrs Henry Scott, who had married as widow and widower. Enhancing their cordiality was the undoubted attraction of Mrs Scott's three daughters by her former marriage: Nina Celia, Violet and Hyacinth Cavendish-Bentinck. Their father, a younger son of the fourth Duke of Portland, had been a priest in the Church of England at the time of his death when Celia, the eldest, was only three.

It was on Celia that Lord Glamis focused his keen attention, for she subtly complemented his own particular traits and leanings (though years later she would appear to possess the more forceful personality), and their affection burgeoned for each other in the happy and benevolent atmosphere of the Scotts' home.

The romance did much to counter the tediousness of his duties in the Guards, but nothing less than a family bereavement would release him from them. One wintry day in January 1881, Lord Glamis was informed of the death of his grand-mother. Born Charlotte Grimstead, she was the widow of the eleventh Earl, and had now died aged eighty-three. Her portrait still survives, depicting her as a simple old lady in a lace cap and shawl, yet beneath the innocent naïveté she must have possessed a curious or mischievous mind, as the terms of her will – which were read to Lord Glamis in February – convey. On the other hand, maybe she had a specific reason for what was ostensibly a strange action.

Claude George Bowes-Lyon has been described as Charlotte's first and most favoured grandchild. That being so, it is hard to fathom the wording of her be-quest. In a complex will she left 'to my grandson Claude George my public house known as the Strathmore Arms at St Paul's Walden, the beerhouse known as the Woodman at Whitwell with the paddock adjoining and all my other real estate in the parish of St Paul's Walden or any adjoining parish referred to as my Walden property'.

At this juncture, as he listened in silence, Lord Glamis must have been secretly ecstatic. From the mere status of a subaltern living on army pay and his father's allowance, he was suddenly elevated to the lofty social status of a rich landowner; for in referring to her 'other real estate', it was assumed that the Countess had also embraced St Paul's Walden, a mellow, red brick, eighteenth-century mansion in leafy Hertfordshire, and an extensive acreage of arable land – the greater part of a £40,000 estate, a very substantial figure in those days (today's values would be at least ten times that sum).

But what momentary pleasure his young lordship enjoyed was brusquely de-stroyed as the lawyer read on. After the clauses in dull legal jargon, there appeared a codicil inserted fifteen months after the will had first been drafted. Charlotte, the enigmatic grandma, had changed her mind: she had now bequeathed her Hertfordshire estates to Claude's father for life. To Lord Glamis she assigned an annual income of £400, a useful asset for one contemplating marriage but not enough to rid oneself of uniform.

Dismay, however, was not unduly prolonged. On occasions the law has a subtle knack of bypassing a testator's wishes. Without breaking the terms of the will, Lord Strathmore, as the new owner, allowed his heir the tenancy and income of St Paul's. In addition the young cavalry officer received his annuity. This lately-acquired wealth opened up an entirely different world for Lord Glamis, as well as guaranteeing personal independence. Within months – on 16 July 1881 – he married by special licence at Petersham Parish Church the slim young lady who would dominate his future English and Scottish homes, and mould the character of a potential queen who would be born nineteen years hence. The lineage of

Lord Glamis was extremely lengthy, but so too was that of his bride; the fact that her kinsman, the Duke of Portland, gave her away was testimony too of her ancient ancestry.

The honeymoon concluded, Lord Glamis returned – perhaps somewhat reluctantly – to the regimentation of Hyde Park Barracks, where he was then stationed. But within months he had shed uniform without any misgivings, and left London with his wife for their Hertfordshire estate.

The Waldens, lying some thirty miles from London, have for centuries been marinaded in English tradition. Ethelred, the Saxon king, had chased red deer at King's Walden and in the ninth century someone of the name of Wulfgar gave Abbot's Walden to St Alban's Abbey; from its farms came all the eggs and cheeses needed by the monks. When that bluff monarch Henry VIII dissolved the monasteries, he exchanged the manor for lands owned by the Dean and Chapter of St Paul's Cathedral. Hence St Paul's Walden. It is generally believed that the addition of the word 'bury' merely means manor house.

This rambling mansion to which Lord Glamis took his nineteen-year-old wife dated from the early part of the eighteenth century. Edward Gilbert, a Georgian squire who then owned the estate, had tastefully designed two rococo wings as polygonal pavilions. (In due course, Lord Glamis would contribute extensions in a neo-Elizabethan style.) The perfectionist might regard St Paul's as an architectural hotchpotch but no one could discount its friendly air. Gilbert obviously believed that a mansion was not complete without an enchanting setting. Thus the landscape artistry of André Le Nôtre or one of his pupils: the star-shaped glades – with statuary attributed to John Nost – among the coppices of firs and oaks, beech and silver birch. This informal magnificence, some four miles from Hitchin, merges gently with the soft rolling Hertfordshire countryside and the rich woodlands that clad the horizon.

It was amid the rural charm and peaceful seclusion of St Paul's that Lord and Lady Glamis reared a large family. First came a girl, Violet Hyacinth – named after one of Celia's twin sisters – in April 1882. A second daughter, Mary Frances, was born in August of the following year. Now twenty-two, the tall Lady Glamis gave birth to her first son, John, and then Patrick arrived eighteen months later.

Large families in those Victorian days were eminently fashionable. A third son, Alexander, came on the scene in April 1887 and Fergus appeared in that same month two years later. Yet a further daughter, Rose Constance, entered this world in May 1890, but there would be a gap of three years before the birth of Michael. The time was October, but the joy occasioned by his arrival was quickly clouded by tragedy. He was just seventeen days old when the news reached St Paul's that Violet Hyacinth, then living temporarily at Forbes House with Aunt Violet, had succumbed to diphtheria.

For Lady Glamis, Michael seemed to conclude the long period of childbearing.

To accommodate his offspring and the extra staff required, Lord Glamis had built the neo-Elizabethan wing. It had been imperative. In each of the successive age groups nursemaids had been added to or gradually supplanted by tutors. Lord and Lady Glamis watched their sons and daughters growing up in a noisy and exuberant household, entering into the social life of the locality. The idea of additional children seemed extremely remote, yet to her astonishment Lady Glamis realized there was to be yet another occupant of the St Paul's nursery at the dawn of the century.

The newcomer was a baby girl, who was named Elizabeth after the Tudor Queen, Angela because her father regarded her as an angel, and Marguerite due to her mother's great love of flowers. The future Queen Mother was born on 4 August 1900. It was a Saturday and the month in which Mary Frances, her eldest sister, attained her seventeenth birthday.

There was a large age gap, certainly between the infant Lady Elizabeth and her elder brothers and sisters. It had long been a family rule, however, that the children should show concern for their younger brethren, and among the Bowes-Lyons there was an inbred clannishness and sense of continuity. The nursery itself was a manifestation of this: the high brass fender guarding the young from the fire, the old scratched furniture and the well-handled toys that bore the traces of wear and tear caused by other small hands. One day Elizabeth's own daughters would amuse themselves in this nostalgic childhood domain. They would also receive the devoted care of their mother's nursemaid, Clara Cooper Knight, the daughter of a tenant farmer on the St Paul's estate and nicknamed 'Alah' by the Royal Family.

When the tiny Lady Elizabeth was fifteen months old she was joined in the nursery by a baby brother. On 2 May 1902, Lady Glamis, then in her fortieth year, bore her tenth and last child. He was christened David, and in that nursery setting there developed between Elizabeth and her brother – dubbed by their mother the 'two Benjamins' – a long and intensely close friendship which would end only in David's death in manhood.

Together they savoured the joys of childhood in their delectable Hertfordshire home. To the young mind, St Paul's Walden bore the charisma of fairyland. Apart from the sounds and cries of wildlife, the dairy in the exquisite gardens offered its fund of delights, as did the garden temples, a dilapidated barn where the hens deposited their eggs, and the harness room and its stables. Memories would linger through life, not only of the sights and the sounds but also the scents and the smells of those childhood scenes. Fountains recklessly cast their diamonds in the sunlight and roses blazed in the shelter of yews. Peacocks of clipped hawthorn added grace, and there were the ilex and the mulberries heavy with lush fruit. But it was the centuries-old pleached-lime alley trained into Latin mottoes that led young feet into the heart of fairyland. No one could describe more vividly the magic of this enchanting world than the Queen Mother herself. In her late

Mary Eleanor Bowes, the 9th Countess of Strathmore, who was the Queen Mother's great-great-grandmother, invested the Lyons of Glamis with her surname. Part of her vast inheritance was the Hertfordshire estate of St Paul's Walden Bury.

St Paul's Walden Bury where the Queen Mother was born. In these peaceful grounds Prince Albert's proposal of marriage was accepted. Here Princess Elizabeth (now Queen Elizabeth II) and Princess Margaret spent much of their childhood.

twenties, as the Duchess of York, she graphically reminisced for Lady Cynthia Asquith on these early escapes into wonderland:

At the bottom of the garden, where the sun always seems to be shining, is *the wood* – the haunt of fairies, with its anemones and ponds, and moss-grown statues, and the *big oak* under which she reads and where the two ring-doves, Caroline-Curly-Love and Rhoda-Wrigley-Worm, contentedly coo in their wicker-work 'Ideal Home'.

There are carpets of primroses and anemones to sit on, and she generally has tea either in the shadow of Diana or near another very favourite one called the 'Running Footman' or the 'Bounding Butler' (to grown-up people known as the Disc-Thrower). These statues live in cut-out grassy places, and sometimes there are wild strawberries around them, sometimes bee-orchises.

Whenever – and this is often – a dead bird is found in this enchanted wood it is given a solemn burial in a small box lined with rose leaves.

Her small brother David is always with her and usually a tiny Shetland pony called Bobs. Bobs will follow her into the house and even walk up and down long stone steps, and she has to be very careful that he does not tread on her little brother's toes.

Now it is time to go haymaking, which means getting very hot in a delicious smell. Very often she gets up wonderfully early – about six o'clock – to feed her chickens and make sure they are safe after the dangers of the night. The hens stubbornly insist on laying their eggs in a place called the *flea house*, and this is where she and her brother go and hide from Nurse.

Nothing is quite so good as the *flea house*, but the place called the *harness room* is very attractive too. Besides hens there are bantams – whose-eggs-for-tea-are-so-good. Also Persian kittens and tortoises. . . .

As can be seen, the decrepit Flea House, once used for brewing, was a cherished haunt, especially as an escape from authority. A dirty cobwebbed attic was approached by a ladder which was so dangerously dilapidated that no adults would attempt to climb it. It was up this ladder that 'the Benjamins' decided to 'run away'. Recollecting the incident in later life, David Bowes-Lyon once remarked:

A great resort of ours was an old and half-ruined Brew-house. . . . This attic could only be reached by a very rotten ladder, the rungs of which would certainly have broken if an adult had attempted the ascent. Consequently our nurse was unable to come up and retrieve us. This attic was considered our very own parlour, though I must admit that a good many fleas intruded. In it we kept a regular store of forbidden delicacies acquired by devious devices. This store consisted of apples, oranges, sugar, sweets, slabs of chocolate Meunier, matches and packets of Woodbines. Many other things there were besides, and to this blissful retreat we used, between the ages of five and six, to have resource whenever it seemed an agreeable plan to escape our morning lessons.

In the main, these two young hedonists created their own pleasures, but once a year they were taken to experience the unforgettable thrill of the Drury Lane pantomime, 'where we sat enthralled from start to finish, usually with insufferable headaches from the unaccustomed glare'.

2

The Bowes: A Change of Name

The young Lady Elizabeth would learn later that St Paul's Walden was not just a haven of domesticity; actually it formed an integral part of the family history, little of which is generally known. Indeed, as subsequent pages disclose, St Paul's had been the setting of misery and tragedy; it was also the key to her family's one-time wealth and, for that matter, the current surname, Bowes-Lyon.

Over the centuries the Lyons in Angus had waxed in power, but their affluence could scarcely match that of the rich English aristocracy. The Bowes changed all that.

The first Bowes of any note was Sir Adam, a fourteenth-century lawyer, who augmented his own appreciable fortune by marrying the heiress of the Traynes of Streatlam Castle in County Durham. In 1691 Sir William Bowes wed the Blakiston heiress of Gibside, also in Durham, and his son George, a man of both artistic taste and commercial bent, consolidated the vast fortune. As a pioneer colliery owner he engaged in price cutting on a scale which roused his competitors' wrath, but lavishly swelled his already huge income.

George Bowes was twenty-one when he received the gargantuan inheritance. He had been a childless widower for twenty-two years when this handsome Whig Member of Parliament for Durham (and doubtless a connoisseur of art, architecture and landscape gardening) took as his second wife Mary Gilbert, the daughter of that Georgian squire who originally owned St Paul's Walden.

Only one child resulted from this union but, as will be realized, with the exception of the Queen Mother (her great-great-granddaughter) she was the most conspicuous personality in Lyon annals since the eighteenth century. In character she would be the very antithesis of the Queen Mother and, to some extent, the tragic victim of human foibles. After bringing wealth to the Lyons, she came near to losing it in what can be classed as one of the most outrageous of British scandals.

Her name was Mary Eleanor, to whom Mary Bowes gave birth on 24 February 1749. Eighteen years later, as the ninth Countess of Strathmore, Mary Eleanor Bowes would not only invest the Lyons of Glamis with her name but with the Bowes' fortunes that in their entirety amounted to some millions of pounds. Her inheritance included some £21,000 in rents alone (an enormous sum in eighteenth-century England), coalmines and ironworks, no less than 43,000 acres of land and Streatlam, Gibside and St Paul's Walden. But such riches for a while would be inseparable from opprobrium and great personal suffering.

To explain the significance of this episode in the Queen Mother's family history, one must recount Mary Eleanor's story in some detail.

Unlike her descendant the Queen Mother, the Countess was never sustained by religious faith. She wrote with a brutal frankness in her *Confessions* that she was 'convinced that a want of a proper sense of religion has been the original cause of all my errors; all the grounds of this mischief were laid before my father died, and then I was only between eleven and twelve years old.... As he was uncommon handsome and a great rake in his youth, he grew very pious in his advanced years.' But her father confused her by having her instructed 'in the mythology of every heathen nation that ever existed.... My mind was so puzzled with such a variety of religions that, except the firm belief of a God, I knew not which of all the modes of worship to adopt from real conviction, as to the weak judgment of a child all appeared supported by tradition.'

Her father's whole care, she explained, was channelled into improving her knowledge in whatever 'I showed a genius for, and in acquiring a good stock of health, hardening and strengthening my constitution by every possible means, often the most rigid ones'. The father seemed to possess uncanny foresight, for events would tax to the extreme his daughter's hardiness. Unfortunately George Bowes was never once heard to say 'that chastity, patience and forgiveness of injuries were virtues; and he was passionate'.

If she had accepted the advice of her mother and Mrs Parish, her governess, Mary Eleanor would have rejected John Lyon, heir to the eighth Earl of Strathmore, and the Queen Mother's ancestry would have consequently taken another course. But Mary Eleanor Bowes could not resist John Lyon's 'beauty which was then very great and a dream, or rather a vision to which I was foolish enough to give more credit than it deserves'.

The marriage settlement took eighteen months to complete, during which time she had qualms and wished to retract, 'but my pride and sometimes my weakness would not let me'. Thus she entered the Lyon family, adding her own lurid chapter to an already arresting history, and appreciably enhancing their fortunes.

Human foibles can have a potent effect on other people's lives, and even on history. But for Mary Eleanor's pride, the Queen Mother's family surname would doubtless still be simply Lyon. Certainly she would never have been born at St Paul's Walden; neither would her children, Queen Elizabeth II and Princess Margaret, have spent much of their childhood there. Furthermore, the Lyons would have been denied the Bowes' wealth. Not that, rather curiously, the Lyons of that time enthused over accepting either Mary Eleanor or her riches.

Mary Eleanor Bowes and John Lyon were married in London on 24 February 1767 at St George's, Hanover Square, and travelled to St Paul's Walden for the honeymoon. As part of the marriage settlement John Lyon, now Lord Strathmore,

Elizabeth when seven years old. Even in childhood she enchanted with her tact and charm.

had agreed to 'take and use the surname of Bowes next, before and in addition to his titles of honour' and assured that any offspring 'should use the surname of Bowes in addition to any title of honour to which they might have right'.

The nine-years-old marriage (which yielded three sons and two daughters) had inbuilt pitfalls from the outset. Lord and Lady Strathmore were grossly incompatible, a shaky foundation for marital bliss. Family hostility, precipitated by Thomas Lyon, the Countess's brother-in-law, made it flimsier still. One can find no trace of the cause of this resentment. It appears to be odd considering that Mary Eleanor, in a financial sense, was a decided attraction. For George Bowes had left the enormous sum of £600,000 in trust for her; and from her mother she could expect to inherit St Paul's Walden and other lucrative properties in Middlesex.

Yet in her *Confessions* the Countess complained that Thomas Lyon 'publicly and causelessly ... insulted me in the public rooms in Edinburgh when I was with him and Mrs Lyon, who was just married, all the race week without Lord Strathmore, during which time he behaved in such a manner as scandalized the whole town of Edinburgh, who at that time hated him as much as they liked and pitied me'. Regrettably, and one suspects somewhat fatuously, Lord Strathmore ruled in the family quarrel that his brother 'could not err'.

Unlike the Queen Mother, Mary Eleanor disliked Glamis. This and the lack of mutual interest between husband and wife offered fertile soil for planting seeds of flirtation. Indifferent to his wife's intellectual pursuits, the Earl has been described as 'a hearty Scotchman and a good bottle companion', but Jesse Foot, a surgeon and contemporary chronicler, claims that he imposed no restraints on the Countess, an attitude which doubtless enabled her relationship with James Graham, brother of the Laird of Fintry, to thrive. She also caused the eyes of Robert, an elder brother – for a while the factor at Glamis – 'to dart fire and sparkle like diamonds'. But the Countess spurned his advances and so he quit Glamis 'in a pet'.

For James, however, there would be a serious relationship, and when he left Scotland to join his regiment in London Mary Eleanor devised a code in correspondence with his sister to get news of him. But the Countess 'received one letter only from him which I burnt to ashes, and drank them up for fear of any accident'. Even when Graham left England, her passion for him did not vanish immediately. Yet, getting no message, she wrote angrily to his sister and broke off the liaison.

By now the thread that bound Lord Strathmore to his wife was tenuous. Tragically, he was consumptive and his life was on the wane. The Turf and the stud at Streatlam (which might have accounted for debts totalling some £30,000 at his death) typified his interests, completely different from his wife's probing of natural history, for which he admonished her for purchasing 'stuffed animals and other useless and absurd extravagances'. Neither did the Earl approve – and the evidence implies some justification – of some of the people whom the Countess chose as friends. Certainly two people would enter this circle, bringing the Countess much misery and degradation.

While on medical advice Lord Strathmore took the waters at Bristol and Bath, the Countess remained in London with her children and governess, Mrs Parish. In these unhappy circumstances the lonely young woman fell prey to George Grey (or Gray), a lazy, amorous adventurer who, it is conjectured, might have been the person whom Clive of India dismissed for corruption from the Council of Bengal in 1765. Grey met Lady Strathmore in 1774 and, in the early part of the following year, she wrote that it was not 'till after many months of constant attention, and many marks of sincerity and friendship, that just as I was going to St Paul's Walden for two months, Mr Grey ... expressed ... his regard for me'. The friendship ripened on their return to London.

Unknown to Grey, others were to aid him inadvertently in his nefarious plan. The Countess received 'a letter from Mr Lyon in which he refused, very uncivilly, to send me a small sum of money I told him I had written for by Lord Strathmore's directions; and another letter from Miss Graham, in which I found she had received a letter from her brother ... who never so much as mentioned me but spoke with the highest commendations of a lady at Minorca where he was arrived'. While resenting Lyon's behaviour, and determined to sweep Graham from her mind, 'a servant brought me a letter from Mr Grey who ... had pitched upon that very day to see how far he might venture.' The outcome was her acceptance of Grey's dubious love. 'I saw him three times when I knew Mrs Parish was at the Museum, and met him for a short time, as if by accident, at the Ring.' For clandestine meetings at her home they had to rely on the trust and prudence of George Walker, her footman.

The Countess promised Grey her entire affection if Lord Strathmore died 'but if he recovered he must give me up'. To this extent, time was the devil's disciple. The Earl embarked for Lisbon, to which in those times the affluent sick were prone to resort, but during mid-February 1776, not long before he left England, the Countess was seduced by Grey. She revealed: 'I was off my guard and ever after that I lived occasionally with him as his wife.'

Lord Strathmore never even reached Portugal alive; he died on the voyage early in March and a month later his widow received a letter he had written on board. The forthright contents indicate that, whatever the Earl's shortcomings, Mary Eleanor could never justifiably escape her husband's strictures. 'As this is not intended for your perusal till I am dead,' he wrote, 'I hope you will pay a little more attention to it than you ever did to anything I said to you while alive. . . . I freely forgive you all your liberties and follies (however fatal they have been to me) as being thoroughly persuaded they were not the produce of your own mind, but the suggestions of some vile interested monster.'

Lord Strathmore was convinced that the prejudices she had conceived against his family were entirely without foundation.

I must also earnestly desire you would endeavour to give up your foolish partiality for your daughters, and that most unnatural prejudice you have against your eldest innocent son. All children should rank equally in a parent's mind. . . .

I will say nothing of your extreme rage for literary fame. I think your own understanding, when matured, will convince you of the futility of the pursuit. . . .

I come now to a point very essential to your ease and comfort, and allow me to say that no one ever studied with more attention to promote the happiness of another than I have constantly done to promote yours. If I have not succeeded it is my misfortune, not my fault. What I mean to speak of relates to your Estate, the management of which, as you have never known about it, it is impossible you should understand. For which reason I should advise you most earnestly to appoint some person you can confide in, to fix with your son's trustees for a certain sum payable quarterly or half yearly as you shall approve.

How Mary Eleanor reacted to her husband's letter one does not know. To have mourned the loss of her husband would have been hypocritical. His death had liberated her. With an annual income ranging somewhere between £16,000 and £20,000 she could create her intellectual coterie without hindrance and from now onwards lead a carefree life. She had already identified herself with a group sarcastically nicknamed the 'Male Literati' or 'Bloomsbury Jilts'. In all fairness, despite the pseudo element some of its members were genuine intellectuals, especially Daniel Carl Solander, the Swedish botanist of international note, who had accompanied Captain James Cook on one of his voyages of exploration. Qualified, too, in botanical knowledge was the brother of Mrs Parish, Joseph Planta of the Natural History Department of the British Museum.

The Countess's situation, however, was not without its anxieties. Made pregnant by Grey, she had suffered the indignity of an induced miscarriage – a fact known to Mrs Parish, whose loyalty was now in question. Since Lord Strathmore's death Mrs Parish had been badgered by both Mrs Bowes, the Countess's mother, and the Lyons for intimate details of Lady Strathmore's affair with Grey. Bribery is suspected but why the Countess despatched her old governess from her service has not been clarified, beyond the disclosure that she 'had displeased me so much, and . . . determined to part with her. . . . Therefore I resolved to raise £2,000. . . . This, I thought, would be sufficient to make her easy in circumstances.'

Lacking the incumbrance of Mrs Parish, the liaison flourished. Yet the Countess saw Grey 'only every other night'. It had been agreed that 'by the intervention of one night, we might meet the next with more pleasure and have less chance of being tired of each other. Not to mention that it was often four or five in the morning before he went away. . . . I saw him some part of every day, or when I did not, by any accident, he never failed writing. . . .' As if seeking divine approval of her licentiousness, Mary Eleanor plighted herself most solemnly to Grey in the holy environs of St Paul's Cathedral, 'to marry none but him'.

These words, however, were soon to be challenged, with dire consequences.

Lady Elizabeth, aged fourteen. The serene
childhood years ended in the cataclysm of
the First World War. Hostilities awakened
in her qualities which had been dormant.

With her father, the Earl of Strathmore.
Deeply religious, he doubtless influenced
his daughter in her early life. He deplored
distasteful morals.

Meanwhile, there was a good reason for atonement and marriage. She had succeeded in effecting a second induced miscarriage but failed with yet a third pregnancy: the child was due to be born in August 1776. Undeterred, the enterprising
Countess announced her betrothal to George Grey, planned to leave England
in April and wed abroad, then return home with the child after several years.

Unfortunately for Mary Eleanor she omitted a scheming, callous rogue from
her calculations. Andrew Robinson Stoney, a sadistic, contemptible fortune-
hunter, had first entered her life the previous autumn, an Irishman from Kings
County who had received a commission in the Army. For his description one
turns to Jesse Foot, who drew attention to the connection of Stoney's nose 'with
his upper lip; he could never talk without the nose, which was long and curved
downwards being also moved ridiculously with the upper lip. . . . It was seen much
more in serious discourse than in light conversation. It was when he meant to
be emphatic that it was most discovered. In light conversation he avoided it, by
not employing the upper lip beyond a certain extent; and in that case he was
necessarily forced to lisp.' Some five feet ten inches tall, this fair, quick-witted
trickster flashed a ready smile.

It is astonishing how some women of wealth will yield to bogus charm. Such
a person had been the woman he married – Hannah Newton, a Durham colliery-
owner's daughter, whose fortune, lying somewhere between £20,000 and
£30,000, was augmented by a house and landed property known as Cold Pike
Hill in Durham. From Foot's account of Stoney's treatment of his wife, this dreadful blackguard was bent on destroying her to seize her fortune. Cunningly he broke
her heart, provoking and humiliating her before guests. He even brutally knocked
her downstairs. The final and most cruel act was to imprison her in a tiny, stifling
cupboard for days, restricting her to a solitary meal of one egg daily. Hannah
Stoney died soon afterwards and her ruthless husband acquired her wealth.

Not unexpectedly, Andrew Stoney was drawn to London's St James's area and
its gambling, drinking and cock-fighting clubs. Describing the contemporary
scene, Jesse Foot explained that the types frequenting such establishments were
of similar ilk, exchanging their horses, dogs and mistresses 'for the capricious ac-
commodation of one another; and keep a sharp look-out for the opportunity of
obtaining money and improving their fortunes from heir or heiress, by play or
marriage, no matter which'.

With cold, calculating guile Andrew Stoney decided to ensnare his second
heiress. With the skill of his breed, he quickly familiarized himself with Lady
Strathmore's weaknesses and cleverly played on them. As it was public knowledge,
he obviously knew of her liaison with Grey. And as in some Victorian melodrama,
one visualizes the nose and upper lip curving in a contemptible sneer as he plotted
to oust him from her ladyship's affections. Stoney had the advantage. He was
ten years younger, more artful, and 'bred up more regularly to the trade'. Moreover, he had 'the superior aid, the air, and the necessary art of a man of the St

James's Coffee House. There was no antiquated, dissipated, impudent and profligate nabob a match for him'. So wrote Jesse Foot.

As for Lady Strathmore, the fact that she wallowed in the flattery of poseurs, and was so gullible as to put her faith in the predictions of fortune-tellers, led to her downfall. No doubt at Stoney's instance, one soothsayer, pretending to foretell her future, strongly advised her to marry an Irishman. The Countess was still unsuspecting when she received letters which, purporting to have been written by someone in Durham, condemned Stoney for jilting her in favour of Lady Strathmore. It seems apparent that they emanated from the Irishman's own pen, like the letter which the Countess received while staying at St Paul's Walden. Writing in a servile style, Stoney declared:

> ... I am all impatience to see your ladyship; I really cannot wait till Saturday; I must have five minutes chat with you before that time. You will think me whimsical; but upon Thursday next, at one o'clock, I shall be in the garden at St Paul's Walden. There is a leaden statue, or there was formerly, and near that spot ... I shall wait; and can I presume that you will condescend to know the place? Eliza [who had taken over the duties of Mrs Parish, her sister] shall be our excuse for this innocent frolic....

Although she was engaged by now to marry Grey, Lady Strathmore foolishly yielded to the wiles of her bogus lover. The spectacular climax would be reached during January 1777, exploding in a scandal which became the cardinal item of gossip in the salons and coffee-houses of Georgian London.

A primary figure in this sensation was the Reverend Henry Bate, an intimate of the Prince Regent. Parson Bate, who eventually received a baronetcy as Sir Henry Bate Dudley, belonged to that unique, versatile breed which, ebullient and even violent, characterized the essence of Georgian England. He was a man of both town and country. In Essex he attended to the spiritual needs of his parishioners at Bradwell-juxta-Mare, a region of farmlands and sea-girt marshes. As an agriculturist, he reclaimed areas of windswept saltings. In sport, he was adroit with the sword and a doughty pugilist in the ring. Certainly he was not a person to trifle with or confront in a duel.

It was, however, his capacity as editor and founder of the *Morning Post* that concerns this story; for it was in Bate's newspaper that the scandal – in which Lady Strathmore was the central figure – suddenly erupted. The letters that Bate published vehemently condemned the Countess for her callous treatment of her husband, more so during the period of his incurable ailment. No one knows exactly the author of those letters. One can merely surmise. Could it have been Stoney himself? Perhaps, because he made it widely known that in defence of his honour – and doubtless of Lady Strathmore's – Grey should challenge Bate to a duel.

George Grey knew his limitations; he was no match, no matter what weapons were chosen, with the owner of the *Morning Post*. Maybe this had lurked in Stoney's evil mind, but whatever had been his intention he now issued a challenge himself.

Accounts of the duel tend to confuse; there are certainly no clear-cut facts. Stoney and Bate met in an upper room of the Adelphi Tavern near London's Strand, but what happened precisely no one knows. One has to resort again to Jesse Foot who reveals that, on the night of Monday, 13 January 1777, he was hurriedly summoned. In the room were a Doctor Scott, a servant, Stoney (who until then was a complete stranger) and Bate (with whom he was already acquainted). The latter bore a trifling wound but Stoney, extremely crestfallen, had been stabbed three times, twice in the right breast. Foot noticed two swords in the room and one was bent. A pistol shot had shattered a mirror.

On hearing shots, a man explained that when he and others broke down the door the room was in complete darkness. Consequently, what actually transpired is difficult to reconstruct, but it has been suggested that Stoney extinguished the candles either by pistol shots or sword, imagining that darkness would offer protection. It has also been implied that Stoney wounded himself, but all this is speculation. Unfortunately Parson Bate made no attempt to expose the truth.

What is factual is that Grey was dishonoured and supplanted by Stoney as Lady Strathmore's lover. Moreover, marriage between the Countess and her Irishman occurred quickly – on 17 January, only four days after the odd episode in the tavern. And like the Earl of Strathmore before him, under the marriage terms formulated by the Countess's father, the Irishman was compelled to accept the surname of Bowes. Henceforth he would be known as Stoney Bowes.

The disconcerted Grey was eventually awarded £12,000 for what he rightly argued was breach of promise, but Stoney Bowes, much to his chagrin and astonishment, learnt that the Countess's estate was beyond his reach, being in trust for her life whether she married or not. The words were stark. Whatever monies accrued from the trusts were 'for her separate and peculiar use and disposal, exclusive of any husband she should thereafter marry with; and wherewith he should not intermeddle, nor should the same be anyways subject or liable to his debts, control or management'.

To appreciate the significance of Lady Strathmore's action, one must realize that it was an age when a husband was normally empowered to control his wife's estate. The Countess's lawyer, however, declined to supply the deeds unless Bowes catered for the Countess out of his own wealth. But that was contrary to the reason he had married Lady Strathmore. Bowes refused, and for the Countess it was the beginning of years of abuse, torment and even extreme brutality. Humiliation started at once; she could neither be alone with her daughter nor use her carriage without his consent. He also instructed the servants to hand him her mail.

Bowes now hastened to try and capitalize on his new name. With the political slogan 'Bowes and Freedom', within weeks of his marriage he campaigned for a parliamentary seat for the Radicals at Newcastle-upon-Tyne. Sir John Trevelyan won after a spate of vitriolic innuendo and bribery – the main ingredients of eighteenth-century elections. From the window of an inn the Countess dropped jewels or trinkets, for which voters received money on returning them. Scathingly, his opponents sneered that, if Lady Strathmore should die, Bowes would return 'to his original insignificance. Would it be decent . . . to entrust our rights and proper- ties to a man who, in a few hours, may find himself divested of the very appearance of an estate?'

However, on 1 May, Bowes using, it is suspected, terror and personal violence, gained legal control of Lady Strathmore's wealth. From her estate her ruthless husband defrayed huge debts incurred in the election.

When a daughter, Mary, was born in August it was an unhappy reminder of Lady Strathmore's sinful past with Grey, and a further excuse for more calumny from Bowes, perhaps the vilest person in Georgian England. The Queen Mother's great-great-grandmother distinctly lacked any saintly qualities, yet Bowes's sad- ism towards her was inexcusable. Apparently it was during this period – in 1778 – that Bowes compelled his wife to write her *Confessions*, his motive probably being to use them, if necessary, in litigation. According to Foot, they were a miscellany of falsehoods and truths.

Gibside was now in frequent use for entertaining when Bowes was appointed High Sheriff of Newcastle in the following year. Then in February 1780 he gained a seat in the House of Commons, but neglected his duties on failing to wheedle from the Prime Minister an Irish peerage. Within twelve months of his election – in January 1781 – he found new interests; his mother-in-law died, bequeathing the St Paul's Walden estate to her daughter. With the death of Mrs Bowes, this Hertfordshire mansion would figure more in the marital strife of Bowes and his wife, and be the scene of seduction and even rape. For as at Gibside and Streatlam Castle, few females were safe from his amorous attentions.

Typical was the eye-witness account given by Foot while staying at St Paul's. At that time Bowes was obsessed with spying at night on a tenant farmer's wife and daughters. After dinner, Bowes asked Foot to stroll with him.

He took me to the farm [related Foot] and peeped into the windows where they were all sitting and preparing for bed. Everything, in their innocent custom, was undoing. The dog barked, and I returned and left him there, where he was for a long time.

He told me there was no danger from the dog, as he had made the farmer tie him up, because, as he said, he had been caught killing some of his sheep. He went thus to the window almost every night. In a week after my return to London he sent for me in haste, as he had met with an accident. The farmer, finding that his dog barked thus every night, suspected thieves and determined to let him loose; and the dog, revenging himself against Bowes in one of these excursions, fastened upon his leg, and bit it severely.

Bowes's peculiar antics expose a repulsive character. On 8 May 1782 the dis- consolate Countess had given birth to a boy, William Johnstone Bowes. Her hus- band raped Mrs Houghton, the child's wet nurse, and made her pregnant, and Dorothy Stevenson, the nursery-maid, was likewise assaulted, as was her successor, Elizabeth Waite, a poor girl whose father was incarcerated for debt in the King's

Bench Prison. Posing as a charitable master, he promised to pay her father's debts but instead sexually assaulted her in her bedroom. Rushing in terror from St Paul's, she was eventually admitted to Magdalen Hospital, a haven for London waifs.

Yet another serving-maid was the object of Bowes's evil attentions. Spying on her from the garden one dark night, he saw a manservant enter her room. Unknown to their master, they had married in secret but Bowes rushed furiously upstairs and ordered them out of the house. The next day the lodge-keeper at the park gates was summarily dismissed for letting them stay with him for the night. The family chaplain protested, more so considering that the hypocritical Bowes had wished to seduce the maid himself. With that he quit St Paul's, refusing to give Bowes the satisfaction of dismissing him, but Bowes spitefully withheld his luggage until the parish constable intervened.

As was usual, Lady Strathmore bore the brunt of her husband's fiendishness, as would be disclosed long afterwards when she strove to gain her release. Bowes, the High Court would learn, rained many violent blows on her chest, head and other parts of her body, and 'even kicked her and sometimes pinched her ears nearly through'. Once he hurled hot potatoes into her face, followed by a drenching of wine.

During one of his visits to St Paul's Walden, Jesse Foot thought Lady Strathmore was altered and dejected, pale and nervous,

and her under-jaw constantly moved from side to side. If she said anything, she looked at Bowes first. If she was asked to drink a glass of wine, she took his intelligence before she answered. She sat but for a short time at dinner, and then was out of my sight.

I did get one morning's walk with her . . . into the once beautiful pleasure garden where, in spite of the ruinous state of it, much was left for admiration; because the taste that gave it a creation was not yet totally obliterated. The Countess pointed out to us the concern she had formerly taken in the shrubs, the flower beds, the alcoves and the walks of this most delectable recess. She even pointed out the assistance her own hand had lent to individual articles.

In observing her during her conversation, the agitation of her mind was apparent by its action on her mouth. She would look for some time, hesitate, and then her under-jaw would act in that convulsive manner, which absolutely explained her state of melancholy remembrance beyond all other proofs abstracted knowledge could confirm or technical teachers could demonstrate.

To be deprived of her daughters, Lady Maria Jane and Lady Anna Maria, by her first marriage greatly intensified her dismay. For some unexplained reason, Lady Strathmore adored her daughters but was indifferent to her sons. Determined to safeguard the young Bowes-Lyons, their relatives at Glamis succeeded in having them made wards of Chancery, and the Lord Chancellor chose Thomas Lyon and a Scottish lawyer as their guardians. Taken from their town house in Grosvenor Square, John and George were admitted to a boarding school at

A portrait of Lady Elizabeth as a bridesmaid at the wedding of Princess Mary and Viscount Lascelles.

Neasden in Middlesex and the sisters were sent to a similar establishment in London's Queen's Square.

Lady Strathmore was anxious that her daughters should live with her at St Paul's Walden. When, therefore, Lady Anna wrote on 12 May 1784 requesting the pleasure of spending the Whitsun holiday with her, the Countess eagerly awaited the reunion. But Thomas Lyon prevented it, pin-pointing the possible harmful influence of Bowes. Lady Jane was instead entrusted to the care of Lady Anne Simpson, an aunt who resided in Harley Street.

Because of his consistent cruelty to his wife, there must have been an ulterior motive to account for the reason that Bowes now wished to assist her. On his instructions, Lady Strathmore wrote to Mrs Carlisle, the headmistress at the Queen's Square school, requesting a visit from Lady Anna before the Countess departed allegedly for Bath. This was agreed to, and in response to a similar request Lady Simpson asked her sister-in-law, Mrs John Ord, to conduct Lady Jane to the Bowes's London home. Yet when the time came to return to Harley Street, Lady Jane withheld.

Sensing mischief, Mrs Ord tried to speak to Lady Strathmore in her dressing-room but found the door secured, and on returning to the drawing room she was handed a letter from the Countess, who wrote:

> ... I conclude that you have some written orders ... from a majority of her [Jane's] guardians; if thus authorized I should not choose to interfere in regard to her returning to you today. But if you cannot produce such sanction, you will, I hope, excuse my detaining her till, by representing my case and laying my grievance before my Lord Chancellor, I shall be honoured by his Lordship's command.
>
> However inhuman may be the behaviour I have experienced from those who never paid the slightest intentions to my feelings as a mother, and whose professed regard for my children ought to have taught them a very different lesson; yet I hope you will be so obliging as to believe that nothing can be further from my wishes than to treat you with the most distant degree of impoliteness, especially in my own house; but that goodness of heart that I have the pleasure to know you possess will I doubt not, fully excuse the liberty I now take, and lead you to sympathize in the sufferings of a parent whose children have, for many years, been entirely secluded from her sight, an affliction which, though you have never been so unfortunate as to experience, yet you may easily conceive the severity of; and from your own sensations upon inferior occasions, will form a just idea how impossible it must be ever to exist under such cruel and unnatural control.

Clearly a lady of some resourcefulness, Mrs Ord promptly sent a messenger to her husband, then sat outside Lady Strathmore's room, making it obvious that she would not leave without the child. Her stubbornness succeeded; the door opened and out walked Jane. But there was no Anna. When, after several days, the Lyons requested the Lord Chancellor to compel Bowes to produce the girl, it was found that he, Lady Strathmore and her daughter had crossed to France.

In correspondence from the Hôtel Luxembourg in Paris, Bowes tried to excul-
pate his action which was tantamount to abduction. Evading the Lord Chancellor's order to return to England, for some months Bowes treacherously attributed the delay to her ladyship's refusal to release her daughter. At the end of
October, however, the party travelled to St Paul's Walden. Only then was it disclosed how Bowes had savagely treated his wife. Mrs Morgan, her maid, unhesitat-
ingly exposed how, on the outward journey, she had noticed at Calais an ugly
bruise on the Countess's arm. In the coach to Paris the following day, Bowes,
anxious not to be recognized, had kicked and punched his wife when she peered
through the window. This torturing of his wife persisted. Bowes scratched her
deeply behind one ear causing much bleeding and struck her when she refused
to write in French his letter to a Frenchwoman he was trying to seduce. To Lady
Anna's distress, she witnessed Bowes sadistically pierce her mother's tongue with
a quill and also thrust a hot candle into her face. Not surprisingly, in her agitation
the Countess began to take laudanum.

Back in England, Bowes dismissed Mrs Morgan from his wife's service but the
Countess, aided by a housemaid, sent a message to Mrs Morgan enlisting her
help to escape. She was convinced, the Countess pleaded, that Bowes was determined to murder her. It so happened that Mrs Morgan had a cousin named Shutter, a London barrister, who readily collaborated in a plot.

On 3 February, while Bowes was dining away from home, the Countess fled
from the house in Grosvenor Square, her domestic staff willingly cooperating to
release their mistress from so much suffering. Yet the scheme almost foundered.
In the dash to freedom no hackney carriage was available until they reached
Oxford Street. Soon afterwards Stoney Bowes hurried past, furiously searching
for his terrified spouse. Reaching Shutter's premises in Cursitor Street near Chancery Lane, the Countess was met by Mrs Morgan and Ann Parks, her housemaid,
who accompanied her to Dyers Buildings, Holborn, where, in the name of Mrs
Jefferies, she enjoyed the protection of a High Court tipstaff. In her modest sanc-
tuary Lady Strathmore instituted the slow-moving action to end her marriage,
citing adultery and cruelty, and to try to regain the control of her estate. She
would endure much suffering before either was achieved.

As the months dragged by, Stoney Bowes faced the unpleasant fact that the
tedious machinery of the law was grinding in his wife's favour. If she won her
divorce suit, his plot to grasp her fortune would undeniably collapse. The prospect
conjured up in his distorted mind bizarre notions that terminated in one of the
most stupendous dramas in English society. He planned to kidnap the Countess,
compel her under threat of death to abandon the suit and cohabit again. The
scope for her abduction had widened. Now more confident, she had taken more
commodious premises in Bloomsbury Square, whence – now in possession of her
coach – she sometimes dared to drive about London. This fashioned the pattern
of Bowes's fantastic plan: to lull Lady Strathmore into a false sense of security

by pretending to be dead. Thus deceived, she would move about more freely and broaden his chance to abduct her.

Journeying north to Gibside, Bowes induced a coal-miner named Chapman to inform Dr Brown, the Countess's doctor in Newcastle, that he (Bowes) had fatally shot himself the previous night. Next Joseph Hill, Bowes's groom, acquainted the doctor of the same story, asking him to persuade her lady-ship to retain his services. When, however, some Gibside miners called on the doctor to ascertain who would from now onwards pay their wages, Brown grew suspicious.

With his scheme abortive, Bowes, accompanied by Chapman and a fellow miner called Pigg, as well as a coal merchant named Peacock, returned to London, renting 18 Norfolk Square. Assuming the name of Colonel Maddison, Bowes, spy-ing on his wife, posed as a Justice of the Peace, affecting an extensive wig and big spectacles. Sometimes he attired himself in sailor's dress. But the ruse was ineffectual; his excursions in and around Bloomsbury Square betrayed him, and his wife reported his antics to a barrister.

Thwarted again, Bowes, leaving his fellow conspirators at Norfolk Square, tra-velled to Streatlam Castle to feign suicide a second time. Lending their services were Henry Bourne, the estate agent, and Hobson, a surgeon. The idea was to pretend that Bowes had been thrown severely by his horse and to embroil an independent witness to bear testimony. Thus, accompanied by Bourne and Pre-vot, his French valet, Bowes rode past another horseman named Thomas Colpitts. Some minutes had elapsed when Colpitts recognized Bourne galloping madly to-wards him; Bowes, Bourne shouted, had encountered a serious mishap and was in a critical state. Colpitts, who arrived in haste, thought Bowes was dying; and as part of the plan, after Bowes had been borne away in a carriage, it was reported that he would not be available to anyone for months.

Yet a week later he had rejoined his ruffians in London. At the Pyed Bull in Russell Street off Bloomsbury Square, Edward Crook, the landlord, believed them to be thieves until, to dispel his fears, they presented him to the bewigged and bespectacled 'Justice Maddison'. Bowes so convinced him that he was search-ing for criminals that Crook introduced him to Edward Lucas, a constable who had served under Mr Justice Walker.

Bowes's corruptive powers were stronger than Lucas's desire to uphold the law. Yielding to bribery, he approached Lady Strathmore under the pretence that her house was under the surveillance of rogues. The alarmed Countess promptly engaged him to protect her for twelve shillings a week. Unwittingly she had admitted her husband's agent into her home.

Stoney Bowes now operated with speed and guile. On 8 November, Chapman swore before Mr Justice Walker that his life was endangered by her ladyship's coachman, footman and maid-servant. Their arrest was ordered at once. Two days later, quite oblivious that she was being shadowed by Lucas and his hirelings,

Lady Strathmore, accompanied by Mrs Morgan and Captain Henry Farrer, her solicitor's brother, drove in her carriage to Oxford Street to an ironmonger named Forster.

No sooner had the carriage stopped than Lucas's henchmen dragged down the coachman and footman, ostensibly arresting them to appear before Mr Justice Walker. Meanwhile the startled Countess and her companions dashed into the shop, seeking refuge in an upper room, which they bolted. However, on hearing Lucas's reassuring voice she unsuspectingly opened the door. To her horror, her so-called bodyguard took her prisoner, adding: 'I must take you at once to Lord Mansfield [the Lord Chief Justice] at Caen Wood [Ken Wood]. It is as much as my life is worth not to execute this warrant.' Rather foolishly, as circumstances turned out, Lucas allowed Mrs Morgan to go free. Despite her fright, this sensible woman hurriedly informed Farrer and Lacey, the Countess's lawyers, of her mistress's curious arrest.

By this time Lady Strathmore and Captain Farrer believed themselves to be on their way to Caen Wood. Instead, the carriage bowled along to Highgate, stopping at the Red Lion Inn. As she was led upstairs the Countess was shocked to see confronting her none other than her terrifying husband. Her pleas were to no avail; they must, she was told, proceed to Lord Mansfield.

Eventually both Farrer and the Countess realized they were following another route and when the captain protested, Bowes angrily ordered him from the coach. From that moment there began one of the most notorious abductions in English history. Throughout the country it eclipsed the news of the day and galvanized the nation to a peak of excitement. As the mileage grew on that northward dash, the situation developed into a hunt for the money-crazed Bowes. On his instructions Peter Orme, a postboy at the Adam and Eve at Barnet, had hired a chaise, but before the party could start the Countess, frantically smashing the coach window, shrieked: 'Murder!' Ostlers and others stared in amazement, but Bowes brusquely explained that the woman was mad; they were taking her home.

Travelling both day and night along the Great North Road, thirty-three hours had elapsed by the time the steaming horses reached The Angel in Doncaster. Cold and miserable, Mary Eleanor also bore the marks of physical violence. At The Bell at Stilton, Bowes had thrust a pistol to his wife's head, threatening to pull the trigger unless she signed a document renouncing her suit for divorce.

One admires her unconquerable spirit. Defying him, she was beaten on the face, and in the coach he cruelly tried to batter her into submission. But she endured his brutality, even after he had struck the bruised face with his watchchain and seals. Indeed, she still resisted when, crossing into County Durham, the horses eventually came to a halt at Streatlam Castle. The time was about midnight.

The last coach had been hired at Greta Bridge and now, shouting agitatedly to the postillion, the Countess appealed to him to make it known that she had been abducted. Characteristically, Bowes bribed the man with guinea coins, urging him to say that the Countess had been left temporarily demented after the carriage crashed into a ditch.

In the dining-room Bowes again held out the document to his wife, but, despite her terrible distress, she courageously told him to kill her. In consternation, Bowes ordered Chapman and Pigg to carry her to her bed.

It appears that Bowes planned to keep his wife prisoner in Ireland. In that event the Countess would have been in serious difficulties. Fortunately James Farrer, her lawyer, was already active on her behalf. The Lord Chief Justice ordered a writ of Habeas Corpus, despatching a tipstaff called Ridgeway to Streatlam Castle. Arriving there on Monday, 13 November, he pushed the writ beneath the door on being refused admission.

Farrer reached Streatlam two days later but by now Bowes was in hiding, taking the Countess with him. In darkness, at about midnight the previous Monday, they had hurried to a cottage occupied by the father of Mary Gowland, a maid at Streatlam and a concubine of Bowes.

All the while the persecution continued as the pressure to coerce the Countess to accept Bowes's terms intensified. He threatened to have her certified as mentally unsound, but still her resistance refused to snap. Her wretchedness must be set against spiteful wind and cold, for the countryside lay under snow.

Such was the weather when, on the Thursday night, she was conducted over Bowes Moor to the cottage of Matthew Shields, a gamekeeper at Argill. The party included Chapman, Pigg and Mary Gowland. On the following day they were moving again. The fact that Bowes was taking a tortuous route perhaps suggests that his nerves were now too jangled to think clearly. Whatever the truth, at about 4 am on Sunday, 19 November, Bowes and his confederates entered his lawyer's house in Darlington.

From this time onwards Bowes's movements were highly erratic, the behaviour of the hunted. On 20 November, James Farrer issued a notice offering a reward of fifty pounds for Bowes's arrest, then in the city of Carlisle calmly awaited results. A further notice circulated the next day described Bowes as 'above the middle size, sallow complexion, large nose which stands rather one side, and lisps in his speech.' Lady Strathmore was depicted as 'a little woman, a longish Face, with fine dark brown Hair, rather Bulky over the Chest – Mr Bowes gives out that she is Dumb, and sometimes Disordered in her Mind – Her Ladyship does not speak.'

Town and countryside now buzzed with excitement, throwing Bowes, then at Newcastle, into a state of panic. Hurrying the exhausted Countess and Mary Gowland into a chaise, Bowes drove off furiously along the road to Durham, Prevot, his valet, following on horseback. Bowes, however, could not escape; shadowing him was Abraham Dunn, who had been engaged by Lady Strathmore's aunt, Mrs Liddell, to prevent inn-keepers from releasing fresh horses to Bowes.

Lady Elizabeth Bowes-Lyon attending to some of the telegrams and letters of congratulation at 17 Bruton Street, her parents' London home (since demolished), on her engagement to Prince Albert, Duke of York.

Bourne must have known of his master's whereabouts for at Aycliff, near Darlington, he galloped up, shouting that the area was on the alert. Detaching a horse from the shafts, and with the Countess clinging behind him, Bowes rushed away across the frozen countryside, with Dunn and a man called Robert Thornton, who had recognized Bowes, in close pursuit. At Neasham Christopher Smith, the parish constable, and some of the villagers likewise gave chase.

In his subsequent affidavits, Smith described how the alarm

was given by a man on horseback that Bowes had killed his wife and the country was in arms to take him. I had seen a man ride past with a woman behind him, without a pillion, attended by another man on horseback, wanting a hat or any covering on his head, and a bare sword by his side, and took them for pickpockets.

Upon this, I ran to the door and said to my brother, 'Let us each get a stick, and we will go and take him.' We went after them, as did several of the village, about a mile into Sockburn Lane. Upon our coming up, Mr Bowes said, 'What do you want?' I said, 'The country is alarmed with a bad report, we are come to take you.' Mr Bowes presented a pistol and said he would blow out the first man's brains that dared touch him. I said, if he would surrender, we would not hurt him. He again said he would shoot anyone that came nigh him, and that he would pay anyone who would take him to Northallerton....

Mr Bowes turned about his horse, seeming to go away, when the woman slipped off from behind him and, clasping her hands together, said, 'I am Lady Strathmore, for God's sake assist me.' I said, 'Are you indeed Lady Strathmore?' She said, 'I am, and am forced away contrary to every inclination by that man' (pointing to Bowes). I said, 'If you are Lady Strathmore, we will secure your person, and take him' and bade the men get sticks and we would set upon him, and take him at all events.

Seeing Bowes rest one pistol on the other, Smith rushed upon him and snatched them both. In the struggle 'one of the pistol handles broke in my hand ... I threw that pistol away, and with the other gave Bowes a blow upon the right side of his head which knocked him from his horse.' A surgeon was sent for to dress the wound, then Bowes was carried away to his lawyer's house in Darlington. Some days later, three men accompanied him to London, arriving there on 27 November 1786.

Cunning to the last, he contrived to buy ipecacuanha on the way, consuming it 'in order that his appearance might excite commiseration and avoid if possible being committed to prison' when law officers took him to a hotel in Dean Street, Soho. In court at Westminster Hall, his counsel pleaded that he was too ill to be imprisoned. To general amusement the Marshal of the King's Bench Prison offered to accommodate Bowes in his house at St George's Fields. There Bowes paid rent for a suite of rooms.

At the trial on 30 May 1787, Bowes and his ruffians answered charges of abducting Lady Strathmore to try and make her discontinue her divorce suit, and for assaulting and imprisoning her without stating a conspiracy. Mr Justice Buller delayed sentence for twenty-seven days. In that time Bowes revealed himself as the contemptible scoundrel he was; despicably he drew public attention to the Countess's *Confessions* by announcing: 'Preparing for the press and shortly will be published, an account of the life of M. E. Bowes, including a Narrative of her Conduct from the age of thirteen till a short time previous to her elopement from her present husband. Written by herself.'

Bowes and his minions were sentenced on 26 June. As the arch-conspirator he was fined £300 with three years' imprisonment, at the end of which he was bound over for fourteen years in securities totalling £20,000. Lucas received a three-year sentence and was fined £50. Peacock was jailed for two years and fined £100, and Prevot was imprisoned for one year. Six months in jail and a fine of £50 was Bourne's sentence.

Apart from being a chapter of Bowes-Lyon history, the Stoney Bowes case conveyed a facet of Hanoverian justice. This loathsome scoundrel continued to reside in the Marshal's house with his mistress, Mary Gowland, his small son, William Johnstone Bowes, and servants, who included Peacock and his wife. Stoney Bowes would be an inmate in the Marshal's house, or live nearby, acting under prison regulations, for twenty-two years. In spite of this strange mode of incarceration, for the moment Bowes was still legally in control of his wife's income and estates. Meanwhile, however, James Farrer was preparing the law suit for the Countess's divorce.

Given considerable care and attention in her lawyer's London home, at first it did not seem that the great-great-grandmother of the Queen Mother would survive her wretched ordeal. Yet in December 1786 this note appeared in the *London Packet*: 'Lady Strathmore returns her sincere and hearty thanks to her friends . . . for their humane and spirited exertions towards the restoration of her liberty, and the preservation of her life. . . . She is able to inform her friends that she is at length in a fair way to recovery from the painful and alarming effects of her late sufferings, and gains strength daily.'

Bowes, who had secured the controlling interest in the newspaper, the *Universal Register*, abused both Lady Strathmore and her lawyer, whom he accused of having amorous designs on his client. Amazingly, he conducted these journalistic sallies from his prison suite. Indeed, Bowes did much more; he immersed himself in much legal wrangling in his desperate struggle to retain some of the Countess's riches. He claimed that no one had the

right to receive the Streatlam Estate rents except the receiver or receivers appointed by the Court of Chancery under the claim of a mortgage for the sum of £6,500 raised by the late Earl of Strathmore and that when the transfer of the mortgage is made (as it will be soon) then the rents of the estate will revert to me or Mr H. Bourne. Lady Strathmore never can or will possess any power over, or any right to receive, the rents of the said estate during the term of my life. I will only give her an allowance or alimony unless she quits the society of artful, interested attorneys and menial servants . . . or unless some respectable persons among her relations or former friends will take her under their charge and protection. No debts incurred by Lady Strathmore or Mrs Morgan, since Lady Strathmore's elopement, will be paid by me or, according to my firm belief, by any other person whatever.

Maybe this was the bluff of the confidence trickster, or over-confidence, or self-deceit, for after bitter legal entanglement the Lord Chancellor finally gave over the estates and income to the Countess. Bowes was instructed to refund £10,295 11s 1d as well as Lady Strathmore's taxed costs. His Lordship spoke contemptuously of the sordid union; they 'seemed to have been pretty well matched.... Marriage in general seemed to have been Lady Strathmore's object; she was disposed to marry anybody but not to part with her fortune.'

As a blackguard, Stoney Bowes could have had few peers. While Mary Eleanor could never truthfully deny the accusations of being irreligious or immoral, it is unlikely she was guilty of the debauchery which Bowes attributed to her. He even accused her of misconduct with George Walker, her footman, contended that she preferred cats to her children, and protested that before their marriage she had accumulated debts due to the indulgence and gratification of her 'lusts and other profligate means'.

Thus Bowes lost again in his marital tussles. On 2 March 1789, the Lords Commissoners declared that he had committed the acts of cruelty complained of and the 'heinous crime of adultery'. He and the Countess were to be divorced and live apart, and neither was allowed to marry during the natural life of the other.

Bowes – 'mauled, stripped, disgraced and blasted', according to Foot – continued to wallow in his life of degradation which finally consumed him. As well as Mary Gowland, he took a second mistress, Jenny Sutton, who met Bowes when she visited her father then imprisoned for debt. During 1800 he was permitted a occupy a house provided that he complied with prison rules. With him went Jenny Sutton and their illegitimate offspring, as well as cats and dogs. He installed another mistress in a house nearby – a sempstress who had caught Bowes's attention when visiting her sister in the King's Bench Prison.

Harassed by creditors, it is intriguing how he managed to exist. His home was reduced to a slum. His children and Jenny Sutton, who, it is said, was allowed merely one meal daily, lived in dreadful squalor. Yet even Jenny's loyalty reaped Bowes's calumny and treachery. In January 1810 as he lay dying, Jesse Foot learned from a tearful Jenny how Bowes callously proposed to leave her and the children entirely destitute. Bowes's sister and Mr Sampson Perry, who had treated Bowes medically, were already at the death-bed scene when Foot and Bowes's lawyer, a Mr Robbins, met to mediate on Jenny's behalf. Bowes's sister had also called in the parish clergyman. Foot recorded:

... all were devoted to see if Bowes could be prevailed upon to give anything to Miss Sutton.... With these powerful engines, with the particular address of Mr Sampson Perry, with the intercession of all around him, with the begging of the children advancing to the bedside one after the other, Bowes at length gave way, opened his mouth, and consented to Miss Sutton having one hundred pounds per annum. This being avowed to Mr Perry by Bowes, and legally put down by Mr Robbins, witnessed by him, his friend and myself, we took our leave. I ought to observe there was not a shilling in the house, till Mr Robbins left a sum ... a ready display of direct humanity upon this necessitous occasion.

Stoney Bowes – 'hypocritical, tyrannic, mean, violent, selfish, jealous, revengeful, inhuman and savage' – died on 23 January 1810. His remains lie mouldering in the vault of St George's, Borough, in south London.

Lady Strathmore had already been dead ten years. Happily in the last eleven years of her life her existence had been placid. Some of her traits were scarcely praiseworthy. Her maternal instinct had never been pronounced, certainly in the case of her sons. And one is somewhat nauseated by her fetish for publicity, recapturing her sensational days by pasting in an album news cuttings describing her experiences and litigation and the scandal with Bowes.

The relationship with the Lyons grew a trifle more congenial. In her *Confessions* she had written about 'my unnatural dislike to my eldest son, for faults which, at most, he could only be the innocent cause and not the author of. Of this I have repented many months ago and am most sincerely sorry I did not sooner, in compliance with most sincere and disinterested advice.' Her attitude had indeed changed. When her eldest son, John Bowes-Lyon, reached his majority in 1790 as the tenth Earl of Strathmore, she transferred the estates and their income to him. She did not neglect, however, to provide for Mary and William Johnstone Bowes whose custody she had secured. Spared her father's squalid environment, Mary wrote to her mother: 'When I parted from you I was much too young to know the loss of a mother.... I long very much to see you and hope there is nothing more now wanting to complete my happiness.... Although I have been almost five years absent from you I have not forgot any place where I spent my infancy and believe I could find my way over one half of Paul's Walden and Gibside houses etc.'

Rather in the maternal mould, Lady Anna defied her mother, crossing precariously by means of a ladder from her room to a house across the street, and eloping with a law student called Jessup. But the marriage ended in his early death after Anna had borne two daughters. For the rest of her life, she resided at Bird Hill House in the grounds at Gibside where she was maintained by the Earl.

After transferring St Paul's Walden to her second son, George, in 1792, Lady Strathmore occupied Purbrook Park, near Cosham, with two of her daughters. She lived quietly, her preoccupation now being pets, especially dogs.

One wonders who made the choice of her burial dress. When Lady Strathmore died on 28 April 1800, she was buried in Westminster Abbey in her wedding attire. If the choice were hers, one likes to speculate that it was a trace of sentiment for her Strathmore Earl. Her son William Johnstone Bowes, then a naval officer, died seventeen years later, drowned in the *Blenheim*. When his sister Mary died as a spinster in Bath, it concluded the grotesque story of Stoney Bowes and the Queen Mother's unusual ancestor.

As for Mary Eleanor, even in death her spirit seemed to persist. John Strathmore inherited his mother's weakness for romance. The Countess was still alive when he succumbed to the charm of the daughter of Sir John Hussey Delaval of Seaton Delaval, who at sixteen had married her father's friend, Lord Tyrconnel. But the illicit liaison ended in tragedy. By coincidence, during the year of his mother's death Lady Tyrconnel, then at Gibside, died of consumption in Lord Strathmore's arms. Her ghost is said to haunt the mansion – now a roofless decaying ruin.

Driven to distraction by his loss, Lord Strathmore spent a colossal sum on his mistress's funeral. 'Her face,' it is recorded, 'was painted like the most brilliant life. He dressed her head himself! And then, having decked her out in all her jewels and covered her with ruffled lace from head to foot, he sent her up to London, causing her to lie in state at every town upon the road and finally to be buried in Westminster Abbey.'

The Earl of Strathmore reacted irrationally to Lady Tyconnel's death: he became almost crazily obsessed with Lady Susan Carpenter, her daughter. That he saw in the daughter the regeneration of his mistress had been given as the reason for this incongruous behaviour. In the end there was no betrothal. For a while Lord Strathmore occupied himself in the breeding of thoroughbred horses, and developing Gibside into one of the most 'exquisite works of English classical architecture ... a fragment of the majestic landscape conception of which it formed the culmination'.

It was, however, at another estate that Strathmore's passion was rekindled. Mary Milner, a market gardener's daughter, worked as a housemaid at Wemmergill Hall, the Earl's shooting box on the Yorkshire moors. Described as possessing intelligence, natural dignity and charm, Mary Milner cohabited with the Earl at Wemmergill and at an address in Chelsea. After the birth of a son, who was christened simply John Bowes, the 'son of John and Mary Milner', on 29 June 1811, Strathmore and his mistress lived eventually at Streatlam before returning to London. There the folly of the father would reap the severity of the law for the son, and by this quirk of fate leave its imprint on history. But for this, the Queen Mother would not have been the daughter of a Strathmore earl or the future consort of a king and the mother of a queen. In 1817, John Strathmore bequeathed his English estates to his son, but the boy would be deprived of the family titles. When he was dying three years later, John Strathmore strove to make his son his legitimate heir. At his request, in the early hours of 1 July 1820 the banker, Mr John Dean Paul, sought to secure a special licence so that Strathmore's mistress could become his legal wife. When the Archbishop of Canterbury declined to assist, the banker obtained one through Doctor's Commons. Only a day had gone by when, borne in a sedan chair to St George's Church, Hanover Square, the dying peer made Mary Milner his lawful wife. A messenger on horse-back hurried to John Bowes, then a scholar at a school in Ealing, informing him that he was now Lord Glamis. The boy's distinction, however, was short-lived. John Strathmore lay dead the following day, but it was not his son but his brother, Mary Eleanor's third and only surviving son, who became the eleventh Earl of Strathmore and Kinghorne and the Queen Mother's great-grandfather.

In the House of Lords he challenged his nephew's legitimacy. Unfortunately for John his birth had occurred in England. Had he been born in Scotland his parents' marriage would have legitimatized him. But not so under English law, a disparity which resulted in young Bowes's loss of a Scottish earldom. In turn, the Scottish side of the family were deprived of the Bowes's riches. For though the law had ruthlessly snatched a coronet from his grasp, John Bowes's lifestyle would surpass that of most peers; he was left in possession of the Bowes inheritance. Educated at Eton and Cambridge, he resided at Streatlam in a state of rare mag-nificence. As well as the landed estates, vast revenue resulted from coal-mines, ironworks and a thoroughbred stud. His income from coal alone exceeded one thousand pounds daily. Business interests included ship-building at Jarrow, and his activities on the Turf were exceptionally profitable.

Sitting in Parliament as the Member for South Durham, one might have assumed that with such enormous commercial assets and political ties, he would have soared into the realm of government office. Instead John Bowes – a man of exquisite taste, who surrounded himself with works of art – was enticed away by the theatre. To satisfy his penchant for the stage, he purchased the Théâtre de Variétés in Paris. Probably his finest acquisition was his wife, Josephine Benoite Coffin-Chevallier, Contessa di Montalbo, a French actress. Although she was merely the grand-daughter of a Lyons clock-maker, her parents accumulated great wealth and bought their title from the tiny republic of San Marino.

Mrs Bowes, an admirable artist and a connoisseur of *objets d'art*, proved to be a loyal and worthy spouse. After their marriage in 1854 at St Marylebone Church, London, Bowes and his wife lived in Paris at 7 Rue de Berlin. Another home in France was the Chateau de Louveciennes, the mansion which Louis XV had erected for Madame Du Barry. On selling the chateau in 1862 Bowes had the contents conveyed to Streatlam. This was the period when he built up his collection of pictures which few private collections, if any, could rival.

H. M. Thackeray, the writer, a contemporary of Bowes at Cambridge, explained that he visited him in Paris. His friend received £40,000 a year and had 'palaces in the country, and here he is manager of the Théâtre de Variétés – and his talk was about actors and *coulisses* all the time of our interview – I wish it could be the last, but he had made me promise to dine with him and go I must, to be killed by his melancholy *gentlemanlikeness*.'

While at Streatlam it is suspected that Thackeray read Foot's *Lives* – which depicts the bizarre career of Andrew Stoney Bowes – adapting the story for his novel *Barry Lyndon*.

It is, however, Augustus Hare's account in *The Story of My Life* which really creates the atmosphere of Streatlam, to which his cousin, John Bowes, welcomed him in 1861. Streatlam lay in a hollow,

an enormous building of the last century, enclosing a medieval castle. I sleep in the ghost-room, looking most grim and weird from its black oak with red hangings, and containing a tall bed with a red canopy.... The long galleries are full of family portraits – Hyltons, Blakistons and Bowes – one of them, Miss Bowes of Streatlam, was Mrs John Knox! More interesting to me is the great picture of Mary Eleanor, the unhappy Countess of Strathmore, walking in the grounds of St Paul's Walden.

... This is the oddest house I ever was in! Everything is arranged for you, from the moment you get up till the moment you go to bed, and you are never allowed to deviate from the rules laid down: I even write this in time stolen from the half-hour for dressing. We are called at eight, and at ten march into breakfast with the same procession as at dinner, only at this meal 'Madame Bowes' does not appear, for she is then reclining in a bath of coal-black acid, which 'refreshes her system' but leaves her nails black.

After breakfast we are all set down to employments appointed for the morning. At twelve Madame appears, having painted the under-lids of her jet-black eyes with belladonna. At two the bell rings for luncheon, and we are fetched if not punctual to an instant. At three we are all sent out driving (the coachman having exact orders where to take us) immense drives (twenty-four miles today) in an open barouche and pair. At seven we dine in great splendour and afterwards we sit in the oak drawing-room and talk about our ancestors!

John Bowes and his Josephine left to posterity one of Britain's greatest treasures. Not far from Barnard Castle a chateau-like structure stands in stately magnificence on the fringe of bleak Bowes Moor. It is called the Bowes Museum.

3

Ancestral Influence at Glamis

After those tempestuous scenes in an earlier age, life for Lady Elizabeth Bowes-Lyon at St Paul's Walden was, by comparison, a halcyon time. Little happened to cast a shadow over the sunshine of childhood. Now and again there was the minor, isolated incident as, for instance, when Bobbie, a cherished bullfinch, who had been in the habit of eating off her plate at mealtimes, was killed by a cat. Carefully placing the mauled bird in a cedar-wood pencil-box, she consigned him to the grave, fervently intoning burial rites of her own creation. Distressing, too, was the sad tale of Lucifer and Emma, two Berkshire pigs. Elizabeth and David were upset to learn that Lucifer had been taken away to be offered as the prize for a raffle at a local bazaar. Anxiously they pooled their savings and frantically bought roughly half of the tickets. But their enterprise turned out to be quite abortive; Lucifer, won by a stranger, disappeared for ever from the childhood scene.

The vivacity and grace of manner, as well as the genuine hospitality and regard for others which would one day enchant millions, had its incipience even in infancy. For instance, totally devoid of shyness, she was only three years old when, detaching a notable guest from other visitors at Glamis, she took him to a room near the drawing-room and asked: 'Shall us sit and talk?'

Guests of the Bowes-Lyons commented on the child's tact and skill at putting others at ease. As if foretelling her future elevation to royal status, she explained that she called herself 'the Princess Elizabeth' when, dancing with her brother David in fancy dress, she was asked by a visitor to Glamis to describe the character she portrayed.

An intimate of the Bowes-Lyons has revealed that for an unaccountable reason he never failed to address the future Queen as 'Princess Elizabeth', kissed her hand 'and invariably made her a low bow, which she acknowledged haughtily and courteously'. Another contemporary, who resided in London, was more explicit. As a boy at a party at Lansdowne House, he was introduced to a little girl called Elizabeth Lyon. 'I turned and looked and was aware of a small, charming, rosy face, around which twined and strayed rings and tendrils of silken hair, and a pair of dewy grey eyes. Her flower-like mouth parted in a grave, enchanting smile, and between the pearly teeth flowed out tones of drowsy melting sweetness that seemed to caress the words they uttered. . . . Here was the true heroine. She had come. I had seen and she had conquered.'

For the next two summers she figured largely in his life. He remembered her 'playing in the park, racing beside her yellow-haired brother, her hair flying in the wind, her cheeks bright with the exercise, her clear infectious laugh ringing out; or sitting demurely at the tea-table; or best of all, at a fancy-dress party dressed as a Vandyck child, with high square bodice and stiff satin skirts, surrounded by a bevy of adorers. I thought she was like the princess of every fairy-tale I had ever read.'

He didn't see her again until he was ten years old

living in London because I was too ill to go to school. Then she came to tea with her governess. Outside the short November day was fading to a close. I lay upon a sofa, watching the gale blow about the tops of the plane trees, listening to the patter of the rain on the window and feeling very small and lonely. The door was thrown open and a lady came in with a little girl. It was over three years since I had seen her ... and in the dim light I hardly knew her for a moment. She was taller and paler and darker than I remembered. But her charm was the same: the drowsy, caressing voice, the slow sweet smile, the delicious gurgle of laughter, the soft eyes glowing with sympathy as she leant forward in the firelight; that had not altered. At the first silvery words all my depression fell from me. And when she went I felt it worth being ill a thousand times over so to be visited.

One recalls this idyllic interlude to illustrate that the charm which would captivate throughout the world years hence was never false but innate.

There were lessons, of course, as well as pleasure. First came the French governesses and by the time she was ten little Elizabeth could converse in French almost as well as in English. The Countess of Strathmore shunned the new trend of banishing daughters to boarding schools, an attitude which seems to have been endorsed by Elizabeth herself. Attendance at a London day school lasted only two terms, but long enough to win the school's literature prize awarded for an essay.

In London her father owned an Adam house in St James's Square and it helped to broaden her horizons, for visits there enabled her to develop her talents. She received lessons in dancing and music, both of which delighted her, although one senses there were also aberrations. Madame Matilde Verne, her music mistress, once recalled an incident in her studio in what was known as the Paderewski Room.

I heard someone being taught an exercise that all pupils, old and young, detest. It seemed to me that the struggle was going on too long, so I went into the Torture Chamber and found that little Elizabeth was the victim. 'We have only just begun,' said the teacher firmly.

I looked at the child. Though reverent in face, there was a warning gleam in her eyes as she said to the teacher: 'Thank you very much. That was wonderful,' and promptly

Ancient Glamis. The centuries-old fortress is on the left; a more recent addition on the right. This ancestral home developed Elizabeth's keen sense of history.

The crypt in Glamis Castle with its mementoes of past wars. The Queen Mother's ancestors supported the Jacobite cause against the Hanoverians although, ironically, she married one of their descendants.

slid off the music-stool holding out her tiny hand in polite farewell. She always had perfect manners. I am glad to remember that she was easily coaxed back to the piano, and that the practice lesson ended happily.

Not only was there the London home and St Paul's Walden to roam in. When Elizabeth was four years old her father had succeeded to the earldom. Simultaneously he became Baron Bowes of Streatlam Castle and of Lunedale and it was by these English titles that he took his place in the House of Lords. Thus, like the Royal Family, the Bowes-Lyons adhered rigidly to a system of seasonal migrations to their estates, temporarily vacating St Paul's or the London house before travelling to Streatlam and then on to Glamis.

Occasionally there would be the excitement of Continental night travel and restaurant car meals on visits to the now widowed maternal grandmother, Mrs Scott, who had chosen to live at the Villa Capponi that overlooked Florence. Permanently inscribed on the young Elizabeth's mind would be the beauty of the Florentine scene; the massive drawing-room boasting an organ at one end and a huge fireplace in the centre of the dark panelled walls; the exquisite harmony of artistic furniture, flowers and books; and the red damasked walls of the chapel adorned with paintings.

It was customary to arrive at Glamis in August. Coincidental or deliberately planned, it was the time when the Royal Family made its perennial sojourn at Balmoral. House parties were commonplace at Glamis. Lord Gorell, editor and author, recalling those days with some nostalgia, claimed that no house parties

were ever so altogether friendly as those of the summer holidays.... The ostensible reason for the assembly was cricket, jolly cricket on the castle ground or in the neighbourhood, not too serious cricket.... There was always incident and excitement in plenty over cricket at Glamis: once we all subscribed for a Panama hat for our captain, Lord Strathmore, in honour of his doing the 'hat-trick' against the Dundee Drapers.

And then when this serious-non-serious cricket was over for the day, came cricket again in the evening, very serious indeed, with Elizabeth and David in rivalry for the perpetual right to bat.

In between the matches were days on the moors after grouse and blackcock, and other days of picnic – nominally rest days – when Elizabeth would sally forth bestriding an aged donkey, reputed to be at Glamis for a quiet end, 'and the unfortunate slaves on foot, to please their imperious and delighted little mistress of the ceremonies, instead of sauntering leisurely along beside her as they had planned to do, had to run breathlessly at her stirrup and then exert all their tired muscles to prevent donkey and rider from plunging ... headlong into the stream.'

The old castle echoed with fun and laughter. The evenings were joyfully abandoned to charades, or, gathering round Lady Strathmore at the piano, family and guests sang songs in an atmosphere of oil lamps and candlelight. Such was the pleasant atmosphere at Glamis, 'a great and historic house, no stiffness, no aloofness anywhere, no formality except the beautiful old custom of having the two pipers marching round the table at the close of dinner, followed by a momentary silence as the sound of their bagpipes died away gradually in the distance of the castle'.

That was the environment in which Lady Elizabeth Bowes-Lyon was reared. It can be argued that a child's future character is moulded by early domestic influences and physical surroundings. This contention is decidedly confirmed by a life study of the Queen Mother. Although the pleasance of St Paul's Walden perhaps stimulated the tranquility and even gaiety of temperament, it was the trim fortress in the sweeping valley of Strathmore which awoke and reinforced the romanticism and keen sense of history.

As the years went by, Elizabeth increasingly delved into the tangled skein of Scotland's past – an activity which later appealed to Queen Mary and Elizabeth's future husband, Prince Albert. A recurring strand in that skein would be Glamis and her ancestry. Over the years this ancient Scottish fortress, with its long tradition and centuries-old power, has in its subtle way imposed a predominant influence on her character.

At Glamis there was one subject which Elizabeth was debarred from discussing. The Dowager Lady Granville, the late elder sister of the Queen Mother, is on record as saying: 'We were never allowed to talk about it . . . our parents forbade us ever to discuss the matter or ask any questions about it. My father and grandfather refused absolutely to discuss it.'

This was the so-called 'monster' of Glamis, a subject which occupied the lively pens of Victorian writers. Hidden in one of the castle's secret chambers in the fifteen-feet thick walls, tradition claims that he lived to an enormous age. His identity was strictly guarded, a secret rigorously confined to the Earl, his heir, the family lawyer and the factor, or agent, of the Glamis estate. When he came of age, each eldest son was confronted with the monster who apparently was the lawful Earl.

Successive earls were noted for their sadness. Augustus Hare, commenting on a house party at Glamis in 1877, wrote:

Only Lord Strathmore himself has an ever-sad look. The Bishop of Brechin, who was a great friend of the house, felt this strange sadness so deeply that he went to Lord Strathmore and, after imploring him in the most touching fashion to forgive the intrusion into his private affairs, said how, having heard of the strange secret which oppressed him, he could not help entreating him to make the most use of his services as an ecclesiastic, if he could in any way, by any means be of use to him. Lord Strathmore was deeply moved. He said that he thanked him, but that in his most unfortunate position, no one could ever help him.

Charles, Viscount Halifax, a relative of the Bowes-Lyons, related a conversation in 1870 with a Miss Virginia Gabriel who had been residing at Glamis. She revealed 'that after [his] brother-in-law's funeral the lawyer and the agent initiated Claude [the Earl of Strathmore] into the family secret. He went from them to his wife and said: "My dearest, you know how often we have joked over the secret room and the family mystery. I have been into the room; I have heard the secret; and if you wish to please me you will never mention the subject to me again".'

Lord Halifax further explained that while Lord Strathmore and his family were residing at their London home 'a man working in, I think, the Chapel, came upon a door opening up a long passage' which he explored. Lord Halifax does not describe what alarmed the man, but he quickly drew it to the attention of the Clerk of the Works who suspended the operation until the Earl of Strathmore and Mr Dundas of Edinburgh, a lawyer, had travelled to Glamis to question the workman on what he had observed. The fact that the man and his family 'were subsidised and induced to emigrate' implies a graphic and maybe gruesome discovery. Whatever the revelation, after the secret was exposed 'Claude was quite a changed man, silent and moody, with an anxious, scared look on his face.' The transformation was such that his son, the father of the Queen Mother, adamantly refused to be admitted into the secret on attaining his majority.

Mr James Wentworth Day has mentioned another theory to account for the so-called monster. He referred to Mr Paul Bloomfield, who, after minute research, concluded that this strange creature was the first son of Thomas, Lord Glamis, who married Charlotte Grimstead; indeed, the Queen Mother's great grandparents. Consulting *Burke's Peerage*, Mr Bloomfield points out that Charlotte, who was married on 21 December 1820, bore an heir, Thomas George, on 22 September 1822; he would succeed to the Strathmore title as the twelfth Earl. Mr Bloomfield however, stresses that, from the time of the marriage to the day of his birth, there lapsed twenty-two months – a period in which a first-born child had escaped Burke's observations. Mr Bloomfield consulted Douglas' *Scots Peerage* for clues and to his surprise noticed that a son was born – and died – on 21 October 1821. Confirmation of this offspring lurks in Cockayne's *Complete Peerage* but the date is a few days earlier – the eighteenth.

This revelation has roused the suspicion that the first-born child was so grotesque that Lord and Lady Glamis deliberately pretended that he was dead, conscious that he could never inherit the earldom. The second son, Thomas George, succeeded to the title and he was followed by his brother Claude, whose heir was his son Claude George, father of the Queen Mother. Doubtless the story of the monster will always be shrouded in mystery and the subject of speculation, for no precise records appear to exist.

For Elizabeth, when at Glamis, there was always the excitement of a chance encounter with ghosts. Viscount Halifax, who probed the eerie world of the supernatural, did not doubt that the castle was haunted. He recalled in a book the experience of Mrs Munro of Lindertis. Sleeping in the Red Room with her husband, she awoke to the touch of a beard brushing her face. In suffused moon-light she noticed a figure move into the adjacent dressing-room occupied by her young son. Suddenly the boy screamed in terror and told his parents that he had seen a giant.

Glamis's most eminent bewhiskered wraith is the notorious Earl Beardie, other-wise Lord Crawford, who long ago quarrelled with the current Lord Glamis while gambling in the early hours of a forbidden Sabbath. One suspects that time has embroidered fact with fantasy, yet one member of the domestic staff at Glamis is on record as having heard Beardie and his companion 'rattle the dice, stamp and swear'. Lord Halifax has also told how a guest at Glamis, the Hon Mrs Wingfield, disturbed in her sleep, saw 'in front of the fire, a huge old man with a long, flowing beard. He turned his head and gazed fixedly at her, and then she saw that, although his beard rose and fell as he breathed, the face was that of a dead man.' Many people might be sceptical, but the Viscount entertained the belief that Beardie haunts the Blue Room at Glamis. We have his written account of a visitation during a nightmare and Beardie's revelation that he had been weighed down by irons ever since 1486.

During Elizabeth's childhood, when Viscount Halifax sometimes visited Glamis, he noted that 'Rose, the second girl [later the Dowager Countess of Gran-ville] and David, the youngest boy, often [saw] shadowy figures flitting about the Castle. They [were] not alarmed by them, but Rose said she would not like to sleep in the Blue Room.' In adult life the Dowager explained how, when she lived at Glamis, 'children often woke up at night in those upper rooms screaming for their mamas because a huge, bearded man had leant over their beds and looked at them. All the furniture was cleared out.... No one sleeps there today.'

A strange assortment of spirits is associated with Glamis. Once on visiting the Bowes-Lyons with his wife, Viscount Halifax discovered the household in tremen-dous excitement 'as the White Lady had been seen by Lady Strathmore, her nieces and Lady Glasgow, from different windows at the same moment. Their descrip-tions were exceedingly vague and incoherent.'

Mr Wentworth Day, allowed to peruse ancient family papers in the Charter Room – a cell in the castle wall – chanced upon hand-written sheets of paper signed by Mrs Augusta Maclagan, wife of the Archbishop of York. The writing revealed how the Dean of Brechin, Dr Nicholson, 'was once sleeping in the room on the central staircase called, in my sister Charlotte Strathmore's time, "Earl Patrick's room". He locked the door before going to bed. Suddenly he became aware of a tall figure in a cloak, fastened with a clasp, standing by his bed. Neither spoke. Presently the figure disappeared in the wall, where there was no door. The door on the staircase was still locked.'

The Bishop of Brechin, Dr Forbes, teased him on being told of the incident. But in the following year 'the two met at Glamis for the Chapel festival, with the Provost of Perth. Passing Earl Patrick's room, the Provost told the Dean he had once seen a ghost there. They compared notes. Both had seen the same ghost.' No longer sceptical, Bishop Forbes offered to exorcize it, but Lord Strathmore – Elizabeth's grandfather – was 'afraid to agree to it'.

In her childhood, tales of Glamis's legendary ghosts must have impressed the young Elizabeth. There is the Mad Earl who stalks the leaded roof, the woman running across the park pointing to her tongueless mouth and the Black Boy who is alleged to occupy a small stone seat near the door of the Queen Mother's sitting-room; probably a servant or page boy, a story describes how he was treated harshly some two centuries ago. Her bathroom has been 'exorcized'. Originally a little bedroom or dressing-room adjoining what is today the Queen Mother's sleeping quarters, occupants experienced creepy sensations, as if something tugged at the bedclothes. But once it was converted into a bathroom all uncanniness ceased.

Because the great stone pile of Glamis oozes with history, Shakespeare not unnaturally (but quite inaccurately) chose it as the gory setting for *Macbeth*. Sir Walter Scott, the novelist, after his first stay at Glamis in 1793, put the record straight, writing:

It was the scene of the murder of a Scottish King of great antiquity, not indeed the gracious Duncan, with whom the name naturally associates itself, but Malcolm II. . . . Peter Proctor, seneschal of the Castle, conducted me to my apartments in a distant part of the building. I must own that when I heard door after door shut, after my conductor had retired, I began to consider myself as too far from the living, and somewhat too near the dead. We had passed through what is called the King's Room, a vaulted apartment garnished with stags' antlers and other trophies of the chase, and said by tradition to be the spot of Malcolm's murder. . . .

In spite of the truth of history, the whole night scene in Macbeth's Castle rushed at once upon me. . . . I experienced sensations which . . . did not fail to affect me. . . .

His experience at Glamis influenced some of his later writings, notably in *The Antiquary*.

Doubtless the royal tragedy weighed heavily on the young mind, for Lady Granville once explained that when 'my sister, the Queen Mother, and I were children we would sometimes be sent downstairs to fetch something. We always raced through Duncan's Hall and the Banqueting Room. As for King Malcolm's Room, where Malcolm was murdered, there was a bloodstain on the floor which would never wash out. So my mother had the whole floor boarded over.'

A nearby room had its full measure of spookiness. The door possessed a mystifying habit of opening at night. Lady Granville, pinpointing this phenomenon, said that one 'could bolt it, lock it and even stick a chest of drawers against it – it was still open in the morning'. To counter this nocturnal oddity, Lord Strathmore had the wall taken down and removed the door to an upstairs room.

An element of the macabre is unavoidable when it is realized that for centuries the Lyons were the Thanes of Glamis. As such, the Scottish kings empowered

The wedding of Elizabeth and Albert at Westminster Abbey. Near by stand the Prince of Wales (the future King Edward VIII), Queen Mary and others who, with the Yorks, would figure in the abdication crisis.

The Duke and Duchess of York acknowledging the cheers of guests as they left Buckingham Palace for their honeymoon.

them to maintain law and order throughout Angus. The Hangman's Chamber is a memento of those days when the Lyons kept a private hangman to dispose of the condemned on Hangman's Hill. To add to Glamis' story of death, a butler once chose to hang himself in this very room.

In contrast to the gruesome backcloth of Glamis's chequered past, can be cited the ghost of the gentle and unobtrusive Grey Lady. In this case scepticism must concede the possibility of authenticity, for various Bowes-Lyons claimed categorically to have seen her. Lady Granville admitted that, while playing music in the chapel one sunny afternoon, she experienced a disquieting sensation that she was being observed by 'someone or something'. Kneeling in one of the pews 'was our little Grey Lady. She was praying. I distinctly saw the detail of her dress and the outline of her figure but the sun, shining through the windows, shone through her and made a pattern on the floor. No one knows who she was, but several people have seen her. She is a sweet little person and harms no one. I have not the faintest idea why she comes here. When I had finished playing my music she vanished.'

Her nephew, the Earl of Strathmore, also confirmed the existence of this mild, diminutive apparition. In the chapel, among a number of paintings by the Dutch artist de Wint, there is one portraying Christ in the likeness of Charles I. Entering the chapel one afternoon to scrutinize some detail of the painting, he was amazed to see the Grey Lady kneeling in prayer.

Childhood and adolescence are impressionable years and Glamis's legends must have influenced the thoughts and character of the young Elizabeth. Certainly her years at Glamis were infused with a sense of history. It was inescapable, for the Lyons are inextricably entwined with Scotland's richly colourful and bloody past.

What is seemingly incongruous is that Lady Elizabeth Bowes-Lyon was classed as a commoner from birth because she is not of the blood royal. Yet she can trace her impressive lineage to Scottish kings. Indeed, by a remarkable coincidence Robert II, the first of the Stuart sovereigns, was an ancestor common to both herself and the royal prince she would marry. Robert, the hereditary High Steward of Scotland, ascended the Scottish throne in 1371 by virtue of his mother, Marjorie Bruce, the daughter and heiress of Robert Bruce, hero of Bannockburn. The death of Margaret, the Maid of Norway, while returning to her native Scotland in 1290, had terminated the central line of Scottish sovereigns, thus enabling Robert Bruce, a descendant of a minor offshoot from the twelfth-century David I, to wear the Crown. Further into Scottish history beyond King David drift the shadowy figures of the McAlpine monarchs – among them Shakespeare's Duncan – until the line vanishes in hazy legend.

James V of Scotland and his fateful daughter, Mary Queen of Scots, as well as those Stuarts who wore the English crown, were likewise descended from Robert. With such a glittering pedigree, it was hard to classify Lady Elizabeth

Bowes-Lyon as a commoner. Moreover, on the maternal side, the Countess of Strathmore could trace her ancestry not merely to Dutch aristocrats who accompanied William of Orange to England, but also to the union of the Lancastrian Henry VII and Elizabeth of York.

Directly or indirectly, Glamis has long been connected with royalty. Kings of Scotland held court there from the eleventh century (and perhaps earlier) until the fourteenth century, since when – as Elizabeth would learn – it had been owned by her family. For in 1376 John Lyon of Forteviot married Lady Jane Stuart, the widowed daughter of Robert II, whose dower was Glamis. But royalty still arrived with their retinues. James V and his Queen, Mary of Lorraine, sometimes held court there, after incarcerating the widowed Lady Glamis with her son, a mere boy, and her second husband, a Campbell of Skipnish, in Edinburgh Castle. The King feared this granddaughter of the notorious Earl of Angus who was widely known as 'Bell the Cat'. The trumped-up charge was witchcraft, for which she was burnt alive – 'suffering all . . . with a manlike courage, all men conceiving that it was not this fact [witchcraft] but the hatred which the King carried to her brothers'.

Campbell died while trying to escape, but the young Lord Glamis's life was spared; he was kept in prison until the King's death, then returned to a depleted home – for James had ransacked the castle of most of its treasures. The Exchequer Rolls of 1513–40 record: 'Twelve great silver flaggons melted down for the mint, each of seven pounds weight.'

James's daughter, Mary Queen of Scots, called at Glamis in 1562 during the journey to subdue Huntly's rebellion. Like her father, she issued royal documents under the Privy Seal from Glamis. Mary's son, James VI of Scotland and I of England, knew the castle well during the days of Patrick, the ninth Lord, and the first Earl of Kinghorne. Earl Patrick was one of the Queen Mother's most oustanding ancestors. Both he and his son Earl John effected great architectural changes at Glamis, surprisingly when Scotland was harassed by war. It was a critical period for the ancestral home; father and son were compelled to raise money for the 'exigencies of war by borrowing the security of their real estate, and every available piece of ground . . . was mortgaged or pledged in some form to numerous creditors throughout the land'.

Earl John bequeathed a precarious inheritance to Patrick, his four-year-old son. Matters worsened when Lord Linlithgow, the child's hard-hearted stepfather, stole from the boy's estates, and Oliver Cromwell, the Lord Protector, levied swingeing fines; some of his troops, billeted at Glamis, left their marks of barbarity.

Most probably the Queen Mother would never have known Glamis as an ancestral home but for the fortitude of young Earl Patrick; indeed, the family might have declined into anonymity. The first Earl of Strathmore and third Earl of Kinghorne, he looms prominently in Scotland's cavalcade of exceptional men.

Patrick Lyon was seventeen on taking over the vast estates and equally vast debts of some £400,000 – a catastrophic figure exceeding four million pounds in modern values. Glamis was virtually barren, the lands in ruin and Castle Lyon – another seat, in the Carse of Gowrie – was uninhabitable.

The colossal and seemingly impossible task of regaining solvency would have been too daunting to many. As he later wrote in his *Book of Records*: 'I had a verie small and a verie hard beginning and if I had not done so great and good things as I might or willingly would have done I desyre that my posteritie whom God has bless'd me with may excuse these my endeavours....' What illustrates his early privations is the disclosure: '... att that time I was not worth a four-footed beast, safe on little dog that I keeped att and brought with me from St Andrews.' Briefly, his byres, barns and stables were pathetically empty. How different from the affluent scene in Elizabeth Bowes-Lyon's childhood.

Initially Patrick went to Castle Lyon where he lacked even a bed. Out of altruism, the minister of Longforgan lent him one until his simple furniture arrived from St Andrew's where he had recently completed his studies. In his enforced austerity, he had no option but to live at Castle Lyon, being devoid of the means to make Glamis habitable. From deserted Glamis, he and his sister, Lady Elizabeth Lyon, collected 'some old potts and pans which were verie usefull', then with their own hands gradually restored their stone-floored prison-like castle.

His sister remained with him until his marriage in 1662. Like his descendant, the fourteenth Earl, the father of the Queen Mother, Patrick derived immense moral courage and strength from his wife, Lady Helen Middleton, second daughter of John, first Earl of Middleton. There seems to have been a striking parallel between herself and the fourteenth Countess. Both had a keen sense of domesticity and around each revolved the family's life. Married at the Abbey of Holyrood in August 1662, Patrick and his bride wintered in Edinburgh before leaving for Castle Lyon in the following March, remaining there for seven years before they left to renovate Glamis.

Endowed with keen acumen, Patrick Lyon tenaciously set about reducing the debts that ironically he himself had never incurred. Simultaneously he redesigned his two castles, to the point that Glamis gradually grew into one of Scotland's most magnificent stately homes. The enormity of the task and the degree of accomplishment are reflected by the fact that, though he had to borrow considerably, by shrewd dealing the debts had shrunk to £175,400 at the time of his death.

Thus he rescued Glamis for his descendants. Employing mostly local craftsmen, he also commissioned two Dutchmen who had been assigned to work at Holyrood Palace in Edinburgh: Jacob de Wet, an artist, and Jan Van Santvoort, who executed paintings and carvings. Patrick not only stabilized the fortunes of the Lyons, but by a charter dated 1 July 1677, he ordained that his heirs should be designated for all time Earls of Strathmore and Kinghorne, Viscounts Lyon, and Barons Glamis, Tannadyce, Sidlaw and Strathdichtie.

The Duke and Duchess of York on honeymoon at Polesden Lacey, Surrey, where Edward VII and his clique had once played golf and backgammon.

Patrick was not inclined to emulate his father and grandfather by dabbling in wars. Such intrigues and alliances had brought them ruin. Early in the Glorious Revolution of 1688 Patrick Lyon opposed the Prince of Orange by cooperating with such stalwart Jacobites as Callender, Southesk and Breadalbane. But their expeditionary force soon dwindled to nothing. James II fled to France and it was clearly imprudent – perhaps risking imprisonment and even execution – to oppose the Prince. The restoration of his castles and estates was far more paramount than involvement in dynastic machinations. At a Privy Council meeting in Edinburgh he was selected to attend the Prince of Orange in London, but he found an excuse so that his eldest son travelled in his stead.

Jacobism would not die, however, at Glamis, but would erupt with tragic outcome when the Stuarts strove to wrest their rightful crown from the Hanoverians who had replaced them. It seems ironical now that, more than two centuries later, Lady Elizabeth Bowes-Lyon should be united in marriage with a descendant of those German princelings. Their elder daughter, today Queen Elizabeth II, with the blood of both Stuarts and Hanoverians in her veins, would in a sense symbolize the reconciliation between these conflicting factions.

Much hatred and contempt for the Hanoverians would be engendered before that time. John, the fifth Earl, and his uncle, the Hon Patrick Lyon of Auchterhouse, rallied to the standard of the Chevalier de St George, better known in history as the Old Pretender, at the 'Rising of the Fifteen'. When the Earl of Mar, who led the Jacobite troops, marched into Perth, the young Earl and his Strathmore regiment – a force composed of retainers and tenants – marched with him. With four of his companies, Strathmore took part in the attack on an English flotilla blocking the Firth of Forth. When the attempt proved abortive, the Earl and some two hundred Jacobites fled to the Isle of May before reaching the mainland.

The climax of the rising was on 13 November 1715, the day of the calamitous Battle of Sherrifmuir. Like his uncle, Patrick Lyon ,the gallant young Strathmore fell in this gory struggle. The Master of Sinclaire wrote:

On our left, the brave younge Strathmore was killed after being wounded and taken.... When he found all turning their backs, he seized the colours, and persuaded fourteen or some such number to stand by him for some time, which drew upon him the ennemie's fire, by which he was wounded, and going off was taken and murder'd by a dragoon, and it may be said in his fate that a millstone crusht a brilliant. He was the younge man of all I ever saw who approached the nearest to perfection ... and his least qualitie was that he was of a noble, ancient family, and a man of qualitie.

Still extant at Glamis is the Household Book in which Elizabeth, the widowed Countess of Strathmore, sadly wrote: 'I sent my Chaplain, Mr Balvaird, to see my son' (the dead Earl), and subsequently records how she sent for his equipment and 'paid for my son's coffin and the journey of his body to Glamis'.

His successor, an artless boy of sixteen, was host to the Chevalier some two months later. With the Pretender was Mar who, circulating a letter from the castle to the Highland chiefs, wrote:

Glames, 5th Jan. 1716. I met the King at Fetteresso, on Tuesday Sen'night, where we staid till Friday, from thence we came to Briechin, then to Kinnaird, and yesterday here. The King design'd to have gone to Dundee today, but there is such a fall of snow, that he is forced to put it off till tomorrow, if it be practicable then; and from thence he designs to go to Scoon. There was no haste in his being their sooner, for nothing can be done this season, else he had not been so long by the way.

A large retinue of officers and gentlemen accompanied the Chevalier; indeed, the youthful Lord Strathmore was called upon to provide eighty-eight beds. So devoted were the Lyons to the Stuart cause that for years the bed that the Chevalier occupied was shown to visitors with unconcealed pride. So, too, was his sword which was inscribed: 'God save King James VIII, prosperitie to Scotland and No Union.' His watch also came to be in their possession but in a roundabout way. Inadvertently leaving it beneath his pillow, a maid purloined it but must have confessed her guilt to her family; after some years it was returned to the Lyons by her great-granddaughter.

To the adolescent Strathmore, the Chevalier 'was a very cheerful, fine young gentleman and a lover of dancing; also of great and uncommon understanding, punctual to his word, very religious, modest and chaste'. To ordinary folk he was believed (as indeed were all the Stuart sovereigns) to be endowed with the divine attribute of curing victims of the disease known as scrofula. The chapel at Glamis was the picturesque setting for one of those ceremonies called 'touching for the King's Evil'. Father Lewis Innes, Principal of the Scots College in Paris, who journeyed with the Chevalier as his private chaplain, described the scene. The original document was lost earlier this century but a copy survives. He wrote:

The King (!) knelt upon a cushion, and the assistants, as well as those who were to be 'touched', knelt upon the floor of the chapel. The King's Confessor [Father Innes], wearing cotta and stole, recited certain prayers to which His Majesty responded. The priest then read the Gospel of Christ's ordering his disciples to go and teach all nations and afterwards using the words *Super egros manus imponent et bene habebunt*'.

When these words were being said one of the King's aides-de-camp led the patients, some of them being children, one by one to His Majesty, who was now seated, and who laid his hands upon each, the priest meanwhile repeating *Super egros*', etc.

The King then knelt and recited certain prayers, after which, resuming his seat he hung a silver medal, bearing St Michael on one side and a three-masted ship on the other, round the neck of each patient. The King performed the ceremony in a saintly manner, with great devoutness and recollection of mind. The office used was that of King Henry VII, revived by King James II.

All the patients, each bearing the sores of the disease in varying degrees, recovered. A silver touch-piece, which the Chevalier hung round the necks of the diseased, still exists at Glamis, a relic of the Chevalier's audience.

The Chevalier was profoundly impressed with the nobility of Glamis, and in the grounds where Elizabeth Bowes-Lyon would play with her brother David many years later the figures of the Stuart kings testified to Lyon allegiance. An account of Glamis, written most probably by Defoe a few years after the Chevalier's visit, propounds that

when seen at a distance the piles of turrets and lofty buildings, spires and towers, made it look like a town. The palace, as you approach it, strikes you with awe and admiration by the many turrets and gilded balustrades at the top. The outer court has a statue on each side of the top of the gate, as big as life. On the great gate of the inner court are balustrades of stone finely adorned with statues; and in the court are four brazen statues bigger than the life on pedestals; the one of James VI and I of England in his stole; the other of Charles I in his boots, spurs, and sword, as he is sometimes painted by Vandyke; Charles II is in Roman dress, as on the Exchange in London; and James II in the same as he is in Whitehall.

In the 'Rising of the Forty-Five' some of the men of Glamis took up arms for Bonnie Prince Charlie, the Chevalier's son; but not their lord. Leading the Hanoverian forces, the Duke of Cumberland – nicknamed the 'Bloody Butcher' for his brutality – stopped at Glamis on his northward march. One can only speculate on Lord Strathmore's reaction to Cumberland's stay. Perhaps there was a sense of humiliation and embarrassment but his subsequent action indicates anger and hatred. When, to his relief, his unwelcome visitor left, he instructed that the bed he had occupied should be smashed.

Later, to Lord Strathmore's dismay, Stuart aspirations would be shattered for all time in the ghastly massacre at Culloden. Some of his relatives and friends would face vicissitudes and even death. Robert Fletcher, a grandson of Elizabeth Lyon of West-Ogil, who married a Lyon of the same cadet family of Glamis, escaped with Lord Ogilvy from Broughty Ferry. Embarking at night, they landed at Bergen in Norway where, at the instigation of the English government, they were seized and confined to the castle there, until they were liberated to make their way to France.

The lot of Patrick Lyon of Ogil who fought as a lieutenant in the Ogilvy regiment is vague, but death was the fate of the Rev. Robert Lyon, an Episcopalian clergyman in Perth who, defraying his expenses out of his personal funds, joined the Jacobite adventure on religious grounds. Butcher Cumberland maintained his reputation for savagery; Robert Lyon was tried, condemned and executed at Penrith on 28 October 1746.

Lyon's altruism was implicit in his actions before he died. He administered the Sacrament to the condemned before they were taken away for execution. And even on the scaffold he conducted divine service, during which he unrelentingly espoused the Stuart cause. Still at Glamis, and in a way spanning the years between that melancholy day and the present, is the Prayer Book of Miss Stewart

Rose, daughter of Bishop Rose of Edinburgh, who was to have been the bride of Robert Lyon. Inside it is a copy of that final speech.

The Lyon family of those perilous days gradually resigned themselves to the inevitability of Hanoverian rule. But the relics continue to linger as memorials to a lost but romantic venture.

4

The Commoner and the Prince

The serene years at St Paul's Walden ended abruptly. The sun which had always seemed to shine on Elizabeth's childhood was dramatically eclipsed by the sombre clouds of war. It was her fourteenth birthday and in celebration Lady Elizabeth was taken to a variety show at the London Coliseum – a night that would be unforgettable. With members of her family, from a theatre box she witnessed the excitement and hysterical outburst when the audience frenziedly demonstrated its patriotism at the declaration of hostilities. By the time Elizabeth was in bed at the family home in St James's Square, Britain was at war with Germany.

It was the end of an era. Inevitably, in its cataclysmic effects, war would lead to drastic social changes. Six months before the birth of Lady Elizabeth Bowes-Lyon, the British Labour Party had opened its headquarters in London's Farringdon Road. Hostilities would give impetus to the tempo of the social revolution that had begun in the reign of George v. The King was reactionary, disliking change, and one suspects that Lady Elizabeth later regretted much that became reality in the war's aftermath. Gone were the leisurely times which, perhaps, were more in harmony with her character. Yet as the years would convey, the changes evoked forceful qualities which until then had been concealed.

For Elizabeth, war's stridency sounded at first on the domestic scene. Four brothers were of military age and within days Patrick, John, Michael and Fergus had joined their regiments – the Black Watch and the Royal Scots. Their young sister was caught up in the eddies of excitement, participating in 'the bustle of hurried visits to chemists for outfits of every sort of medicine and to gunsmiths to buy all the things that people thought they wanted for a war and then found they didn't'.

Within a week of the outbreak of hostilities, Elizabeth was travelling in a crowded train to Scotland. Already the disruption caused by war had spread to peaceful Glamis: the castle was in the process of being transformed into a hospital. Strange and empty seemed that particular August to the young Elizabeth. There was no longer the sound of ball on bat; the cricketing Augusts were mere memories. Even the billiard table was crammed with 'comforts': mufflers, thick shirts and socks, body belts and sheepskin coats to be cut and treated with a type of varnish.

At least there was some slight compensation for Elizabeth; for the moment, lessons could be neglected 'for during these first few months we were so busy knitting, knitting, knitting and making shorts for the local battalions – the 5th Black Watch. My chief occupation was crumpling up tissue paper until it was so soft that it no longer crackled, to put into the lining of sleeping-bags.'

The first car loads of wounded – veterans of trench warfare in France – came over the Sidlaw Hills in December from a hospital in Dundee, some few miles away. Elizabeth was among the first to greet the 'boys in blue', so named because of their blue flannel hospital suits. For the next five years neat beds arranged in ordered rows along the panelled walls of the extensive drawing-room would always be occupied. The crypt was converted into a dining-room, and at Christmas time – the first Yuletide that Elizabeth had spent at Glamis – she distributed presents from a huge tree whose glow from numerous candles was mirrored in shining armour redolent of ancient wars.

Elizabeth's older sister, Lady Rose, having completed her nursing training in a London hospital, travelled northwards to take control of the patients at Glamis. Elizabeth was too young to appear officially on the roll of hospital staff, but she was in constant demand as the soldiers' companion, messenger and amateur entertainer. But her mere presence, the flashing smile that was destined to be internationally known, was a tonic to the patients' morale. As one man wrote: 'She had the loveliest pair of blue eyes I'd ever seen – very expressive, eloquent eyes that could speak for themselves ... her smile was a refreshment.'

Written by a Sergeant Pearne, he further illustrated Elizabeth's profound concern for people. 'Taking photographs', he wrote, 'was a favourite hobby of hers, and it was the result of one of her productions that caused a little misunderstanding at my home. When my parents visited me at Dundee while I was so ill, they were warned not to be surprised should they hear that my arm had been amputated. I didn't know of this. Lady Elizabeth gave me a photograph she'd taken of me and I sent it home, not thinking that ... with my right arm being in a sling, and I sitting right sideways, it didn't show at all.'

When, the parents received it, they were convinced that the arm had been removed, causing them such acute distress that a friend wrote asking him to tell his parents the truth – 'it was kinder to let them know the worst'. Unable to understand the contents of his friend's letter, Sergeant Pearne showed it to Lady Elizabeth – who wrote off 'straight to them saying exactly how my arm was progressing and how sorry she was to think "they had been mislead". Then she sent for me to come to the garden ... to have ... myself photographed so that my arm and the sling could be seen.'

The Bowes-Lyons did not escape their share of anxiety and grief. Elizabeth, already an aunt, acquired a new niece when in July 1915 a daughter was born to the wife of her brother Fergus. During September, Captain Fergus Bowes-Lyon of the 8th Battalion, The Black Watch, managed to secure a brief leave at Glamis.

Yet, tragically, returning to his unit on the evening of Monday 20 September, he fell in the Battle of Loos that commenced six days later. He was killed in the taking and holding of the Hohenzollern Redoubt.

The fear of receiving yet another telegram haunted the Bowes-Lyons until the early weeks of 1917, when Michael was reported by the War Office as being dead. Broken-hearted by the latest tragedy, David was summoned from Eton to give solace to his parents. To their surprise he refused to wear mourning. Told by the minister of Glamis that he should not be so finely dressed so soon after his brother's death, David protested that Michael had not died: he had seen him twice in dreams. 'He is in a big house surrounded with fir trees,' he confidently explained. 'He is not dead, but I think he is very ill because his head is tied up in a cloth.' David's second sense was proved to be correct three months later, when Michael was discovered to be in a German prison hospital suffering from a wound in the head.

Meanwhile, Elizabeth had resumed her studies, one suspects rather erratically. To reach her schoolroom she had to climb the great, winding stone staircase. From the windows she overlooked the courtyard where a bell announced the time for chapel and meals. It was not in this family chapel that she was confirmed (although the Bishop of Brechin would by tradition have conducted the ceremony there) but with other young people at St John's Church in nearby Forfar. Elizabeth was identifying herself more closely with local life. One activity – the Girl Guide movement – would lead to significant repercusssons, ending in a close friendship with Princess Mary and the Royal Family. It was an association which would help to create the conditions that would foster her marriage.

From now onwards fate seemed to direct the steps that eventually took her to the throne. During May 1916 Elizabeth assumed greater domestic responsibilities when her sister, Lady Rose, left Glamis to marry the Hon William Leveson-Gower, RN, at St James's, Piccadilly. The domestic strain increased not only due to the absence of sister Rose but because Lady Strathmore, still affected by the shock of Fergus's death, now suffered from indifferent health. The outcome was a burgeoning and an annealing process which strengthened Elizabeth's character.

The keen presence of mind which had been so apparent over the years was noted in December. Fire broke out in the upper part of the central keep which stands some ninety feet high. First, Elizabeth telephoned for the fire brigades at Glamis, Forfar and Dundee before she called her brother David and domestic help. The hoses of the Glamis brigade were much too short to raise water from the nearby River Dean and the Forfar brigade was little better equipped. Soon a lead water tank on the roof burst under the intense heat and the water rushed in a deluge down the staircase where Elizabeth and David, deploying their force with brushes and mops, prevented it from sweeping into the drawing-room and other apartments.

The Duchess's initiation to many official foreign visits was the christening of the son of King Alexander of Yugoslavia and the wedding of Alexander's cousin, Prince Paul, to Princess Olga of Greece.

A historic photograph. From the left (standing) King George v, the Duke of York (who succeeded after the short reign of his brother, Edward VIII, as George VI) and the Earl of Strathmore; (seated) Queen Mary, the Duchess of York (later Queen Elizabeth) and the Countess of Strathmore. The baby girl would become Queen Elizabeth II.

By now villagers had been attracted by the fiery glow, and the young chateleine of Glamis arranged them in line to pass paintings, furniture and other valuables to safety. The damage was excessive before the Dundee force arrived, and it would take years to repair. Ancient Glamis, however, might have been completely gutted but for the quick-wittedness of the future Queen.

Even after the Armistice was signed, Glamis remained a hospital until 1919 and the Bowes-Lyons were the hosts of Australian and New Zealand officers awaiting return to their homeland. Lady Elizabeth was now nineteen. There had been the metamorphosis from girlhood to young womanhood under the stress of war. For Lady Elizabeth a new world had begun to open up, but it was much more gradual than many suppose. She now visited country houses, the normal routine in high society.

At that particular stage, this appeared to be the blueprint for her future life, marrying in due course a fellow aristocrat and following that unfettered private existence which the Bowes-Lyons were keen to preserve. Yet in retrospect, the first indication of her future niche in history was visible in May 1920. Lady Elizabeth Bowes-Lyon met Prince Albert, King George v's second son, in London at a dance given by Lord and Lady Farquhar at 6 Grosvenor Square. Lady Annaly, a close friend of Lady Elizabeth, and her husband were other guests and perhaps introduced Lady Elizabeth to the Farquhar set.

Then seventy-six, Lord Farquhar was an eccentric and described as possessing 'a fierce expression, a firm chin and a military moustache'. Bonar Law, as Prime Minister, thought he was 'so gaga' that he had no idea what to make of him. In the reign of Edward vii Lord Farquhar, widely believed to be a man of enormous wealth, had been Master of the King's Household. Possibly his greatest eccentricity was in drawing up a will leaving grandiose bequests to most members of the Royal Family, only to die deeply in debt. With the legacies never paid, there is a touch of irony in that funds that he had controlled for Prince Arthur of Connaught were never satisfactorily accounted for; indeed, no adequate explanation was ever forthcoming, apparently, for their disappearance.

Doubtless his finest contribution to the monarchy was in supplying the setting where a royal romance began. Prince Albert, who would ascend the throne as King George vi, had already met his future consort. But that had been fifteen years ago – in London in 1905, at a party given by the Countess of Leicester at Montague House. She was five and he was nine and in what is now a legend describes how she gave him the crystallized cherries from her sugar cake.

There would be no such time gap between their next meetings. Indeed, the Prince, whom the King had recently created Duke of York, paid his first visit to Glamis within months – in the autumn of 1920. At that time his sister, Princess Mary, was the guest of a lady-in-waiting to Queen Mary, Lady Airlie, who, living in nearby Cortachy Castle, was also an old friend of the Bowes-Lyons. Lord

Strathmore therefore arranged a large house party to meet the Duke – who was staying at Balmoral – and greet the Princess.

Prince Albert was captivated by the gaiety and conviviality of homely Glamis. Here he was free to relax from the rather stilted formality of the court. Unlike Lady Strathmore, one could hardly visualize Queen Mary seated at a candle-lit piano, the focal point of merry-making. The King's consort was not an emotional person and Mr James Pope-Hennessy, her biographer, claimed that her 'withdrawn, reserved manner, her cool, even temperament, made it unlikely that [she] would ever inspire a violent emotion'.

Bertie's mode of living in his early years was to a high degree the antithesis of that of the person he would marry. His birth and childhood setting was York Cottage on the Sandringham estate. Sir Harold Nicolson, who was familiar with it then, described it as 'a glum little villa, encompassed by thickets of laurel and rhododendron ... and separated by an abrupt rim of lawn from a pond, at the edge of which a leaden pelican gazes in dejection upon the water lilies and bamboos. The rooms inside, with their fumed oak surrounds, their white overmantels framing oval mirrors, their Doulton tiles and stained glass fanlights, are indistinguishable from those of any Surbiton or Upper Norwood home.'

As the family increased, gables and horizontal turrets and beams were added so that York Cottage 'became a rabbit-warren of tiny rooms connected by narrow passages, in which royal pages and tall footmen would sit or stand, blocking the way'.

This smacks somewhat of an extremist, even biased view, just as the alleged unhappy childhood of the offspring of George V and Queen Mary (then the Duke and Duchess of York) has on occasions been grossly exaggerated. There was much to amuse and foster enjoyment for the royal children at Sandringham. But against this one has to set parental temperament and consider the characteristics of Bertie and his elder brother, David.

In Bertie's case, misfortune even attended his birth. He had been born at the outrageous hour of three o'clock in the morning on 14 December 1895, sacrilegiously intruding by a few hours into the 'terrible anniversary' of the death of Prince Albert. Queen Victoria's consort had departed this life thirty-four years previously, yet the Queen-Empress still recalled her bereavement with grief and profound solemnity. The Duke of York had dutifully telegraphed his aged grandmother, apologizing for Bertie's violation of such a hallowed day. Ever ready to put pen to paper, Victoria had recorded: 'I have a feeling that it might be a blessing for the dear little boy, and may be looked upon as a gift from God.' But apparently the Duke was never wholly convinced that he had escaped reproach; more than once he ruefully confided that Queen Victoria looked on the birth as 'a personal affront'.

Five sons and a daughter would be born to the Yorks, yet even when David and Bertie had been joined by their sister Mary, the nursery merely consisted of two rooms; the three children and their nurse occupied one by day and slept in the other at night. In keeping with the strict domestic pattern of upper-class families of those days, the children were reared in isolation from their parents, being entrusted to the mercy of a nanny. Like many of the families in this social station, the children usually saw their parents only once, or at the most twice, a day when specially groomed to meet them.

In reflective mood David, writing as the Duke of Windsor, referring to his child-hood frankly confessed to the absence of that affection normally bestowed on a child in any good home. Even when servants displayed warmth, he was never certain if it was genuine or because of his unique status as the heir apparent. The affection of his nurse was certainly questionable; indeed, the after-effects were perhaps traceable into manhood. It seems that this neurotic woman was so obsessed with her young Prince that she could not bear to release him from her care. Whenever she took her charge to his parents she would secretly twist his arm so that the tearful David was returned to her more promptly.

It is quite likely that this childhood torture influenced his later temperament. After three years the nurse was dismissed owing to her mental instability. But in that time the consequences of her behaviour had had a serious effect on Prince Albert. So badly did she neglect him that this is the suspected cause of his lifelong delicate constitution. Like some ritual torture, each afternoon Albert was bottle-fed during the nursery carriage outing which has been referred to as resembling a Channel crossing, 'and with corresponding results'. Done wittingly or not, the Prince's acute gastric complaint, which developed into a torment, originated from that time. Also, in common with his father and brothers (save David), he endured another disability: knock knees. Consequently he was fitted with corrective braces which he wore during the night and part of each day. The splints generated such pain that a manservant removed them out of kindness to avoid the nocturnal agony, until the King happened to hear of it. Summoning the valet, he drew up his trousers to reveal his own knock knees. 'Look at them,' he thundered, 'if that boy grows up to be like this, it will be your fault.' Albert wrote to his mother with childish resignation: 'I am sitting in an armchair with my legs in the new splints ... I have got an invalid table, which is splendid for reading but rather awkward for writing at present ... I expect I shall get used to it.'

The legs would be straightened, but the terrible stammer that also originated in childhood would not be overcome until his marriage. Albert was what is labelled in modern terms a shifted sinistral; in short, he was left-handed, a natural trend which – foolishly labouring in the Victorian belief that left-handedness was virtually unseemly – his father ordered the boy's tutor to 'correct'.

One visualizes the depressing sight of a sensitive child in corrective splints at an invalid table, struggling against natural inclination by trying to write with an awkward right hand. Dogged by these terrible handicaps, moments of despair and rebellious, mercurial temper (such as the time he angrily tugged his German

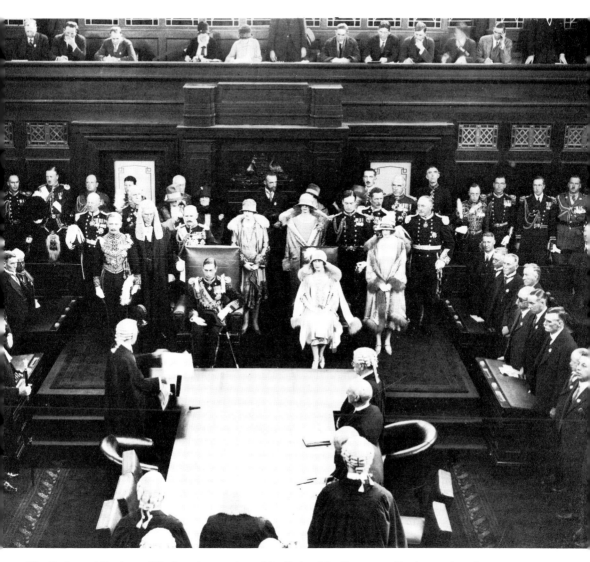

The Duke and Duchess of York at the opening of the Federal Parliament at Canberra, then the new Australian capital.

tutor's beard) were inevitable. Instead of inspiring sympathy, these tearful out-bursts merely evoked parental annoyance, and often wrath.

Albert undoubtedly felt keenly the repressive influence of his father. To his subjects George v was not merely an institution; his image as a dutiful father struck a reverberant chord in the people's hearts. Yet he was a strange combination of qualities. Pious (he read the Bible daily) and punctilious in fulfilling his royal duties, he exemplified kingly and personal virtues. He was affectionate towards children and doted over his own in infancy, but as they grew older, even though he adored them they became the victims of his severity. This former naval officer was, according to one biographer, Mr John Gore, 'impetuous by nature [and] he gave vent to his feelings instantly and without reserve'. George v ensured that his household adhered to the timetable precision of a ship and demanded the utmost obedience. He possessed the temper – and the vocabulary – of a salty old sea-dog, and when his children were summoned by him for an alleged mis-demeanour, the encounter could be a nerve-racking experience.

As Duke and Duchess of York (and later as King George v and Queen Mary), they were profoundly conscious of their roles and their majesty, and their children were compelled to be conscious of it too. But apart from this, the Duke in particu-lar seemed incapable of exhibiting parental affection. This was exacerbated by a genuine anxiety for his children. Moreover, he was a reactionary by nature and did not care for change. As was seen in his later dealings with his eldest son, he could tolerate only the customs of his own childhood and youth. In his own words he claimed to be 'devoted to children and good with them, but they grow up, and you can only watch them going their own way and can do nothing to stop them'.

The result of this attitude was that the King and Queen never really succeeded in their relationship with their children; indeed, it can be argued that on tempera-mental grounds alone they were unsuited to parenthood. Queen Mary resented pregnancy and possessed an utter detestation of the physical aspects of childbear-ing. It is generally known that, as the Empress Frederick explained, Queen Mary was 'very cold and stiff and very unmaternal'. Neither could she stand between the children and 'the sudden gusts of their father's wrath'. Like King George v, she was extremely conscientious in meeting the demands of her royal calling, and her role and duties as consort overwhelmingly took precedence over the slightest maternal instinct.

As subsequent reigns would testify, it was an unimaginative attitude to adopt. Years later, in his official biography of King George vi, Sir John Wheeler-Bennett would reveal: 'The relations of Lord and Lady Strathmore with their children and the happy badinage and affection of a large and closely-knit family were a revelation to him [Prince Albert], providing a climate of ideas to which he in-stantly responded, and in which his own personality throve and blossomed.' In-deed, through their daughter Elizabeth, the Strathmores would indirectly have a bearing on the Royal House. The happy domestic relationship that they engendered would filter into the court of George VI and Queen Elizabeth.

In the spring of 1921, Prince Albert made his first proposal of marriage to Lady Elizabeth, but to his dismay it was declined. It is believed that in her mind lurked the paramount fear that if the Prince of Wales were to die childless Prince Albert would become the King and she the Queen. The prospect of being shackled to constant public duties and the inflexibility of royal routine and protocol appalled her. There was the Prince's acute impediment and unstable health as well to consider. But towering above all other reasons, she was essentially a private person who wished to safeguard that privacy.

Probably finding parental domination somewhat irksome, as well as being rather lonely at court, doubtless the Prince was downcast, evoking the sentiment of Lady Strathmore who informed a friend: 'I hope he will find a nice wife who will make him happy,' adding with unconscious insight, 'I like him very much and he is a man who will be made or marred by his wife.'

Queen Mary also bore sympathy towards her son. It is irrelevant whether the visit was contrived or not, yet in the summer the Queen and Princess Mary were the guests of Lady Airlie. Lord Strathmore again invited Bertie to Glamis for his favourite pastime – shooting. 'It is delightful here and Elizabeth is very kind to me,' he wrote to his mother some days before she came to tea. He added, as if it was an afterthought: 'The more I see of her the more I like her.'

As her mother was ill, Lady Elizabeth was again the chatelaine at Glamis and impressed the Queen with her flawless efficiency as housekeeper and hostess. It is strongly rumoured that both King George V and Queen Mary had included Lady Elizabeth's name in the short exclusive list from which to choose a bride for the Prince of Wales. Assuming this to be true, it is intriguing to conjecture on the outcome of such a union; undoubtedly the course of history would have been different, for there would have been no abdication.

Although marriage had as yet eluded Bertie, a royal wedding was in the offing. In November there came the announcement of the engagement of Princess Mary to Lord Lascelles. Because their friendship had blossomed, not unexpectedly Princess Mary invited Lady Elizabeth to be one of her bridesmaids. To Westminster Abbey, on 28 February 1922, Lady Elizabeth rode for the first time in a state procession. Within fifteen months she would repeat the journey, this time as the bride. The state coaches would rumble again for coronation fifteen years later. Yet it seems unlikely that anyone could have predicted this on that February day.

Elizabeth sat next to the Duke of York at the luncheon at Buckingham Palace but a hiatus now developed in their friendship. That spring Lady Elizabeth visited her friend Diamond Hardinge (whose brother was fated to be embroiled in the drama of the abdication) in Paris, where the widowed Lord Hardinge attended to Britain's affairs as ambassador. It was Lady Elizabeth's initiation into Parisian life. There was the sightseeing and the shopping to enjoy, and drives to Fontainebleau and Malmaison, but the climax of her programme was an Embassy ball. One guest recorded: 'The most charming sight there was Lady Elizabeth Lyon, a bewitching little figure in rose colour ... with an absolutely enchanting smile ... she stood out as an English rose, sweet and fresh as if with the dew still on it.' It has been rumoured that one Embassy official proposed marriage later that summer, but there is no confirmation. Certainly there were proposals during the year, but all were rejected.

In court circles it was well known that the Duke of York's affection for Lady Elizabeth had never waned. In August he journeyed again to Glamis. The Countess, who had recovered appreciably from her illness, noted that her daughter was worried and ill-at-ease. 'I think she was torn between her longing to make Bertie happy,' she subsequently explained, 'and her reluctance to take on the big responsibilities which this marriage must bring.'

This self-debating ended in January of the next year. The date was the thirteenth and, to the superstitious, full of portent. But as the young Duke of York drove in his car through the wintry Hertfordshire countryside to St Paul's Walden, one thing predominated in his mind. Ostensibly he was merely a guest at a house party but in reality he was determined to seek Lady Elizabeth's hand in marriage. Being the thirteenth of the month it might have augured failure, yet the Prince refused to be deterred. For two years he had been a persistent suitor in spite of what appeared to be Lady Elizabeth's apathy. His parents were aware of his intentions and George v, with typical bluffness, had told him: 'You will be lucky if she has you.'

But the King secretly hoped that his son's suit would succeed. He was a sovereign of incurable habits. Expounding on this point, David Duff in his book on the Queen Mother explains that the King rose at precisely the same time each morning, and 'straightened his hair with the same brush that he had used as a boy at Sandringham. Even the collar stud was the same (when it broke he had it mended). Breakfast was at 9, and that meant 9. He had it alone with his wife. It was better that way, as throughout the meal his parrot Charlotte roamed the table, sticking her beak into the sugar and marmalade. Ritual followed ritual.'

In this little pen picture of the King, it is clear that there was no place in his ménage for the young cigarette-and-cocktail women then prevalent in society. The mere notion of having them as daughters-in-law really troubled him. 'I hope that we shall be as lucky with our daughters-in-law as Lady Holford has been,' he wrote in August 1922. 'I must say I dread the idea and always have.'

Lady Elizabeth however was different; she was feminine and not modern in either fashion or behaviour. Indeed, between them there would develop a close rapport. Few people, if any, were more attuned to the King's idiosyncrasies, and on George v's death in 1936 she would write to Lord Dawson of Penn, the royal

Waving farewell to the crowds at the railway station in Melbourne after the Yorks' visit to New Zealand and Australia in 1927.

The face of the Duke of York (right) reflects the strain of the mounting Abdication crisis. In contrast, the Duchess conveys calm.

physician: 'I miss him dreadfully. Unlike his own children I was never afraid of him, and in all the twelve years of knowing him as a daughter-in-law he never spoke one unkind or abrupt word to me, and was always ready to listen and give advice on one's own silly little affairs. He was kind and dependable!'

To the King's delight, on Sunday 14 January 1923, while the rest of the guests at St Paul's Walden were at church, Bertie and Elizabeth strolled down to The Wood which, now stripped of the livery of autumn, had wrought its magic in childhood. There, with the agonizing stammer that could leave him speechless, the Prince proposed and to his joy was finally accepted. 'It was my duty to marry Bertie and I fell in love with him afterwards,' Lady Elizabeth is said to have confided in a friend some years later.

To the King and Queen then at Sandringham, the ex-sailor wired with delight: 'All right. Bertie.' In the letter that followed he revealed: 'I am very, very happy, and I can only hope that Elizabeth feels the same as I do. I know I am very lucky to have won her over at last.'

At that precise moment the Prince did not realize how incisively history would echo that last sentiment. The strength of character and the captivating charm of 'the smiling Duchess' would be significant in the destiny of the throne. Temporarily the crown would tarnish, but she would help to restore its lustre, thus ensuring not only her husband's reign but that of Elizabeth, her daughter. Resilience born of moral strength and coolness in crises would enable her influence to be far-reaching, both as the consort of a king and the mother of a queen.

The welter of publicity sparked off by the engagement announcement two days later shattered for ever Lady Elizabeth's hopes for a private life. From now onwards she would grow in public prestige, finally becoming a personality of world stature. Rather than provoking criticism, Lady Elizabeth's unacceptance of modernity endeared her to press and public alike. They saw in it a person who could courageously think for herself and shun the dictates of others. Certainly she was no slave to fashion or any of the oddities of the twenties. *The Times* summed up:

Lady Elizabeth is essentially unmodern – and that is her charm. She is like a picture by Sir Peter Lely. Her figure is that of a woman, not the flat boyish outline so much admired today. She has wonderful skin and eyes and hair. But her greatest charm is her voice. It is like cream and honey turned into sound, and the listener is hypnotised by its musical quality. Although serenity is the key-note of Elizabeth's character, as with all the women of the Strathmore family she has also a Scot's shrewdness. She is intensely home-loving. Perhaps that is one of her chief charms for her husband-to-be. From her mother she inherits the house-wifely qualities of the Dutch.

Motoring to London, Lady Elizabeth felt 'happy but quite dazed' by the torrent of favourable publicity. She saw her name on the ubiquitous newspaper placards and realized that she was the most discussed woman in the British Empire and Europe, too. It was a tribute to her mental equilibrium and marked leavening of humour that she refused to allow herself to be affected by the newspaper adulation.

In 1920 the Strathmores had dispensed with 20 St James's Square and transferred to 17 Bruton Street off Berkeley Square. It was here, at the family's town home, that Lady Elizabeth demonstrated the composure and diplomacy which she would exhibit over the years. Harry Cozens-Hardy of *The Star* requested to interview her.

The Bruton Street butler [he revealed in his memoirs] did not give me a particularly warm welcome, and Lady Strathmore ... seemed quite ready to assist the servant in his efforts to get rid of me. But just behind the Countess was her daughter, with the most radiant face that the purlieus of Bond Street had even seen. 'Mother, leave this gentleman to *me*', Lady Elizabeth was heard to exclaim. Seated at a little writing desk, pen in hand, with letters and telegrams before her, she tactfully remarked: 'I suppose you have come to congratulate me? How very kind of you.' When Mr Cozens-Hardy asked if, as reported, the Duke had found it necessary to propose three times before getting her acceptance, she replied gracefully: 'Now look at me. Do you think I am the sort of person Bertie would have to ask twice?'

There were to be no more interviews – on the instructions of the King.

5

"Truly British to the Core!"

Change – both technical and social – was inevitable after the turmoil of war. Neither did its impact leave the Royal Family untouched. A generation earlier, Prince Albert, Duke of York, would have been debarred from marrying the daughter of an earl. Although Lyon ancestry meandered back over the centuries to the early Scottish kings, Lady Elizabeth Bowes-Lyon, in the eyes of royalty, was a commoner. Thus inflexible royal dictates would have presented an insurmountable barrier.

When the Hanoverians sat on the British throne their omnipotent code forbade such marriages. Thus developed the tacit understanding between the British and German royal houses that brides and bridegrooms should be restricted to their own courts. George I had set the seal on the tradition that only royalty could wed royalty, but it was George III who made this ruling absolute. Doubtless left to his own choice, he would himself have proposed marriage to the titled commoner who had intrigued him, but instead, complying with the royal decree, he dutifully accepted the princess who had arrived from Germany. His brothers, the Dukes of Gloucester and Cumberland, defied the ruling, acts of crass folly at that time and more so considering that the King resented their ladies for political as well as social reasons.

Thus out of annoyance and defiance was born the Royal Marriage Act of 1772 which enacted that

no descendant of His late Majesty George II (other than the issue of princesses married or who may marry into foreign families) shall be capable of contracting matrimony without the previous consent of His Majesty, his heirs and successors, signified under the Great Seal. But in case any descendant of George II, being above twenty-five years old, shall persist to contract a marriage disapproved of by His Majesty, such descendant, after giving twelve months' notice to the Privy Council, may contract such marriage, and the same may be solemnized without the consent of His Majesty, etc., and shall be good except both Houses of Parliament shall declare their disapprobation thereto.

By the time of the Duke of York's betrothal, more than two and a half centuries had elapsed since a prince in direct succession to the throne had received a sovereign's blessing to marry a commoner. By a coincidence he, too, had been

The abdication of King Edward VIII thrust the Yorks on to a throne they never sought. The baby Princess Elizabeth was destined to become the Queen.

a Duke of York – the brother of Charles II, later the Catholic James II. James had also married an earl's daughter – Anne Hyde, the offspring of Clarendon, the politician and historian.

Royal attitude to marriage has differed over the centuries. That much-betrothed monarch Henry VIII was the only king of England after Edward IV to marry a subject, yet in the earlier centuries of English history it was not un-common for the sons and daughters of the reigning sovereign to wed commoners. Indeed, such alliances with the great noble houses were even encouraged, to re-plenish the royal coffers.

On 12 February 1923, King George V formally consented to his son's wedding when, at a special meeting of the Privy Council, this document was approved:

> Whereas by an Act of Parliament entitled 'An Act for the better regulating of the future Marriages of the Royal Family', it is amongst other things enacted 'that no descendant of the body of His late Majesty King George II, Male or Female, shall be capable of con-tracting matrimony without the previous consent of His Majesty, His Heirs or Successors, signified under the Great Seal.'
>
> Now know ye that we have consented and by these Presents signify Our Consent to the contracting of Matrimony between His Royal Highness Albert Frederick Arthur George, Duke of York, and the Lady Elizabeth Angela Margaret Bowes-Lyon, youngest daughter of the Right Honourable Claude George, Earl of Strathmore and Kinghorne.

The unyielding Hanoverian practice persisted up to the marriage of George V (then Duke of York) and Princess May of Teck. Queen Victoria had crystallized this absurdity with the words: 'A morganatic marriage is something we would never wish to discuss.' But even in her own eventful lifetime the Queen-Empress – known as the 'Grandmother of Europe' because of inter-marriage and the close family ties which bound her to other royal dynasties – was to appreciate the folly of this rigorous rule.

Europe's royal hierarchy was dominated by the Habsburgs, Hohenzollerns, Coburgs and Romanovs: socially a rarefied set, but inter-marriage within this exclusive circle had taken its sinister toll in the form of the blood disease of haemo-philia. This 'scourge of kings' would destroy even Victoria's own son, Leopold, as well as grandchildren and great-grandchildren. And because this horror was traceable to the female line of these ancient lineages, it was time to inject new blood by broadening the sphere of marriage.

In 1899 the aged Queen sanctioned the betrothal of the Prince of Wales' daughter, Louise, to the Earl of Fife, then at the dining table created him a duke. She could hardly hinder the romance after permitting the marriage of her own daughter Louise to the Marquess of Lorne, son of the Duke of Argyll, eighteen years earlier. Several factors had been involved. To compel the Queen to submit, the Princess, christened the 'Maiden all for Lorne', had threatened to enter a convent. But maybe it was the threatened strife in Europe and Bismarck's belli-gerence that finally persuaded Victoria. The Prussian royal house was incensed by her action but, conveying her fears to Lord Lorne, he calmly replied: 'Ma'am, my ancestors were kings when the Hohenzollerns were parvenues.'

The First World War witnessed the death in Britain of any of these German notions. Even King George v, worried by the mounting tide of public hostility to things Germanic, shrewdly severed all Teutonic connections and assumed for the Royal Family the extremely English name of Windsor. Furthermore, if the younger of the royal children wished to seek marriage outside the exclusive domain of royalty, they could effect unions from among the first three ranks of the nobility: dukes, marquesses and earls. All circumstances considered, the only person who might have prevented the marriage between the second son of the King-Emperor to Lady Elizabeth Bowes-Lyon was the forthcoming bride herself.

In 1923 the House of Hohenzollern did not even exist to approve or not of Elizabeth of Glamis. In any event, Prince Albert, Duke of York, had breached tradition. It was the end of political and dynastic alliances. *The Times* commented on his choice of bride: 'Truly British to the core!'

As so often happens on royal occasions, the engagement and the subsequent marriage at Westminster Abbey temporarily dominated the people's minds, helping for the moment to mitigate the fears of social conflict (which would erupt almost to the day three years later) and international strife which weighed heavily. Such royal events colour the public scene, seeping even into what is normally drab. The wedding of Prince Albert and Lady Elizabeth on 26 April 1923 was no exception. Britain was enduring a lowering phase of terrible depression and in Europe there were even now hints of the bloody holocaust to come. But for a while the people's eyes were directed towards Buckingham Palace, the national hub at times of tragedy and joy. Apart from the popularity of the principals involved, the forthcoming marriage had an added piquancy: Prince Albert was the first of the King's sons to marry. Moreover, there had been no wedding of a royal prince in Westminster Abbey since that of the unfortunate young Richard ii. The marriage of Albert and Elizabeth, therefore, seemed to merit unique treatment. Why not make history and broadcast the event, enthused the progressives? The technique of wireless telephony, as it was then called, had reached a standard whereby programmes could now be heard in most parts of Britain. It was not technical limitations, however, but diehard reaction which prevented it. The Abbey's Dean was in favour but the Chapter, perversely defying all rational argument, objected, claiming that, lacking respect and homage, 'the service might be received by persons in public houses with their hats on'.

Ironically, in the lifetime of Lady Elizabeth Bowes-Lyon the Church hierarchy would welcome not only radio in cathedral and church, but also the more brash medium of television. As for the monarchy, both media would be cardinal assets of the Royal Family, identifying it more closely with the people.

Meanwhile, the formalities and intricate planning that precedes a royal wedding went on. The public, avid for news, was informed that Mr Bull, a veteran clerk at the Archbishop of Canterbury's Faculty Office, would for three days 'stoop over a roll of parchment nearly a yard square in a locked room. He will use nearly twenty quill pens of various thicknesses and will write the licence in old English lettering with black ink.'

Among the spate of presents, there was no longer the bride's dowry of 'half a moonlight', the traditional nuptial gift of the Lyon family to their daughters. This primitive practice dated from the days when plundering was rife and life was inseparable from marauding attacks. Half the booty seized in a nocturnal raid was bestowed on the bride.

Perhaps Lady Elizabeth Bowes-Lyon sensed something of the ancient spirit of her ancestry as she set out for the Abbey on that chilly Thursday morning in April 1923. Whatever her thoughts, despite the old and stirring genealogy she was left in no misapprehension that she was still a commoner. She rode in an unostentatious landau with a modest escort of four mounted policemen, and no troops presented arms along the route.

The day had dawned cold, showery and grey, but as the bride's carriage drew up at the ancient shrine of kings and queens, George v later noted in his diary that the sun suffused the rich colouring of the Abbey's stained glass and scattered the gloom. To the imaginative it might have suggested an augury for the future: the radiance of an endearing personality who would spread warmth wherever she went. Characteristic of this, the bride thoughtfully laid her bouquet of white York roses on the Unknown Warrior's tomb.

Serenity prevailed in the old stone Abbey when the Yorks were married that day, but calm would not always pervade the royal scene. In addressing the bride and bridegroom Dr Cosmo Lang, then Archbishop of York, remarked: 'The warm and generous heart of this people takes you today unto itself. Will you not, in response, take that heart, with all its joys and sorrows, unto your own?' His words might have been a prediction of the event which would swiftly change the lives of the Duke and his bride years hence. Lang, as Archbishop of Canterbury, would be an important figure in the abdication controversy which would culminate in the bleak December of 1936. The Yorks, plunged into kingship, would begin a new partnership between Crown and people.

Nothing existed at that moment to predict this. Indeed, while congratulating the Duke on his choice of fiancée *The Times* had commented: 'There is one wedding to which the people look forward with still deeper interest – the wedding which will give a wife to the Heir to the Throne. . . .' When eventually the Prince of Wales decided on his choice of wife, it would lead to drama.

Some of the principals of those future critical and gloomy weeks were present that day: Queen Mary, regal in aquamarine blue and silver stippled with blue crystals, and the handsome Prince of Wales (to be cast in the part of petulant king) standing immaculate in the uniform of Colonel of the Welsh Guards as the chief supporter (the role nearest to that of best man for a royal groom). The new

Duchess of York, hoping that she and her husband were destined for a royal back-water, was happily unaware of their eventual dramatic projection into history.

When the bride stepped from the Abbey to the boom of bells and the jubilant cries of the crowds, her status had changed. The unglamorous landau had vanished; she now rode in the gilt, ornate coach of state. Gone, too, was the ancestral name. The King's decree and the ritual of marriage had elevated her to the exclusive rank of royalty: she would now be known as Her Royal Highness the Duchess of York. She had discarded the name of Bowes-Lyon, but on that same day an adolescent, serving behind the counter of a humble shop in Kittybrewster – a working-class area of Aberdeen – resolved to acquire it in a court of law.

Some while would elapse, however, before her strange story exploded on the nation, sending its tremors down the corridors of Buckingham Palace and the castle at Glamis. Because of the long secrecy, it is probable that the Bowes-Lyons were innocently ignorant of this skeleton in a dusty cupboard; and maybe it would have continued to moulder but for the marriage of Lady Elizabeth Bowes-Lyon.

Constance Mary Bain, tall and fair-haired, sold fruit, sweets and cigarettes for one J. Smith, newsagent and hairdresser in Powis Terrace. To the observant, how-ever, her lowly status could not belie her air of breeding. The offspring of a romance nineteen years earlier, for some time she had suspected that she was a child of high birth. Connie Bain had read the newspaper account of the royal wedding, and after she had served her last customer that evening she returned home determined to learn the truth about her parents.

To Connie Bain her first five years on earth were a complete void. In her mind the pattern of her life had begun with a woman who had befriended her, but who had died when Connie was twelve years old. Since then home had been a semi-detached house in Elmfield Avenue, a back street in Aberdeen, and the modest address of her guardian, a bookmaker of the name of Bain, and his wife. This kindly, sensible couple had registered Connie in their name at local Sunny-bank School, a state establishment catering for the working-class children in the neighbourhood, but the future did not hold much promise for her, at least not until that night when the Bains unravelled her past.

'Connie, my girl, ye're no Bain. You're a Lyon – a cousin to the bonny leddy that's become a royal duchess today,' revealed her guardian. 'Ye may work in Smith's shop but your right place is in a castle. We'll see the lawyer's aboot it.'

The machinery of the law worked slowly but relentlessly. Fourteen months elapsed before Connie Bain requested the Court of Sessions in Edinburgh to de-clare that she was 'the legitimate, eldest, lawful child of Hubert Ernest Bowes-Lyon, Esquire, grandson of the thirteenth Earl of Strathmore and Kinghorne, and the late Miss Mary Agnes Hay Smeaton.'

The application was simple in itself but the implications were far-reaching – the story of an unwanted child whose existence others had tried to conceal became one of the most discussed topics in Britain. What gave the court proceedings piquancy was that if Connie Bain proved her case she would be acknowledged as a close relative of the Duchess of York. Slowly the truth emerged.

A key witness was Mrs Elizabeth Mackie of Lyon Street, Glasgow, who, described as a 'self-composed woman of forty-seven', explained that in 1904 she and Mary Smeaton – then at variance with her middle-class parents – had shared lodgings in Edinburgh. One night in March of that year Mary Smeaton, then eighteen, met Hubert Lyon, an officer of the Black Watch regiment, at a dance at the local Egyptian Rooms.

Connie Bain's story began that night – a tale of infatuation in which Connie would be the innocent victim. Within weeks Hubert Lyon and Mary Smeaton were cohabiting, and eventually set up home at a house in Blackford Avenue, where for a while Miss Mackie visited them almost daily. While the couple were residing at Blackford Avenue, Mr Lyon resigned his commission, then rented a flat at Tavistock Chambers in Hart Street, London. From there he sent Miss Smeaton fifteen pounds asking her to join him. The furniture travelled there, too, indicating that residence in the capital was likely to be permanent.

To counsel, Mrs Mackie exposed the fact that Mary Smeaton was pregnant before she left Scotland and that Hubert Lyon was the father of the unborn child. In December 1904, on visiting Hubert Lyon and Mary Smeaton, she arranged for a doctor and nurse to attend her friend's confinement. After returning to Edinburgh, Miss Smeaton notified her of the birth of a girl, adding that the child was to be reared in secrecy; neither her own parents nor the Bowes-Lyons were ever to know.

In January 1905, Mary Smeaton, who had legalized her union with Lyon by marriage the previous day, handed over her baby – named Connie – to a Mrs Collie in Aberdeen, arranging to pay her six shillings a week for the infant's upkeep. Mrs Mackie, who accompanied her, noticed that the child's left leg was encased in plaster. From then onwards the parents' link with Connie was extremely vague. Once they had visited her while staying in Edinburgh, and in 1907 Mrs Mackie had travelled with the child to Downey, near Windsor, where the Lyons were then living.

She had visited the couple just once again, and then contact had ceased about 1912. The child had also vanished from her life when she was about five years old. Indeed, time had dimmed the whole episode, to be revived by an advertisement relating to the case now before the court. 'I am sure that this is the girl,' she told the judge, scrutinizing Connie Bain.

Other evidence in testimony was forthcoming. Mrs Margaret Ingrams of Aberdeen explained that she had known Constance in her earlier years. Mrs Collie, her one-time neighbour, had revealed that the child, sent from London, was the daughter of one of the Strathmore's friends.

Connie Bain spoke on her own behalf, informing the court that she remembered

Queen Elizabeth with Princess Elizabeth (left) and Princess Margaret. The Queen was a dominant factor in the training of her daughters, whose upbringing was unpretentious.

Mrs Collie from the time she was about five years old, adding the significant disclosure: 'I have always had trouble with my left leg. I felt pain in it if I walked a lot.' Pleading that although she was born out of wedlock on 24 December 1904, even so she was legitimized under Scottish law by her parents' marriage on 14 January 1905, some three weeks after her birth.

Her action, which was undefended, succeeded. In June 1924 Lord Morrison gave judgment in her favour. The Court of Session declared that Constance Mary Bowes-Lyon (whose mother had died on 5 March 1914) was the legitimate eldest child of Hubert Bowes-Lyon. As such, she was the second cousin of Her Royal Highness the Duchess of York, the future Queen-Empress.

Constance Bowes-Lyon had no aspirations to aggrandize herself or bask in the purple glow that now surrounded her royal cousin. As this quiet, self-possessed Cinderella of an historic house later expressed: 'I was . . . called Miss Bain because Mr Bain had been my guardian for seven years, but I always had the instinctive feeling, from the time I was old enough to entertain such thoughts, that I belonged to a different kind of life from that I am now in. It is only a year ago that my guardian, Mr Bain, took the steps that led to the present legal proceedings. I am quite happy now that my name is cleared. That was all I wanted.' With that she disappeared into self-imposed seclusion.

Why this innocent love-child should have been discarded by her parents – more so after her birth had been legitimized so quickly – one will never know. Maybe the fear of being ostracized, of becoming social outcasts themselves in a society whose rules were then inflexible, was part of the reason. Happily, the discarded waif also met her Prince Charming. In June 1933 she married George Dow of Kilmarnock who took his bride to his vast tobacco plantations in East Africa's Blantyre Hills. There the former shop-girl supervised her servants, and from her small white palace could gaze over an estate that extended far out into the bush.

The day that Constance Bowes-Lyon decided to retrieve her lawful name, her now royal cousin began her honeymoon. In more recent generations the tendency had been to spend royal honeymoons in royal homes. That of Queen Victoria and Prince Albert – a mere four days in duration – had been at Windsor. The future King Edward VII travelled with his attractive consort to Osborne, the home most favoured by his mother. The Prince and Princess of Wales (later King George V and Queen Mary) went to York Cottage at Sandringham, where they resided for many years (although their married life began at Sheen).

The Duke and Duchess of York strayed from precedent, beginning their honeymoon at Polesden Lacey in Surrey, the lovely mansion lent to them by the Hon Mrs Ronald Greville. Sonia Keppel, daughter of that notable beauty Mrs George Keppel, referred to Mrs Greville as 'a small China idol with eyes that blinked'. This suggests something fragile and weak, yet such defects were not present in this only daughter of a Scottish whisky millionaire. Maggie to her intimates, she thirsted for power and exercised it. One of the eminent hostesses of the day, as Sir Osbert Sitwell once remarked, she gathered round her 'celebrated and handsome people'. She has been credited with nurturing the romance of Edwina Ashley and Lord Louis Mountbatten (subsequently Earl and Countess Mountbatten of Burma). It is also claimed that by judicious theatre and dinner parties, she subtly created the fertile soil which enabled the Yorks' romance to root.

Polesden Lacey already had royal connections. In an original house on the site, Richard Brinsley Sheridan had written his plays, but this had been replaced in 1824 by Thomas Cubitt's Grecian villa – the mansion to which Edward VII and his exclusive clique had retired to play golf and backgammon. There, in an exquisite atmosphere of Chippendale, Dutch old masters and painted ceilings it was the discreet setting for discussions on matters of state.

That connection between Maggie Greville and the Royal Family continued over the years. She was even admitted to the select coterie of Queen Mary. Moreover, she had lent Polesden Lacey for an earlier honeymoon, that of the Marquis of Carisbrooke, the son of Princess Beatrice and the grandson of Queen Victoria.

From their rooms the Duke and Duchess of York looked out on to the rolling downs to the south: the same vista which Edward VII had admired years earlier, for he had used this same suite. In what Sheridan had described as 'the nicest place, within a prudent distance of town, in England', the couple enjoyed peace and solitude, sometimes playing tennis and golf. On the third day it was announced that the Duchess had also been created a princess, thus bringing childhood fancy to reality.

Leaving Polesden Lacey the royal couple continued their honeymoon at Glamis. The first-floor suite overlooking the Angles Park that they then occupied is still reserved for the Queen Mother. The sitting-room, hung with eighteenth-century tapestries, predominates. Lattice windows flank the ornate fireplace, with its blue and white Dutch tiles, Adam grate and carved seventeenth-century Dutch chimney-piece. Cabinets exhibit Sèvres porcelain and Canton china, and the Chippendale chairs are adorned with tapestry designs that were worked by Lady Strathmore. Prominent in the main bedroom stands a carved four-poster bed, its hangings embroidered with the names of Lady Strathmore's children and, again, the work of the Countess.

The weather was frightful at the time of the honeymoon – snow, rain and icy winds, and the Duchess (in the words of a castle maid) was 'racked with the coughing'. Bertie wrote to his mother: 'So unromantic to catch whooping-cough on your honeymoon.'

When she recovered they journeyed to Frogmore, a pleasant William and Mary mansion in Windsor Home Park, the house where Queen Victoria had been staying the night that Bertie was born. For the Duke it was a revival of childhood memories, an opportunity to reminisce with his wife. 'So funny being here again,' he wrote to Mr Henry Hansell, his erstwhile tutor. 'Nothing has changed at all. . . .

Old memories come rushing back all the time and our schoolroom is just the same, even to the ink-stains on the writing table.'

George v, predicting the future, wrote to his son: 'You are indeed a lucky man to have such a charming and delightful wife. . . . I am quite certain that Elizabeth will be a splendid partner in your work and share with you and help you in all you have to do.'

Actually marriage for the Duke of York would be seen in the eyes of history as the major step in his life. It liberated him from a court atmosphere that at the time was not lacking in irritations. More important, as his biographer has explained, 'it brought him much for which he had long craved in deprivation – love, understanding, sympathy, support. All these things were now his in generous abundance, and his whole conspectus of life changed accordingly.' The painstaking effort applied to both his duties and his pleasures would go unchanged throughout his life, but the 'tendency to morbidness and introspection and self-pity' would gradually disappear. Now, married happiness and ideal companionship would cast its spell and the 'flower of his natural gaiety blossomed forth and a new spontaneous zest was evident in his whole personality. The world took on a fresh and magical hue for him, and, as the years passed and he became established in his own home with his wife and daughters, his family life came to be his salient joy and comfort.'

King George v had written eulogistically but sincerely of the potentialities of Elizabeth as his partner. She would be the enduring partner not only in moments of joy, but the partner who inspired and untapped his undoubted courage in moments of stress. His consort was a constant reservoir of strength that reinforced him in adversity. The slight touch of the hand, the faintest smile would invest him with determination to struggle with his impediment in public. She too would be the one who quickly assuaged the outbursts of passionate temper which would have done justice to his ancestor, the Duke of Teck.

Yet in that same letter from the King there was a hidden threat to the Yorks' peace. George v had written: 'You have always been . . . ready to . . . agree with my opinions about people and things, that I feel that we have always got on very well together (very different to dear David).' For some time now Bertie had been aware of the growing friction between his father and the self-willed Prince of Wales. What might emerge from this incompatibility of temperament no one could assess at that time. Like the British people, the Duke and Duchess of York lived in the expectation that the Prince of Wales would marry. But the Prince's bachelorhood was tantalizingly lengthy and when marriage came he would quit the throne.

For their first home the King had granted the Duke and Duchess of York the use of White Lodge in Richmond Park. The mansion had begun life as 'a place of refreshment after the chase' for George II but, then christened New Lodge,

It was Queen Elizabeth's interest – when she was Lady Elizabeth Bowes-Lyon – in the Girl Guide movement that brought her closer, through the Princess Royal, to the Royal Family. She is seen here at a Windsor Castle rally.

it became the rural retreat of Queen Caroline, his consort. Hence Queen's Walk, the lush green lime-lined avenue where she liked to stroll. As Ranger of Richmond Park, her daughter Amelia both lived there and enlarged it, calling it White Lodge. Her successor was Lord Bute, whose protectress was the widow of Prince Frederick of Wales.

Then came the long occupancy of Henry Addington, the first Viscount Sidmouth, for more than half a century. His premiership after William Pitt the Younger was brief but White Lodge was the rendezvous of some of the most eminent of the day. On a morning in September 1805 Lord Nelson called on his friend, and touching a finger in wine traced upon a table his plan for an assault which was applied at Trafalgar.

Since that day more than fifty years would pass before Queen Victoria installed her sixteen-year-old heir in one of the wings. Compelled to live in such seclusion, to the Duke of York's grandfather it was akin to incarceration. Throughout the life of the future Edward VII nothing would ever erase the memories of that incubus – the strict disciplinary code which, enforced by two tutors and three equerries, was designed for his military and intellectual advancement.

But of more immediate interest to the Royal Family was that it had been Queen Mary's childhood home. In August 1870 – exactly thirty years before the birth of Lady Elizabeth Bowes-Lyon – Queen Victoria bestowed White Lodge on the Duke and Duchess of Teck. Both had died there, and it was from the old mansion that Queen Mary had left to be married. Sentiment and nostalgia therefore induced the Queen to suggest that this house of lingering memories should be the first married home of the young Duke and Duchess of York. With her daughter-in-law she viewed again her former bedroom and the sitting-room which she had occupied in adolescence.

But the thing which maybe had the greatest appeal to the Duchess – and even poignancy – was the association of her new home with Sir Walter Scott. As Elizabeth Bowes-Lyon she had steeped herself in the Waverley Novels. She knew that it was at White Lodge that Jeanie Deans, in *The Heart of Midlothian*, with the Duke of Argyll as intermediary, begged Queen Caroline to help spare the life of her sister Effie, then under sentence of death for infanticide.

Times had changed since the days of Queen Caroline – and, indeed, of Queen Mary. No longer could White Lodge boast of being a secluded pleasance. Richmond Park, which was enclosed by Charles I for hunting (a decision which provoked widespread anger), was now the haunt of weekend sightseers who arrived in noisy cars and charabancs. Their insensitive inquisitiveness into the lives of the Yorks meant that the royal couple were denied privacy. Furthermore, White Lodge was costly to maintain. But most irksome of all was its unsuitability for the Yorks when coping with engagements.

The public activities of the Duke and Duchess had increased immensely and residence in Richmond was soon to prove impractical. In winter fog often lay thickly over the park and it was difficult for a chauffeur to locate White Lodge. It was clear to the Duke and Duchess that a London address was imperative. However, three years would drag by before that desire materialized. For the times were economically unstable. Only a month before the Yorks' wedding Mr Philip Snowden, the future Socialist Chancellor of the Exchequer, had tried to end the capitalist system with a motion in the House of Commons.

War had also left in its wake both hatred and social upheaval. Ex-servicemen who had survived the holocaust were embittered and disillusioned. The politicians had promised them a land fit for heroes, but for many it would be a land for the homeless and the workless. The tension that prevailed with such dispiriting effect in national life even seeped into the Royal Family itself, as was demonstrated by the King and his eldest son. David was scathing in his contempt for the protocol of his father's court. Doubtless discipline was rather strict, and after the easygoing life at St Paul's Walden and Glamis, it says much for the Duchess of York that she adapted herself to it with consummate ease.

At court the emphasis was on formality. This was reflected by the dress. The King himself set the sartorial standards to which others were compelled to aspire. Like the King, at Buckingham Palace male members of both the Royal Family and the household wore frockcoats by day. The ladies' mode of dress was in keeping. When at Windsor the ladies wore either tailored clothes or full evening dress, according to the time of day. Even when the King and Queen dined entirely alone, the monarch wore tails and his consort a tiara. Formality reached its peak at Windsor Castle during Ascot Week. Before dinner, the guests assembled in the Green Drawing Room, the ladies on one side of the damask room, the men on the other. The Royal Family waited in the corridor outside to receive Their Majesties. The King, his sons and the senior members of his household were attired in Windsor uniform – a dark blue evening dress coat with gold buttons and collar and cuffs of scarlet, worn with knee breeches. (The Windsor colour, it is said, originated because it was in harmony with a mistress of George IV.) After dinner, conversation was somewhat restricted and stiff, but in the later years of his reign George V sometimes introduced bridge or mahjong.

How different would be the royal functions when the Duchess of York became a king's consort. Meanwhile she managed to inject some warmth into the royal atmosphere, a fact which David, the Prince of Wales, would endorse when he recorded: 'She has brought into the family a lively and refreshing spirit.' Even the King, with his fetish for punctuality, would excuse the Duchess's late arrivals, a rare tolerance which was not accorded to anyone else. When someone once reminded him of her unpunctuality, the King blandly replied: 'Ah, but if she weren't late, she would be perfect, and how terrible that would be.'

At the Imperial Conference during the summer of 1923, the Duke disclosed to a dominion Prime Minister the desire of both the Duchess and himself to tour some part of the Commonwealth. But the King forbade it 'because the young people had just been married and must settle down'. Yet quite unexpectedly the Duchess travelled abroad with her husband later that year. The christening of the infant son of King Alexander of Yugoslavia was to be held on 21 October and on the next day Alexander's cousin, Prince Paul, was to marry Princess Olga of Greece. Lord Curzon, the Foreign Secretary, asked that the Duke and Duchess should accept an invitation to be the godparents. Moreover, at both events they would represent King George and Queen Mary.

The Yorks were relaxing on holiday at Holwick Hall, an estate owned by the Strathmores in County Durham, when King George telegraphed his son asking him to accept the assignment despite the brief notice. The Duke and Duchess were annoyed, Prince Albert indignantly replying to Wing Commander Louis Greig, his secretary and comptroller: 'Curzon should be drowned.... He must know things are different now.' His consort had less than three weeks to prepare her wardrobe. On the other hand, it was an introduction to her future duties.

King Alexander now reigned over the new kingdom of the Serbs, Croats and the Slovenes and his wife, a great grandchild of Queen Victoria, was the daughter of Queen Marie of Rumania, who tirelessly sought to underpin the shaky foundations of the Balkan monarchies. Hence the desire to strengthen the link with the British throne. All too vivid was the memory of another King Alexander and his consort, Queen Draga, who had been callously murdered in the royal palace at Belgrade in 1903. Fate would be equally cruel ten years later to the two principals in the October ceremonies. Nazi aggression would compel the godson of the Duchess of York to quit his throne, and the bridegroom, seeking to protect his country, would invoke widespread condemnation.

But there was only happiness at those ceremonies in 1923. The Duke, who received the traditional gift of hand-embroidered underwear from the infant's parents, was temporarily reunited with relatives, participating with his wife in what was also a royal house-warming; for the Serbian Royal Family had moved into a new palace on the site of the old one wrecked by Austrian guns in the First World War. There were still discomforts. To King George V, the Duke wrote: 'We were quite a large family party and how we all lived in the palace is a mystery. We were not too comfortable and there was no hot water!'

For the Duchess it was not only her initiation into the pageantry of a European court, but also her first encounter with the complex family ramifications opened up to her through marriage. Inevitably she was the object of critical gaze, but the Duke reported proudly to his parents: 'They were all enchanted with Elizabeth, especially Cousin Missy [Queen Marie of Rumania]. She was wonderful with all of them and they were all strangers except two, Paul and Olga.'

Domestic snags also awaited the Duke and Duchess on their return to White Lodge. Contractors had been engaged to modernize the antiquated plumbing and install a new boiler, but the Yorks had not reckoned on sluggish workmanship.

Not until the following April would the alterations be completed. In the meantime, to escape from the chills of Richmond Park, the Duke rented The Old House at Guilsborough in Northamptonshire. It was convenient for the Duke's hunting with the Pytchley and Whaddon Chase, but the strain of journeying to London and other parts of Britain was heightened. They were grateful, therefore, when in 1924 Princess Mary lent them Chesterfield House, the Lascelles' home in London, for the season. Because of the inconvenience of White Lodge, this would be the pattern of their lives for some years. The Duke and Duchess leased Curzon House for a while, then 40 Grosvenor Square, before arriving at 17 Bruton Street, the Strathmores' London house.

The Duchess's increasing popularity had bred a gruelling programme of official duties. Moreover, she had suffered from bronchitis during the first year of marriage. Therefore during the subsequent winter the King readily consented to the Yorks spending a holiday abroad. Many women might have chosen the fashionable resorts of Europe, but the Duchess's undauntable spirit preferred the challenge of the African bush. So far the Duchess's foreign travels had been restricted to Yugoslavia, Italy and France. Months of open air life, flavoured with adventure, were to be a new experience.

On 1 December 1924 the young couple left London for Kenya, Uganda and the Sudan. Three weeks later they disembarked in Mombasa. A tremendous crowd of Europeans, Africans, Arabs, Somalis and Indians roared their greeting, and the welcome was devoted to ritual and rhythm: a great dance festival, or *ngoma*, held in their honour, where five thousand men and women – symbolic of the various tribes – danced to the wild unforgettable rhythm from drum and conchshell. Towering over all were the Kikuyu stilt-walkers, adorned with gilt crowns which gleamed with gold candles.

That same night the couple set off by special train for Nairobi. On the journey, some sixty miles to the south, Mount Kilimanjaro raised its snow-capped grandeur, and as the train passed through the Athi Plains and the Game Reserve, the Duke and Duchess sat on a seat at the front of the engine for a closer glimpse of fleeing zebra and ostrich, baboons and wildebeeste. Wrote the Duke: 'A distance of 325 miles through absolutely wild country; untouched as yet by man through lack of surface water ... we saw different animals ... quite near the line. Nearer Nairobi ... the animals roam about just outside the town.'

The royal travellers spent Christmas at Government House as the guests of Sir Robert Coryndon, the Governor of Kenya. What a contrast to the Christmases spent at St Paul's Walden or Glamis.

Vastly different to anything they had experienced before would be their first safari. But first they motored to Embu, into untamed country, where in place of the dry weather that the party had anticipated the heavens opened; five inches of rain poured down in half an hour. The chiefs and their tribes awaited them in the garish grandeur of warpaint and feathers. The Yorks and their companions slept that night in a group of small huts. Early the next morning they drove in lashing rain through the forests of Meru. The cars had to ford swollen rivers and one was so waterlogged that it had to be abandoned, leaving seven people to squeeze themselves into a small Buick.

On 9 January the safari began in earnest, the party rising shortly after 5 am. Soon afterwards they left camp in the cool freshness for the morning shoot. A safari in those days was primitive, undertaken mostly on foot or occasionally on mule-back, and as well as the intense heat there was the torment of the tsetse flies. The royal couple ate in the open at a card table and slept in tents. It was tiring but the natural riches made up for the exhaustion: brightly coloured birds and a profusion of butterflies were always present to excite interest. In their curiosity ostriches often came near the camp and after sunset the cries of wild life would pierce the blue-black of the night.

The Duchess rose early to practise and improve her shooting. But one senses that her rifle, a ·275 Rigby, was carried more out of self-protection, for after proving her proficiency by shooting one animal from each of ten species, she forsook the rifle for the camera.

The safari was spiced with excitement. While the Duke, for instance, was hunting with a single companion, a lioness crossed their path. The Duke fired but the animal dashed into the bush. The dogs were ordered in to force her into the open but instead their barking roused two irate buffaloes. Within seconds the Duke shot twice and brought down both animals dead. Not knowing whether the lioness was alive or dead, Prince Albert and his companion probed cautiously amongst the undergrowth, but found her likewise killed.

Now and again, information concerning the activities of the Duke and Duchess trickled back to the British press, sometimes leavened with distortions. One account falsely described how the Duke was allegedly endangered by a charging rhino. This was not the case. As the Duke wrote in his diary:

> We found one oryx alone . . . and we got up to him within two hundred yards by keeping a tree between us and him. I took a rest off the tree and fired and hit him. He was facing me. He went off and we followed and I hit him three more times when he lay down. I was going to finish him off when we saw a rhino on the edge of a thick patch of bush. . . . We followed him . . . and suddenly came upon not one but two rhinos lying down . . . 8 yds away. One got up towards us and Anderson fired and killed it. . . . The other one ran away. . . . Elizabeth came out with us in the afternoon after tea to look at the rhino.

Prince Albert reassured his parents that he was never at risk, but the report now released pent-up criticism. Some people were antagonistic towards royalty engaging in the futile slaughter of wild animals. They were even more horrified because a woman – the King's daughter-in-law – had involved herself. The Duchess of York, it was argued, should not expose herself to the dangers of the African bush. The severest outcry came from the champions of Sunday

The crowning of Queen Elizabeth at King George VI's Coronation. For the King, the ceremony had its mishaps but the 'little Queen advanced with a real poetry of motion'.

King George VI and Queen Elizabeth riding in the ornate State Coach after a State Opening of Parliament. For such occasions, the Queen helped the monarch to conquer his speech impediment.

observance, who deplored the shooting of game on the Sabbath. The Duke denied the accusation of this last censure.

Leaving the safari for some days, the Duke and Duchess stayed as the guests of Lord and Lady Francis Scott at Rongai. It was there that the royal couple heard of the sudden death of their Nairobi host, Sir Robert Coryndon, and the Duke hastened to the funeral. The safari was abandoned and in mid-February the party carried on to Uganda where the Duchess tested her marksmanship shooting crocodiles, the destruction of which gave her no qualms.

Crossing Victoria Nyanza, the Duke and Duchess stopped at Zinja to see the source of the White Nile at the Ripon Falls. Next day they reached Entebbe on the north-west of the lake where natives greeted them, singing tribal songs in racing canoes. Here they remained for three days, residing at Government House and visiting Kampala, the native capital, to meet the Kabaka of Buganda and receive gifts of ivory and skins.

Next the royal party motored to Fort Portal, lying beneath the Mountains of the Moon. At a *lukiko*, or native parliament, presents and addresses were exchanged, then after a night's rest they set out on a forty-mile trek into the Semliki Valley where King Solomon is reputed to have collected apes, peacocks and ivory for the Queen of Sheba. Here they slept in peculiarly-shaped huts built by the natives from coloured clays, decorated with drawings of animals and hunting weapons.

Uganda was not at its best at that time of the year; natives were burning the tall elephant grass and the smoke shut out the sun. For the Yorks were in elephant country, and the Duke in a letter to King George described his first kill. After calling at Butiaba on Lake Albert, they went on to the next camp for elephant. Because the animals had gone inland, they journeyed in the paddle-steamer *Samuel Baker* down the White Nile, calling at Katengeri after three hours' steaming. There they made camp and in the afternoon 'I went off with Salmon the game ranger and in the evening I shot a very good elephant whose tusks weighed ninety pounds each. It was very lucky as there are not very many big ones left. I got a smaller one two days later.' It was so hot on the steamer that the party slept on deck and all the time there was the scourge of the ubiquitous mosquitoes.

On 5 March they disembarked at Nimule – rapids making the Nile unnavigable at this point – then motored ninety miles to Rejaf. The more luxurious *Nasir* was their home for the five-week passage down the upper Nile. Sometimes they camped ashore for several days in search of good sport and photography. The Duchess would never forget the last of those landings. On the final night her tent collapsed twice under the violence of torrential rain, and she and her belongings were thoroughly soaked.

Unforgettable, too, was the tribal gathering of the Nubas at Talodi. Disembarking at Tonga, the Duke and Duchess motored into the Nuba mountains to witness the march past of twelve thousand Nuban warriors. Highlighting these annual festivities were the spear-throwing and the trials of strength and skill in wrestling.

On 7 April they sighted Khartoum, with its formal triumphal arches and nocturnal illuminations. Two days later they began the voyage home, climbing the gangway of the liner *Maloja* at Port Sudan. But there was still one last adventure: from the banks of the Suez Canal swirled a blinding sandstorm, delaying the ship for twelve hours.

Of the Duchess, an aide would write: 'On several occasions the Duchess, after spending some weeks in camp, wearing the usual safari clothes and living entirely out of doors, had to return to complete and formal civilization – a great change, but one which did not in the least worry her, as she would appear in a quarter of an hour looking as though she had never been motoring miles ... over roads which in England would be considered impassable, or creeping through bush and wading waist-high in a swamp.'

6

A Complementary Loyal Partnership

As historians would be able to evaluate years hence, November 1925 was a significant month. The frail and aged Queen Alexandra sustained a heart attack from which she died. On the nineteenth the Prince of Wales and the Duke of York received a message hastily summoning them to her bedside at Sandringham. David was then in Cardiff and Bertie in Leicestershire. Together these future kings travelled by train to Norfolk the following day – mostly in mist which delayed them – and they were deprived of the chance to bid their grandmother goodbye. She lay dead. The fragile link with the age of Victoria had finally snapped. A new age – as well as a new phase in the life of the Duchess of York – would dawn. In the same month, the nation was told that she was to become a mother in the spring. As the weeks passed, a nursery was prepared at 17 Bruton Street and Clara Knight, who had served the Duchess as nurse, was advised that her services would be needed again.

April 1926 was a cold and wet month – in keeping, it seemed, with the dismal social effects of a national slump. For a while, however, the people could fix their minds on the Strathmores' Mayfair home to which Sir William Joynson-Hicks, the Home Secretary in Baldwin's second government, was summoned. His presence was imperative, an antiquated ritual harking back to the bitter wrangling at the time Mary of Modena, consort of the maligned Roman Catholic James II and believed to be incapable of childbearing, had in July 1688 borne a son. Shocked at the prospect of yet another Papist on the throne, the Protestant Whigs had falsely denounced the offspring as some low-born foundling smuggled into the Queen's bedchamber in a warming-pan.

Even to the most bigoted the 'plot' was barely credible. Yet from it emerged the practice – a quaint anachronism by the twentieth century – for someone responsible to Parliament to guarantee the legitimate claims of anyone eligible for the throne. Thus, in an hour-long vigil, Sir William safeguarded the realm from Jacobite or other nefarious intrigue and announced: 'Her Royal Highness the Duchess of York was safely delivered of a Princess at 2.40 am this morning, Wednesday, April 21st.'

At Windsor Castle, King George and Queen Mary were awakened and given the news. 'Such a relief and joy', entered the Queen in her diary. Had she been

This photograph was chosen by Court photographer Cecil Beaton as his favourite because it captured the Queen's 'light and fairy-book charm' which has won the hearts of millions.

endowed with great percipience she could have recorded more. One of the guests at Windsor that day was Princess Alice of Greece. Twenty-one years hence Philip her son, then aged almost five, would wed the baby girl who was merely some hours old.

To his brother, the Prince of Wales, then recuperating in Biarritz, the Duke sent a telegram happily announcing the birth. When Uncle David's niece was ten years old, he would be the principal in a constitutional crisis. For him the outcome would be lifelong exile; for her parents, an unwanted throne.

Even then there was crisis enough, but of a different character. Industrial strife was imminent and troops were encamped in Hyde Park to cope with an emergency. On 3 May the country was thrown into chaos by a General Strike. For ten days an enfeebled nation was convulsed and then virtually paralysed by the impact. And when the Trades Union Congress capitulated, the miners with traditional stubbornness refused to surrender; sullen and embittered, not until November did they admit defeat. The situation had been explosive, but King George would write: 'Not a shot has been fired and no one killed; it shows what a wonderful people we are.'

The sovereign had been discomfited by the growth of social unrest for some years. On 14 November 1918 the Labour Party, having withdrawn from the Coalition Government, had launched its General Election campaign at the Albert Hall. An almost hysterical outburst had greeted the words of Mr Bob Williams, secretary of the Transport Workers' Union, who cried: 'I hope to see the Red Flag flying from Buckingham Palace,' warning that unless workers' grievances were redressed by constitutional process organized labour would resort to other means.

Nine days later, while reviewing ex-Servicemen in Hyde Park, the King was almost dragged from his horse by the milling mob, who, though loyal to the Crown, were bent on laying their grievances before him. 'Those men were in a funny temper,' remarked the shocked monarch to his eldest son, on later dismounting at Buckingham Palace.

The emergence of Socialism as a third great faction was giving a new dimension to the British political scene. The power that for centuries had been the prerogative of the aristocracy and the well-to-do was slowly but relentlessly being grasped by the working-class millions and their leaders. The situation stirred profound fears and uneasiness at court. Memories of the post-war revolution in which ancient dynasties had perished were too fresh in the mind for complacency. Lord Esher, writing to Lord Stanfordham, the King's private secretary, had stated: 'Some risks will have to be run. The Monarchy and its cost will have to be justified in the future in the eyes of a war-worn and hungry proletariat, endowed with a high preponderance of voting power.' The King and Queen, he claimed, would have to take risks. The strength of Republicanism lay in the personality of Woodrow Wilson, President of the United States.

King George had received with alarm the news of the fall of Baldwin's Conservative Government. With some trepidation he had invited Ramsay MacDonald to form Britain's first Labour administration. Recording the sole authentic account of his father's initial encounter with his Labour ministers, the Duke of York revealed that the King had been horrified by a report that his new Prime Minister had presided over a public meeting at the Albert Hall at which the Bolshevik anthem, the *Internationale*, had been sung.

Fixing MacDonald with a cold eye to show his disapproval, the King asked if the newspaper accounts were true. The Prime Minister admitted with some embarrassment that the song had indeed been sung that evening. '"But that is a dreadful thing to do," said the King. Ramsay MacDonald agreed but added, to my father's consternation, that his followers would in fact have sung it again in the House of Commons in jubilation over the defeat of the Conservatives but for his restraining influence over his militant colleagues. "Good Lord," exclaimed the King, "they will sing it outside the Palace next."'

Fortunately the King had earlier shown wisdom. He had insisted that his family should involve itself in the lives of his subjects, encouraging his sons and daughter to serve as his ambassadors. On the domestic scene a key factor – which would have long-term beneficial results – had been his appointment of Prince Albert to associate himself with industrial affairs. The Rev. Robert Hyde, architect of the Industrial Welfare Society, which was designed to promote human relations in industry, had rightly pointed out that, although Britain was at that time the world's most industrialized power, visits by royalty to industrial plants were rare. Albert, on identifying himself with Hyde's plans, remarked with typical frankness: 'I will do it, but I don't wany any of that damned red carpet.' He immersed himself in industrial causes and after his marriage recruited a stalwart ally in his wife. Together they toured the depressed areas and were genuinely distressed by the social chasm which divided rich from poor. The Duke even financed his own annual camps which provided a rendezvous for boys from public schools and the slums.

Rather than being weakened by industrial upheaval and political change – conditions in which the monarchy might easily have foundered – the mingling of the Yorks with the factory workers, in an atmosphere stripped of ceremony, created a rapport between royalty and people. It is not hyperbole to suggest that from the seeds of goodwill sewn by the Yorks, and their insistence on the human factor in those precarious and impoverished times, they would reap a harvest of tolerance and respect when they ascended an unstable throne. Nicknamed 'The Foreman' by the Royal Family, no monarch could boast of a more sensitive appreciation of the fundamental industrial problems than King George VI.

Meanwhile, the Duke and Duchess were to leave their imprint elsewhere; they were to fulfil their first major assignment together. Mr Stanley Bruce (later

Viscount Bruce of Melbourne), the Australian Prime Minister, had asked King George if one of his sons might open the new Parliament House in Canberra on 9 May 1927.

History was being repeated. On behalf of his father Edward VII, as Duke of Cornwall and York, King George had opened the first session of the new dominion's Parliament in Melbourne. Many might have selected as his representative for this latest ceremony – a climax in Australian history – the Prince of Wales. At a foundation-stone ceremony in Canberra in 1920, Australians had succumbed ecstatically to the Prince's magnetic charm. In such circumstances, the King hesitated in choosing Prince Albert as his deputy on a tour which would embrace New Zealand. Was he equal to a mission of such imperial importance? It has been claimed that official circles in the Antipodes expected that the reception accorded to the Yorks (who lacked the glamour of the heir apparent) would be polite but somewhat lukewarm. Mr Bruce himself had misgivings, having been appalled by the Duke's impediment at the Imperial Conference in 1926.

In spite of his undoubted courage, even Prince Albert, now thirty, had his doubts too. Specialists had failed lamentably to rid him of his agonizing stammer, attributing the cause to a nervous mental state. It had plagued him since childhood as, for instance, during his first term at the Naval College at Dartmouth. Unaware of Bertie's disability, a teacher had asked him in class: 'What is the half of a half?' The Prince strove to say 'quarter' but the word would not emerge. He sat down humiliated by the sniggers of his class-mates. Such instances had bred a nervousness in public and his inarticulation by now was psychological. Further therapy, he considered, was totally useless and he had resigned himself to the idea that his vocal affliction was 'the curse that God has put upon me'.

It was the Duchess of York who 'exorcized' the demon that tormented him. She induced him to make 'just one more try', persuading him to meet Mr Lionel Logue, an Australian speech specialist, who had founded a practice in London's Harley Street. Logue's career was itself phenomenal. His training had never been in medicine but as an engineer. He had originally been made aware of his talent for correcting speech difficulty in the First World War. Logue developed a technique of diaphragm breathing and had effected many cures among handicapped children in his native country.

The Duchess's persuasion would enrich her husband's life. Two days before she gave birth to her first daughter, the Duke had his first consultation with Logue. 'He entered my consulting room at three o'clock in the afternoon,' Mr Logue later recorded, 'a slim, quiet man with tired eyes and all the outward symptoms upon whom habitual speech defect had begun to set the sign. When he left at five o'clock, you could see that there was hope once more in his heart.' Logue listened patiently to the Duke, who wearily explained that he could not easily pronounce his Gs, Ns, Ks and Qs. It was so difficult to articulate the words 'King'

The domesticity created by Queen Elizabeth brought for the King 'much for which he had long craved in deprivation – love, understanding, sympathy, support'.

and 'Queen' that he referred to 'my parents' or 'Their Majesties'. Logue also noted that the Duke was suffering from melancholia. 'There is only one person who can cure you,' stressed Logue, 'and that is yourself. I can tell you what to do but only you can do it.'

Logue's technique was based on correct breathing, if necessary developing the patient's lungs by physical exercises. One of the Duke's problems was a lack of coordination between his brain and his diaphragm. The months ahead would tax Prince Albert's determination and stamina, but always there was the devoted encouragement of his wife. She ensured that he attended the daily hour-long meetings with Logue – often accompanying him herself – and worked with him on his speeches, providing alternatives to awkward words. After a mere month's treatment, the Duke wrote hopefully to King George: 'I wish I could have found him [Logue] before, as now that I know the right way to breathe my fear of talking will vanish.' On the eve of the royal tour, the Duke wrote in gratitude to Logue: 'I am full of confidence for this trip now.'

The Yorks left Portsmouth for New Zealand in the battle cruiser *Renown* on 6 January 1927, taking the route via Jamaica and the Panama Canal. Basking in the sun, the Duchess continued to help the Duke with his therapy until they reached New Zealand on 22 February, the ship steaming into Auckland harbour in a terrific rainstorm. The reception was fantastic – not lukewarm. Nor was the tour a 'pleasure trip' at a time of industrial depression, as described by certain Socialists – to the King's annoyance – in the House of Commons five days earlier. A noted Communist agitator had echoed similar sentiments until, meeting Joseph Coates, the New Zealand Premier, he exclaimed: 'I have done with this bloody Communism', giving the royal couple as the reason for this sudden conversion. 'Why, they're human!' he said. 'Yesterday I was in the crowd with the wife, and one of the children waved his hand, and I am blessed if the Duchess didn't wave back and smile right into my face, not two yards away. I'll never say a word against them again. I have done with it for good and all.'

The radiant personality of the Duchess of York was a cardinal factor in the tour's success, for as one newspaper commented: 'She smiled her way straight into the hearts of the people.' One young Scotsman wrote: 'She shines and warms like sunlight. I never used to believe the stories one reads about people swearing themselves "ready to die" for Mary, Queen of Scots, or Maria Theresa. But if they were anything like the Duchess of York I can easily understand it.'

Unfortunately the strain of the tour of the North Island left its mark. On reaching the South Island, the Duchess became ill with tonsilitis. Outside her hotel the police reduced the traffic noise to a minimum and erected notices requesting motorists to proceed quietly and sound no horns. On medical advice she returned to Wellington to convalesce at Government House, then rejoined the Duke at Invercargill in the south, and on 22 March *Renown* sped through vicious seas en route for Sydney.

You can imagine the arrival of the *Renown* in Sydney Harbour on a perfect autumn morning – brilliant sunshine and just enough breeze to blow the flags out, [reported Lord Stonehaven, the Governor-General, to Lord Stanfordham]. She dropped her anchor under the windows of Admiralty House in Neutral Bay to the minute.... The harbour was filled with craft of all sorts, which however entirely respected the request not to hoot or whistle or make a noise until the anchor was down. The silence added immensely to the impressiveness of the arrival. Once the *Renown* was at anchor the air was made hideous for several minutes by all manner of welcoming shrieks and noises – that was of course inevitable.

This cordial though raucous reception was the keynote of the tour for the next two months. The Duke and Duchess were also profoundly touched by the enthusiasm displayed for their daughter, Princess Elizabeth. At Port Adelaide the Duchess was clearly moved when two little girls scurried from the crowd to the royal dais and handed her two threepenny bits. 'These are for baby Betty's money box,' she was told before the little donors were escorted away. At Melbourne the royal parents witnessed a naval gun salute in honour of their daughter's first birthday. 'It is extraordinary,' wrote the Duke to Queen Mary, 'her arrival is popular out here. Wherever we go, cheers for her are given as well, and the children write to us about her.'

The tour culminated in the opening of the new Federal Parliament House in Canberra. The old Canberra, a meagre township that had grown in the 1840s, had given no signs of ever blossoming into civic greatness, yet curiously an inscription of 1845 on a tombstone in the burial ground of the Church of St John the Baptist would uncannily express that aspiration: 'For here we have no continuing city, but seek one to come.' That simply-worded hope had been fulfilled.

On 9 May 1927, a warm and cloudless day, the Duke opened the new Parliament House with a gold key, then read the King's Speech inside the overcrowded Senate. Silently the Duchess witnessed the results of her efforts to help the Duke. Lady Strathmore had wisely prophesied that he would be made or marred by his choice of wife. Prince Albert could now write to King George: 'I was not very nervous when I made the speech, because the one I made outside went off without a hitch, and I did not hesitate once. I was so relieved as making speeches still rather frightens me, for Logue's teaching has really done wonders for me as I now know how to prevent and get over any difficulty. I have so much more confidence in myself now, which I am sure comes from being able to speak properly at last.'

There was still Perth to visit before the Yorks completed their mission. The voyage across the Great Australian Bight to Fremantle was one which displayed the Duchess's courage. The *Renown* wallowed in a frightening gale that screamed northwards from the Antarctic wastes.

Much damage was caused to picket-boats and cutters [wrote an observer], seats on the deck were smashed to matchwood, furniture was flung about cabins, and mess-decks were flooded. A massive ladder fetched away and crashed on the deck outside the royal apartments.... Though speed was reduced ... she groaned and shivered from stem to stern as, hit by mountainous green walls of water and despite her thirty-two thousand tons, she tossed about almost like a cork ... all the dead lights were down, so that inside the ship one lived by artificial light and in an atmosphere of which the description foetid is hopelessly inadequate.

A number of minor casualties were caused among the members of the ship's company by falls owing to the violent lurching of the ship, and one seaman sustained a fractured rib. Despite the vessel's liveliness the Duke and Duchess were quite unaffected by sea-sickness, and during the wild time the Duchess made several trips up to the bridge with Captain Sullivan, to watch waves breaking their fury on the fo'c'sle and the watery sun forming countless rainbows in the foam.

Less than a fortnight later the Duke and Duchess had embarked on the long voyage home. They had achieved conspicuous success, to which the Duchess had greatly contributed. Her charm and personality had been subtly applied in attracting public attention towards the Duke. Among the encomiums, one which crystallized public reaction was that of Sir Tom Bridges, Governor of South Australia, who informed King George: 'His Royal Highness has touched people profoundly by his youth, his simplicity and natural bearing, while the Duchess has had a tremendous ovation and leaves us with the responsibility of having a continent in love with her. The visit has done untold good.'

Three days out from Fremantle that continent was shocked by a near disaster aboard *Renown*. For the second time in her life the Duchess came to close quarters with fire. On the sweltering afternoon of 26 May an overflow of oil ignited, starting a serious blaze in the boiler-room. Everyone retreated before the gathering inferno, but not before four seamen had been gassed and burnt. Help was very remote. HMAS *Sydney* was some eight hundred miles distant, at least three days' steaming away, and the immediate danger was that the blaze might ravage the main oil supplies. In that event, *Renown* was doomed and everyone would be compelled to abandon ship. The prospect was daunting, for it meant survival for some days in open boats, some of which had been damaged in the Australian Bight.

At one point the fire-fighting party seemed to be losing the struggle. The flames crept relentlessly and plans to flood the ammunition – and even to abandon the ship – were considered. It was half-past ten that night before the crisis was passed and the Duke and Duchess were out of danger.

On Monday 27 June, after calling at Mauritius, Malta and Gibraltar, the Yorks were back in London. Punctilious to the core, for the reunion at Victoria Station the King had enjoined his son: 'We will not embrace at the station before so many people. When you kiss Mama take your hat off.' There was a further injunction to Prince Albert and his staff to wear frock-coats and epaulettes 'without medals and riband, only stars'.

The King and his family gathered round his desk at the Royal Lodge, Windsor, today one of the Queen Mother's homes.

Although thousands of miles had separated them, the Duke and Duchess realized that they could not escape the critical surveillance of the King. In a message to Prince Albert, he had even carped over the position of an equerry in photographs of the Yorks' arrival at Las Palmas. It had been the same during the East African interlude. To the Duke his father's captious attitude was at times quite tiresome. The Duchess, however, was impervious to the critical gaze, yet the King's treatment of his second son would increase her burden in the constitutional crisis of 1936. It was like an echo from the past. The father of George v – King Edward vii – fresh from his triumph, when Prince of Wales, in Canada and the United States, had been virtually rebuked for his recent acclaim. Any personal glory, the Prince Consort flatly informed his son, was merely an offshoot of the fact that he had represented the Queen.

George v's attitude to his son, Prince Albert, was in similar vein. Buoyed by newly-won confidence, the Prince wished to learn the rudiments of statecraft. With some logic, he reasoned that if he was competent enough to deputize for the King, it was not unreasonable to receive some instruction in matters of state. Lurking also in the Yorks' mind was the inexorable reminder that if the King should die, the Prince would at once be the heir apparent.

Opposition to enabling the Duke to peer into the despatch boxes came apparently not from his advisers but from the monarch himself. King George believed that audiences with ministers, and state secrets, were the prerogative of himself and no one else. It was as if the spirit of the old Queen-Empress was abroad in Buckingham Palace again. For years Queen Victoria denied her son the permission to read confidential matters of state. Succeeding as Edward vii as late as his sixtieth year, he had smarted under his mother's reluctance to inform him. Even when a sympathetic Gladstone eventually arranged to furnish him with abstracts of Cabinet meetings, she insisted that the Prime Minister's confidential reports should be seen solely by herself.

To their delight, on returning from the Antipodes the Yorks secured a permanent London home. For three years the Duke had been negotiating with the Crown Estates Office to lease No. 145 Piccadilly, a four-storey stone-faced house in a terrace of similar property. The lofty grey building with balcony and pillared door had long been silent but now life returned. Because the Yorks shunned ceremony and protocol, outwardly there was nothing to denote the presence of royalty. No one stood on duty and two bells – marked 'House' and 'Visitors' – were there for anyone to ring.

Princess Elizabeth – now called Lilibet (the word coined when she tried to pronounce her Christian name) – occupied nursery quarters on the upper floor, close to a glass dome. There, on a circular landing, were 'stabled' her many toy horses. Long lasting would be the memories of the red-carpeted floor, the rocking chair reserved solely for Alah and the glass-fronted toy cupboard which would be used years later by Lilibet's own children. The infant princess looked out on to the privacy of Hamilton Gardens and, beyond, Hyde Park.

The Duchess had inherited from Lady Strathmore her talent for home-making. Domestically she possessed the skill to create an appropriate atmosphere which enabled the Duke's inherent qualities to thrive. In fact, this was the first true home that he had ever experienced, a happy and contented haven – rid of the overshadowing presence of the sovereign and elder brother – that allowed his attributes (which were later so manifest in kingship) to burgeon.

No. 145 Piccadilly was the gentle forcing ground in which the wavering plant strengthened and flourished. At Glamis, domesticity had revolved round the Countess of Strathmore. At the Yorks' London home, it revolved round her daughter. Indeed, the drawing-room of the Duchess of York was the focal point of family life. Much existed in the various rooms to remind of felicitous or exciting moments. In the green, pillared hall hung the tusks of one of the elephants which the Duke had shot in Uganda. A bevy of exquisitely dressed dolls added to the atmosphere of home, as well as Jimmie the parrot, the gift to the Duchess from a working men's club in Western Australia, who squawked with raucous enthusiasm: 'Jimmy have a drink.' Striding the mantelpiece in the morning-room were arresting Highland figures and at intervals came the blare of an astonishing clock – the wedding present to the Yorks from the people of Glasgow. On weekdays, at four three-hourly intervals, a march past burst from this amazing timepiece. And, true to the character of the Scottish Sabbath, the clock was stubbornly silent but for the striking of the hour on Sundays. It was the sole manifestation at No. 145 of royal pomp and ritual, for, at the first tinkling notes of the music, the Duke's ancestor, George III, and his family walked sedately round a dial depicting Whitehall.

The most practical and rewarding action ever taken by the Duke of York was to allow his stubbornness to win the hand of Lady Elizabeth Bowes-Lyon. The nub of her marital success was the nurturing of the Duke's resolute personality which would capture world-wide deference when he became the King. Over the years there would a gradual change of roles. From being her husband's mainstay, the Duchess (by that time the Queen) would lean increasingly on her husband. As a close friend of the Duchess once remarked: 'That was the measure of her greatness as a woman. She drew him out and made him a man so strong that she could lean upon him.'

The domestic atmosphere of those Piccadilly days tended to be quiet rather than spectacular. In contrast to the sophisticated Prince of Wales, the Duke and Duchess shrank from the brittle glitter of life in the frenetic twenties, with the result that the smart socialite set regarded the Yorks as a rather dull pair. Flappers, with their painted fingernails and bobbed hair, dismissed the Duchess as old-fashioned and unstylish, yet the discriminating – like Cecil Beaton, the society photographer – were more observant. Pronouncing on her initial appearance in London society, he had compared her to 'some fragrance from a past age'.

Even if they had desired it, the Duke and Duchess of York could not have entertained on a lavish scale: Prince Albert's allowance would never have permitted it. As it was, the modest home-loving Yorks, outside their many public engagements, adhered to an unruffled simple existence, usually listening to the gramophone or the wireless, reading, or sometimes paying an unobtrusive visit to a nearby cinema.

The Duke's rural recreation was hunting (when the Duchess would follow the chase by car) and both would shoot and fish. In the latter the Duchess excelled, having been instructed in angling skills by the ghillies of Glamis since childhood. Sometimes she would stand for hours, thigh-deep in the waters of the Dee, fishing for salmon.

Occasionally this unassuming couple would relax at the weekend in some country estate; for instance, with Sir Philip Sassoon who still entertained on the grandiose scale at Lympne. Liveried footmen would place drinks on dressing tables as the guests prepared for dinner and the diners would be entertained by musicians of international renown. Lord Boothby has recalled how he was awakened at six o'clock one morning by the crunch of wheels on gravel; below, horses were hauling carts laden with flowering plants, and by breakfast time the gardens around the house were ablaze with colour.

The guests were distinguished – men such as Lawrence of Arabia, Winston Churchill and George Bernard Shaw. 'The Duchess,' claimed the impish Shaw, 'is almost the only member of the Royal Family not embarrassed in my presence.'

The Duke and Duchess of York did not themselves ever entertain so lavishly. Yet their desire to protect their privacy and home life did not deter them from inviting people from public or industrial life. To the library, for instance, the Duke – ever keen to disentangle and smooth out industrial frictions – would invite discussion groups, encouraging representatives of trade unions and managements to try and resolve their problems in the congenial atmosphere of his home.

Serving the nation – short of getting too close in line to the throne – was all that the Yorks desired. That, they hoped, would be the pattern of their life, certainly for some time to come. Yet, haunting spectre or not, a dramatic episode occurred which might quickly have wrecked their wish.

During November 1928, while attending the Armistice Day ceremony at the Cenotaph, King George contracted a severe chill which he unwisely neglected. Within ten days he lay critically ill with septicaemia. The Duchess of York immediately recalled her husband who had recently represented his father at the funeral in Denmark of the Dowager Empress of Russia and was now hunting in the Midlands. The Prince of Wales, then touring East Africa, was also warned of the gravity of his father's condition.

In a letter that enlarged on the King's illness, Prince Albert humorously revealed to the Prince of Wales a story (which had originated in the East End) then rampant explaining 'that the reason he was rushing home is that in view of

During the royal couple's pre-war State visit to France, vast crowds assembled for a glimpse of Britain's White Queen. One newspaper opined: 'Today France is a monarchy again.'

The King and Queen saying farewell to the Rt Hon. Raoul Dandurand, PC, Government Leader in the Senate, on leaving the Canadian Parliament premises in Ottawa during May 1939.

anything happening to Papa I am going to bag the throne in your absence!!!!
Just like the Middle Ages. . . .' Nothing could have been more alien to the minds
of the Yorks. Even when the crown was eventually thrust upon them, they would
resent it.

After a successful operation to his infected lung on 11 December, George V
was conveyed by ambulance to convalesce at Craigwell, near Bognor. The
Duchess of York helped in his recovery by sending young Lilibet – whom the King
adored – to stay with him. When he continued writing his diary, it was to 'our
sweet little grandchild' that he often referred. Not until June was the sovereign
able to resume his official duties in London.

As usual the Yorks made their annual August journey to Glamis. But it would
be the visit in the following year which would hold greater interest. The Duchess
of York was to bear a second child and she was determined that it should be
born north of the Border.

John Clynes, the Socialist Home Secretary, hurried north to confirm the birth.
Perhaps the little Clydesider was over zealous: at least his arrival was untimely.
In some consternation the Duke wrote to Queen Mary: 'I feel so sorry for Mr
Clynes having to be here for so long. I always wanted him to come up when
he was sent for, which would have been so much better.'

A disconcerting situation was averted by the initiative of the Dowager Countess
of Airlie. To the Yorks' relief she invited the Home Secretary to Cortachy Castle,
some eight miles distant. There Clynes's patience was taxed for sixteen days, but
on the stormy night of 21 August 1930, as lightning inflamed the skies, a telephone
call summoned him to Glamis. Driven by the wind, torrential rain streamed down
the castle's rugged walls. Yet nothing disturbed the calm of the Tapestry Room
when a baby girl was born. The time was 9.22. It was the first royal birth in
Scotland since Charles I embarked on a melancholic life at Dunfermline in 1600.
From a turreted window, Princess Elizabeth saw a vast beacon set ablaze high
on Hunter's Hill above Glamis to announce her sister's arrival. The little newcomer would be christened Margaret Rose, the latter name after Lady Leveson-
Gower, the Duchess of York's sister.

The Duke and Duchess had hoped to greet a son. In that case the boy would
have preceded Lilibet in line to the throne. But, son or daughter, as events
materialized one of the Yorks' offspring was destined for the throne.

Before the Duke and Duchess returned to London in October, Bertie visited
Charles Buchanan, the village postmaster and registrar at Glamis, to register the
birth. Superstitious like his consort, the Duke noticed that thirteen would be the
next number in the registration book. The Yorks therefore decided to wait until
another child was born. Actually there was already a boy called George. Some
thirty years later Mrs Gevina Brown revealed in a Sunday newspaper her surprise
at receiving a postcard from the Glamis registrar. He asked her to register her
son without waste of time. She was a trifle unhappy at registering him as number

thirteen, but realized that if she delayed the registration the Duchess would do likewise. She therefore signed the book there and then with no regrets. As she explained: 'The Duchess, as she was then, is a charming person and spoke to us often as we cut through the castle grounds on the way to church on Sundays.'

Lilibet and Margaret lived in an unpretentious and sheltered environment. Happiness was the keynote everywhere. The Duchess insisted that the upbringing of the children should be akin to that of any normal, affluent family, and drew on the experience of her own infancy. Apart from the two terms at a London school, she had been taught entirely at home. Moreover, her mother had supervised the lessons. This would be precisely the educational pattern for the two Princesses. The Duchess taught them about God, and the value of prayer, as well as the Bible tales as her mother had related them to her. The Princesses went early to bed. Pocket money was limited to instil a sense of values, and a visit to the pantomime (as well as a few selected events like the Royal Military Tournament) was an occasion to be awaited with blissful anticipation.

Sometimes Uncle David called to participate in nursery games such as Snap, Happy Families and Racing Demon. A popular pastime was the game called Winnie-the-Pooh. After the Duchess had read from the story book of that name, David and his little nieces enacted the characters in mime.

The Duke of York not only endorsed his wife's training of their children, but years later praised it when writing to his daughter Elizabeth on her honeymoon. He wrote: 'I have watched you grow up all these years with pride under the skilful direction of Mama who, as you know, is the most marvellous person in the world in my eyes.'

Prince Albert would also spare his children the sort of incidents which had scarred his own childhood. While the enforcement of discipline can be commendable, perhaps George v erred to the point of excess. The pockets, for example, on his children's sailor suits were sewn to prevent hands from entering them. And woe betide anyone who let stockings slip below the knees.

Life at the naval training college at Osborne on the Isle of Wight had not been without its traumatic moments either. Never before had he experienced the hurly-burly of so many companions and it had further contributed to his slow scholastic development. He had also acquired the derisory name of 'Batlugs' (owing to the shape of his ears) and felt the pain of pin-pricks from cadets curious to learn if he really possessed blue blood. And in spite of plaintive protests, he was kicked by other cadets who fatuously wished to brag that they had punched the son of the reigning monarch.

Starved in early years of parental affection (although curiously both the King and Queen were, in their particular way, devoted to their children), Prince Albert guaranteed that there was no such omission in the childhood of his daughters.

To give their children the true semblance of normal family life, the Yorks had to escape whenever possible from the prying eyes of public intrusion. At No. 145 Piccadilly inquisitive passengers in the upper decks of passing buses craned their necks, hoping to catch a glimpse of the royal children. And so the Duke and Duchess secured a rural retreat. The decaying Royal Lodge in Windsor Great Park – a grace-and-favour residence – had little to commend it when the Duke and Duchess inspected it in the beginning of 1931. The building was dilapidated but bore traces of former grandeur, and weeds and undergrowth spread in profusion. The repairs, alterations and decorations would take more than a year to complete and George v insisted that it should be known as *The* Royal Lodge ('There can be any number of Royal Lodges but only one known as The Royal Lodge.').

For the Duchess it recalled Lyon Jacobitism, for Thomas Sandby, secretary to the Duke of Cumberland during the 1745 campaign, had resided here when it was known as Lower Lodge. It was rechristened Royal Lodge by another occupant, the ailing George iv who (according to Greville, the diarist) never rose from his bed until six in the evening. He ate breakfast in bed, did whatever business he could be brought to transact in bed, read the newspapers, got up in time for dinner, and then went to bed between ten and eleven (ringing his 'bell forty times in the night').

The Royal Lodge enabled the Duchess to indulge her passion for gardening, a trait also common to Lady Strathmore and Mrs Scott, the Duchess's grandmother. The Duchess's enthusiasm infected the Duke who actually became an expert in landscape gardening and an authority on rhododendrons. 'Now that Bertie has taken up gardening,' the Duchess informed a friend, 'it is almost as if he had invented it himself.' The Duke was a 'dirt gardener' like the Prince of Wales who now resided not far away at Fort Belvedere.

But 1931 was the wrong time to restore the Royal Lodge to a habitable state. A financial crisis wracked Britain. October 1929 was noteworthy for the alarming New York Stock Market crash, and by now Europe was on the brink of financial collapse. Britain ultimately abandoned the gold standard and the country sagged under the oppressive social strain of 2,750,000 unemployed. It was the time of the hunger marches and the means test.

King George v asked the government to reduce his Civil list by £50,000 while the emergency continued, and the Queen and other members of the Royal Family in receipt of parliamentary grants also accepted cuts. That included the Duke and Duchess of York whose expenses increased despite a depleted income. As a further economy, the Duke gave up hunting and sold his six horses.

The Duke and Duchess embarked on tours of the most stricken areas to witness for themselves the social malaise gnawing at the vitals of whole communities. In South Wales they were shocked by the despair on the faces of the men in the dole queues; to see Welsh children singing to try to keep warm; and appalled by the hopelessness of wives and mothers striving to adequately feed their families.

During the pre-war North American tour, Their Majesties also visited the United States. In Washington the Queen was accompanied by Mrs Eleanor Roosevelt, wife of the President.

The Duchess's sentiments concerning the people's plight influenced her husband's report to the King and his Ministers.

In those early thirties, the Duke and Duchess of York might have imagined that their domestic world was inviolate. Even if King George v were to die, they could not visualize any pronounced change. For should his successor remain unwed, in age he was merely eighteen months the Duke's senior, and there was nothing to indicate that David would not enjoy longevity. Anyone who thought along those lines overlooked an important point: David's temperament.

When, as Lady Elizabeth Bowes-Lyon, the Duchess of York had hesitated to marry Prince Albert, David is reputed to have told her: 'You had better take him and go on in the end to Buck House.' The remark had a curious ring. As yet he had never met Mrs Wallis Simpson. Did he therefore doubt, even at that time, his suitability for kingship? Later, as Duke of Windsor, he would firmly deny that he ever wished to quit the throne. Yet had he experienced some pre-monition that, in certain circumstances, abdication might be preferable?

If the words attributed to the Prince are true, it is ironical that, having induced Lady Elizabeth to enter the Royal House – dedicating herself to the public service from which she by nature shrank – he himself forsook the royal duties he had been trained to do from birth. She had told her future husband that she feared she would never again be 'free to think or speak or act as I really feel I ought to think or speak or act'. Indeed, after her marriage the Duchess devoted herself to the nation without question, accepting all the drawbacks without rebellion, and informing her children: 'Your work is the rent you pay for the room you occupy on earth.'

She has never publicly disclosed her reaction to the Prince of Wales's way of life which King George v detested. One can only assume. Both King and daughter-in-law shared a common attitude to royal service: honesty, dignity and sincerity. Bertie, too, was set in his father's mould and as the Prince of Wales commented, both father and brother 'tended to be withdrawn from the hurly-burly of life that I relished'. David's social world was definitely not that of the Duchess of York, and when the throne was imperilled she quickly revealed where her loyalties lay. Maybe David would be surprised by her constancy during and after the Second World War.

The débris after a Nazi air raid on Buckingham Palace. The attack roused anger in North America and assured United States' aid.

7

Anxieties in the Thirties

Almost half a century later, it seems incredible that two vital secrets could be withheld from the British public for so long. These were the deterioration of King George v's health and the love affair between the heir, the Prince of Wales, and Mrs Wallis Simpson. For specific reasons, the Duchess of York would be anxious about both. Indeed, after the lapse of years, it is astonishing how a casual introduction re-shaped British history and revolutionized the life of the Yorks.

The Prince of Wales had exhibited a bias for liaisons with married women. There had been Mrs Dudley Ward, for instance. Between them they had modernized that royal folly Fort Belvedere, a castellated, beautiful house standing high on its hill near Virginia Water. Here the Prince retreated at weekends. Ironically, the Lilliputian fortress, with its battlements and multiplicity of cannon, had been enlarged by Wyatville for George iv, that other headstrong prince who through romance almost wrecked the throne.

But it was neither Mrs Ward nor Lady Furness, with whom the Prince was also intimately involved, who would agitate the peaceful backwater of the Duke and Duchess of York. That person would be an American – Mrs Wallis Simpson, whom Lady Furness, to her ultimate regret, introduced to the Prince at a house party at Melton Mowbray.

Recording this incident which eventually had international repercussions, Lady Furness wrote:

I went over to Wallis, took her to the Prince, and introduced her. This meeting has been the subject of an enormous amount of fiction. It has been written, for example, that the Prince ... asked her if, in England, she did not miss the comforts of central heating, and that she had answered, 'I'm sorry, sir, but you have disappointed me. Every American woman who comes to your country is always asked the same question. I had expected something more original from the Prince of Wales.'

Like so many remarks attributed to the Royal Family, this one is categorized as apocryphal. The claim, moreover, that the Prince was quickly conscious of his destiny with Mrs Simpson – thus placing the Yorks on the inescapable path to the throne – is quite ridiculous. For three and a half years, from either the latter part of 1930 or early in 1931, it is said that the Prince and Mrs Simpson arranged a rendezvous about once weekly. Only from then onwards does it look as though the Prince preferred his friend to the crown. This does not mean that the Royal Family, and perhaps more so the royal ladies, was entirely unalarmed by possible future prospects. As evidence proved later, the Royal House never accepted the association as a fairy tale romance but, in the later stages, considered it a threat to the stability of the thousand-year-old monarchy.

Because of her profound sense of duty and tradition no one could have been more incensed – not merely because she was personally involved – than the Duchess of York. No single person ever changed the Duchess's life more drastically than Mrs Simpson whom, during those 1930s, English society labelled a Baltimore landlady's daughter, an attitude which goaded Mrs Simpson's Aunt Bessie Merryman to observe indignantly: 'You'd think that we'd all come right out of *Tobacco Road*.' Some years later Mrs Simpson – then the Duchess of Windsor – would comment in typical vein on 'the wild canards being circulated that my family had come from the wrong side of the tracks in Baltimore, that my mother had run a boarding-house.'

But it does not appear to have been quite like that, as American genealogists were prepared to affirm. Indeed, if it really existed, the so-called stigma of dubious origin seems to have been completely baseless. To what extent she seriously aspired to attain the status of king's consort, it is hard to assess. There seems to be little doubt, however, that she was ready to accept it. Today one can appreciate that this willingness, combined with a monarch's intractable refusal to reign without the wife of his choice, made inevitable the Duchess of York's future role as consort. As events have confirmed, there was little if anything in the eleven-month reign of Edward VIII to augur years of inspiration from the throne, yet there is much to testify that George VI, with the immeasurable cooperation of his Queen, was the ideal sovereign for his times. To that extent (and because of her influence on the life of the Duchess of York), Mrs Simpson affected the course of the British monarchy and for that reason alone is owed her place in history.

Bessie Wallis Warfield was born on 19 June 1896, four years before the Duchess of York, at Monterey in Maryland. Her parental background linked two American families, both of whom could delve into an ancestry dating from the earliest days of colonialism. Her mother, Alice, was a Montague of Virginia, who married a Southerner, Teackle Wallis Warfield of Maryland. In Baltimore the Warfields attained distinction in banking, commerce and as public servants; the Montagues have been described as being much more worldly. Later in life Wallis Warfield would write: 'If the Montagues were innately French in character and the Warfields British, then I was a new continent for which they contended. All my life, it seems, that battle has raged back and forth within my psyche. Even as a child, when I misbehaved, my mother taught me to believe it was the Montague revelry asserting itself; when I was good, she gratefully attributed the improvement to the sober Warfield influence.'

Some months after Bessie Warfield was born, her father died, leaving her mother virtually penniless. Fortunately there were affluent relatives to rely upon. Foremost was the unmarried Uncle Solomon Davies Warfield, President of the Seaboard Air Line Railway, her late father's brother. Bessie and her mother lived for some years with her paternal grandmother and Uncle Sol, who was 'the nearest thing to a father in my uncertain world, but an odd kind of father – reserved, unbending, silent.... It was my fate to be obliged to turn again and again to him, usually at some new point of crisis for me....'

Friction between mother and grandmother led to a change of address. Now living in a modest hotel, for the first time the child became sharply conscious of her mother's unhappiness, an experience which was somewhat relieved when Aunt Bessie Merryman, who would in due time play a minor part in a king's romance, invited them to share her home.

Bessie Warfield was six or seven years old when her mother sought independence by taking an apartment in Preston Street. This was undoubtedly the origin of the rumours that Mrs Warfield was the landlady of the Preston Apartment House. Years later Bessie Warfield, then the Duchess of Windsor, described how her mother, a skilful cook, created what was akin to a dining club, inviting fellow tenants as paying guests to dinner. Unfortunately her culinary zeal outstripped her sense of business: '... the simple dinners grew into banquets – terrapin, squab, prime sirloin steaks and soft-shell crabs, fresh strawberries, elaborate pastries.'

Again the benevolent Aunt Bessie assumed her protective role, settling the tradesmen's accounts and disbanding the club, and Uncle Sol continued to fulfil what he regarded as his obligation to his brother's child. From a co-educational day school she graduated to Arundell, the second most fashionable girls' school in Baltimore. Now in her teens, Wallis, gay and endowed with charm, quickly learnt that she was like a magnet to the opposite sex.

Her social progress, however, seems to have been temporarily marred by her mother's behaviour; in her penury, she had taken a lover – John Freeman Rasin, a member of a Baltimore family noted for its wealth and prominence on the political scene. He and Wallis's mother would eventually legalize their union but meanwhile the affair provoked the wrath of Mrs Mactier Warfield and Uncle Sol, who tried to transfer Wallis from the maternal influence to his own household. It is worth pondering the subsequent outcome if this proposal had succeeded. Wallis's career would never have taken its now well-known course, thus obviating her influence on the life of the Duchess of York. But Wallis remained determinedly staunch to her mother and a sequence of events ensued which finally enmeshed the Royal Family.

Lady Elizabeth Bowes-Lyon was still enjoying the domestic pleasures of St Paul's Walden and Glamis when Wallis Warfield was entered as a pupil of Oldfields, an establishment resembling an English finishing school. A fellow student,

Their Majesties raised morale in wartime Britain. 'Many an aching heart found some solace in her gracious smile,' commented Churchill of the Queen.

The King and Queen and the Princesses with Sir Winston Churchill. The wartime Premier, who shared with the Queen an interest in art, later counselled her in early widowhood.

Mary Kirk, would figure twenty years later in what would variously be described as a king's romance or a royal scandal.

Oldfields apparently did not nurture thoughts of a professional career but dwelt on marriage. In her memoirs as the Duchess of Windsor, Wallis Warfield would explain that not only was marriage 'the only thing we had to look forward to, but the condition of marriage had been made to seem to us the only state desirable for a woman – and the sooner the better. The fact that few, if any, of us were in love or were even recipients of concentrated masculine attention had nothing to do with the case. It was marriage itself, conceived in the most poetic and romantic terms, that we aspired to.'

In her first marital venture, the 'poetic and romantic terms' would begin a chain reaction of circumstances which would affect others in Britain who were then unaware even of her existence. First Uncle Sol launched her successfully into the social world which would be her metier throughout life, then in 1916 gave her away in marriage to Earl Winfield Spencer Jr, at that time a junior officer in the air arm of the United States Navy. Maybe in reaction to her mother's poverty-haunted widowhood, Wallis had frankly declared that her primary marital consideration would be wealth. But Winfield Spencer could not boast of riches, nor indeed did his career promise the rewards which would guarantee the standards to which she aspired.

Whatever connubial bliss prevailed initially, it gradually disintegrated under the strain of incompatible temperaments. Winfield Spencer, described as an alcoholic, jealously resented the 'gay and flirtatious' behaviour of his wife who, in her own words, 'was brought up to believe that one should be as entertaining as one can at a party.... My gaiety, and even more the response of others to it, made Win jealous.' In retaliation Winfield Spencer is said to have locked his spouse in a room for hours, curious antics which, together with an obvious clash of temperaments, would reverberate eventually about the Duke and Duchess of York. For if the marriage of Winfield and Wallis Spencer had stayed intact, a king might never have cast aside his crown nor would the perturbed Yorks have been thrust onto a rickety throne.

To the consternation of her mother and Aunt Bessie, Wallis decided to end her marriage, a decision that roused the indignation of Uncle Sol; he accused his niece of threatening to bring disgrace to both Warfields and Montagues. The Warfields, he argued, 'in all their known connections since 1662 have never had a divorce.' Unlike her uncle, Wallis did not concern herself with what the people of Baltimore might think.

Spencer and his wife then resided in Washington but when he was transferred to the Far East, Wallis remained behind. It was the neurotic era of the 1920s, when a lonely woman might find herself exposed to risks, especially on sofas and rumble seats. Her code was never to 'drift into light affairs', but the price, she claimed, were evenings alone. Yet it is clear that she did not shun her natural

Like his father, King George V, before him, George VI bestowed the Order of the Garter upon his consort. They attended the Order's 600th anniversary ceremony together.

King George VI and Queen Elizabeth at the thanksgiving service in St Paul's Cathedral during their Silver Wedding celebrations. It was symbolic that they jointly broadcast to the nation.

habitat – society. And in the diplomatic service there was also a surplus of attractive men.

Her heart was 'stirred' by one such person at a Latin-American embassy, for she later revealed: 'For a time he was only a gay escort.... Then he came to mean much more. Perhaps without realizing it he acted both as teacher and model in the art of living. He took me out of the world of small talk and into wider world affairs and diplomacy. This may well have been what was worrying my mother ... I must go through with my divorce or return to Win.'

The upshot was to accompany her cousin, Corinne Mostin, a naval officer's widow, to Paris, where they were soon caught up in the social eddies. Meanwhile, she read her husband's pleas and on returning to America in the liner *France*, travelled to China in July 1924 to rejoin him. Regrettably the marriage collapsed once more and, in retrospect, the next of the episodes that reached their climax in the Abdication and the enthronement of the Yorks began.

Wallis Spencer failed to secure a divorce at the US Court for China in Shanghai, but an introductory letter to an Englishman at the American Embassy gave her the entree to the local social scene. Next she travelled to Peking, to 'shop around for silks and porcelain'. But this oriental lotus-eating had greater significance; at a dance at the Grand Hotel de Peking she met Hermann and Katherine Rogers. They, too, would participate in the drama that would mould the destiny of a king and the Duke and Duchess of York. Wallis Spencer was already acquainted with Katherine Rogers, having met her in Colorado as K. Bigelow, then in widowhood.

Now installed in the Rogers' household, Wallis Spencer savoured the delights of Peking until the 'voice of conscience ... spoke rather severely', reminding her that she 'had better give thought of returning to my own people and winding up the unfinished business of my marriage to Win'.

Returning to Washington, a lawyer – a family friend – instituted a divorce suit at Warrenton, Virginia, but it required one year's residence in this little town in the Fauquier County. Here, again, she encountered an old acquaintance, Hugh Spilman, who led her into the 'social whirl of the local horsey set'. During the period, another acquaintance would have a crucial effect on the life of Wallis Spencer. Indeed, it was a key factor that pointed to the royal upheaval in Britain a decade later. On occasions Wallis travelled to New York and at such times she would be the guest of her erstwhile school companion, Mary Kirk, now the wife of Jacques Raffray. The Raffrays introduced her to Mr and Mrs Ernest Aldrich Simpson whose marriage was then foundering.

Between Ernest Simpson and Wallis Spencer there was a spontaneous attraction. Later she frankly explained that his reserved manner, quiet wit and excellent grooming appealed. A 'good dancer, fond of the theatre, and obviously well-read, he impressed me as an unusually well-balanced man. I had acquired a taste for cosmopolitan minds, and Ernest obviously had one. I was attracted to him and he to me.' That strange alchemy called mutual physical attraction was to result in marriage. Wallis Spencer's divorce suit succeeded in December 1927, and when Mrs Simpson divorced her husband, they were free to marry. After staying with the Hermann Rogers in a villa near Cannes, Wallis Spencer married her second husband in Chelsea in July 1928.

Although he was born in New York of an English father and an American mother, Ernest Simpson's roots were in Britain. In childhood, summer vacations were spent in England (where an older married sister lived) and Europe, travelling there with his father. Later, while at Harvard, this ardent anglophile crossed the Atlantic to enlist during the First World War in the Grenadier Guards as a second lieutenant. A brother officer was the Prince of Wales. Subsequently Simpson became a naturalized Briton, serving in the London office of his father's ship-broking firm. The Simpsons finally settled in Mayfair; indeed, No. 58 Bryanston Square would secure its place in history.

During these early days in London, Mrs Simpson knew comparatively few people to invite to her dinner parties, a problem that her husband's sister, Mrs Kerr Smiley, helped to resolve. One cannot ignore the irony that it was at the latter's house in Belgrave Square that the Prince of Wales had begun his association with Mrs Dudley Ward. That friendship was now to terminate and, one could argue, rather brutally when Mrs Simpson stalked on to the Prince's stage.

Their first meeting occurred in the autumn of 1930. Accounts vary as to the frequency of subsequent meetings. What is factual is that unexpectedly, it appears, the Simpsons were included among the guests at Fort Belvedere in January 1932. Years later Mrs Simpson recalled that, arriving during darkness, 'before the car ground to a stop, the door opened and a servant appeared. An instant later the Prince himself was at the door to welcome his guests and supervise the unloading of our luggage, an attention which I was to discover was a habit with him.' There would be other visits to Fort Belvedere.

By now Mrs Simpson was someone whom the Royal Family could not overlook, for the Prince of Wales's relatives – his brother George and Lord and Lady Louis Mountbatten – were sometimes fellow guests. But it is doubtful if anyone imagined that her shadow would darken the throne. It seemed, at that juncture, to be a matter of rivals seeking the Prince's favour – something to be frowned upon no doubt, but viewed with mild contempt unless it flared up and embroiled the Court. It is generally believed that the Duke and Duchess of York regarded this as remote.

Not even Lady Furness, who was thought to be the current favourite, contemplated that her place in the princely coterie would be challenged. Indeed, the day before she left in January 1934 for a holiday in her native America, she had specifically spoken to Mrs Simpson over cocktails. Recalling that incident years later, Mrs Simpson revealed: 'We rattled along in our fashion; as we said goodbye she said, laughingly, "I'm afraid the Prince is going to be lonely, Wallis, won't you look after him."'

Lady Furness need have had no qualms. In the previous July the Prince had dined for the first time with the Simpsons in the informality of their Mayfair home. Now his visits were more frequent. Whether it was pre-determined or merely co-incidental, the Prince invariably chose evenings when Ernest Simpson would be engaged on business matters.

On her return in March, Lady Furness detected a frigidity in the Prince. By the following month, his affection for Freda Dudley Ward was dead. By May, the friendship of Lady Furness had ceased to be of value to the Prince. Mrs Simpson was now supreme. About this time that inveterate diarist, 'Chips' Channon, made this entry: 'She [Mrs Simpson] has complete power over the Prince of Wales, who is trying to launch her socially.' Others contended that it was Mrs Simpson who was launching the Prince into a society which did not 'provide him with the kind of social intercourse he really needed'.

Sir Harold Nicolson, summing up the situation, wrote: 'I have an uneasy feeling that Mrs Simpson, in spite of her good intentions, is getting him out of touch with the type of person with whom he ought to associate.... Why am I sad? Because ... I think Mrs Simpson is a nice woman who has flaunted suddenly into this absurd position. Because I think the P of W is in a mess.'

The Simpsons were an integral part of the Prince's life by the summer of 1934. This fact could not have assuaged the fears of the Royal House – more so when, to the smouldering resentment of the Prince's staff, Mrs Simpson obtruded into the domestic affairs of Fort Belvedere. More significant as an historical fact was that this was the period when the Duke and Duchess of York, much to their subsequent consternation, were set inexorably in line to the throne.

Visiting Biarritz in August, the Prince invited the Simpsons to join his party. Ernest Simpson declined, having already accepted a business assignment in the United States. Aunt Bessie Merryman was thus recruited as his wife's chaperone, but the Prince and Mrs Simpson spent much time alone. This privacy persisted when the party, chartering Lord Moyne's yacht *Rosaura*, travelled to Genoa. As Mrs Simpson would reveal in her memoirs, this was the occasion when, sitting alone together on the deck on those balmy evenings, she and the Prince crossed the boundary between friendship and love. That short Mediterranean cruise takes its place in history as the time when the Prince declared his feelings. Placing everything into perspective, one can also see that it was the turning-point in the life of the Duke and Duchess of York.

To Mrs Simpson, the Prince was 'the open sesame to a new and glittering world.... It seemed unbelievable that I, Wallis Warfield of Baltimore, Maryland, could be part of this enchanted world.' Sombre clouds would gather to obscure it. In November, a few days before the Prince's brother George married Princess Marina of Greece, Mrs Simpson met the King and Queen at a Buckingham Palace

The King's death wrought a serious rupture in the Queen's life. Her husband's coffin is being borne to its final resting place at Windsor.

reception. It was the first and only meeting. After the wedding the only member of the Prince's family to visit Fort Belvedere with any constancy was Lord Louis Mountbatten.

The Prince and Mrs Simpson left for the winter sports at Kitzbühl in the following February. Ernest Simpson again gave business commitments in New York as the excuse for his unwillingness to go. On her return to Bryanston Square, the Simpson marriage was in tatters. Mrs Simpson, we are told by Lady Longford, advised her husband 'to return to an earlier love, Mary Kirk Raffray, now liberated by a divorce of her own. He eventually took the advice; but without ever denouncing his royal supplanter. In his eyes the monarch was above criticism.' But neither the Prince nor Mrs Simpson were spared the tacit strictures of the monarch himself.

In May of that critical year, 1935, King George v and Queen Mary celebrated the Silver Jubilee of their reign with a state ball at Buckingham Palace. It escaped no one there that the Prince of Wales invited Wallis Simpson. In turn, neither did she evade the iciness of the King's eyes as he observed her. Momentarily, under the withering gaze, she felt a shiver. Perhaps the sensation was reciprocal.

The nation generally was unaware of the anxiety and sadness which tormented their sovereign. His appearance with the Queen in the streets of his capital sparked off such an outburst of public affection, after a tour of the East End of London, that the King remarked to the Archbishop of Canterbury: 'I had no idea they felt like that about me. I'm beginning to think that they must really like me for myself.'

To Britain and the Empire, the gruff King had become an institution, a symbol of stability which could assure and inspire peoples of all colours and creeds in days of crisis. But time was running out for him. During June he appeared to revive from a heavy cold, yet by the autumn the bearded face showed signs of acute weariness. The indomitable spirit was failing, and on 10 December the death of his beloved sister, Princess Victoria, at Coppins, her home near Windsor forest, struck so deeply that he never seemed to recover. His devotion could be measured by the fact that for years he had telephoned 'Toria' each morning. Never before had he allowed personal sentiments to eclipse his official duties, yet now he cancelled the State Opening of Parliament which had been planned for that day.

Oppressive, however, beyond all was his deep distress over David, his heir, whom he wished was of the same firm mould as the self-effacing, domesticated Albert, Duke of York. The gap between the King and his eldest son had widened abysmally, to the degree where conversation was often painfully strained and sometimes almost impossible. The father loathed the son's choice of companions and his flamboyant life. For his part, David was brusquely frank in his wholehearted contempt for his father's regularized mode of living, expressing it by open acts of rebellion. The King confided in Dr Cosmo Lang his anxiousness about the future. There can be little doubt that the Prince's romance with the forthright American was of paramount anxiety to him. There is the claim that it hastened his death. He was much concerned with David's 'latest friendship', which he accepted as being far more serious than previous affairs. He approached the Duke of Connaught to intervene and sought the advice of the Prime Minister, Stanley Baldwin, to whom he conveyed with prophetic accuracy: 'After I am dead the boy will ruin himself in twelve months.'

What in hindsight is amazing is the King's failure to expose his fears to his son. The Prince later submitted weak, even puerile reasons for not speaking candidly to his father. Perhaps the Duke of York came closer to the truth when he suggested that the main obstacle was the King's tendency 'to go' for his eldest son. Beyond casual references to 'my friend Mrs Simpson', neither father nor son had broached the question of the liaison. Doubtless the Prince knew the worst without asking. Indeed, the Royal House would be opposed to him later as king. In his autobiography, written while he was Duke of Windsor, the Prince pondered the court's reaction to the question of Mrs Simpson's proposed divorce. Even then he was starkly aware that, should he perversely marry her, he might have to forsake the throne.

Soon it would be too late to discuss matters with King George v. In his Christmas broadcast from Sandringham many detected in the low, heavy voice the ailing monarch's overwhelming sense of hopelessness. Because the Duchess of York was ill with pneumonia, Lilibet and Margaret journeyed to the Norfolk mansion without their parents. They knew that Grandpa England was a tired and dejected old man, hunched in his room, wearing his fading Tibetan dressing-gown. The King's last Christmas was a dispiriting time. Maybe no one in the house party felt the lowering effect more keenly than Uncle David, worried and irritated no doubt by 'an inner conflict', the consequence of which would vigorously reshape his own and his relations' destiny.

On 15 January, with the devoted Queen Mary walking by his side, the troubled King rode for a while on his old white pony. The next day he was confined to his bed. A telephone call to the Royal Lodge quickly summoned the Duke of York to Sandringham to assist with the guests. On the seventeenth the feeble King, making a final significant entry in his diary, wrote succinctly: 'I feel rotten.' Councillors of State were appointed three days later and on 20 January Queen Mary recorded in distress: 'At five to twelve my darling husband passed peacefully away – my children were angelic.' At that moment the Prince of Wales had become the King, but the Yorks were much closer to permanency on the throne.

At the Royal Lodge the Duchess of York was alone with her thoughts. One suspects that she entertained misgivings about the future in that year of crisis. Between King George v and his daughter-in-law there had existed a genuine bond of affection. And like the late King, she had reason for gloomy thoughts in the months ahead. Reflecting on his dynasty, her father-in-law had vehemently declaimed some weeks earlier: 'I pray to God that my eldest son will never marry and have children, and that nothing will come between Bertie and Lilibet and the throne.' In that event, the Duchess could visualize the enormous task that confronted her. The fate of Prince Albert and herself was now at the mercy of two people: the Prince of Wales and Mrs Simpson. Tragically George V would never know that destiny would grant his dearest wish. Before the year was out, Prince Albert would receive the crown; his consort would be the last Queen-Empress; in time their elder daughter would occupy the throne.

Crystal-gazing and sophistry are precarious ways of predicting royal destiny. Yet in 1903 the Hon Ralph Shirley predicted in a periodical called *The Horoscope* that it was unlikely that Prince Edward would ever reach the throne; if he did he would be swiftly succeeded by the Duke of York. Cheiro (whose real name was Count Louis Hamon), a fashionable clairvoyant and palmist in London before the First World War, was even more precise. Dying in New York a few months before the Abdication, he had written in his *World Predictions*, reprinted in 1931: 'It is well within the range of possibility, owing to the peculiar planetary influences to which he is subjected . . . that the Prince will give up everything, even the chance of being crowned, rather than lose the object of his affections.'

More portentous to those who pinned their faith to omens was the simple procession from King's Cross to Westminster for George V's lying-in-state. As the gun-carriage bearing the coffin rumbled over tramlines in Theobald's Road, the ball of diamonds surmounted by a sapphire cross fell from the Imperial Crown into the roadway. Though it was deftly retrieved, the incident provoked the King's sententious remark: 'Christ! What's going to happen next?' Standing on the fringe of the nearby crowd, Walter Elliott commented to Robert Boothby, a fellow Member of Parliament: 'That will be the motto of the new reign.' To some extent it was an echo of the past. At the coronation of George III, one of the biggest jewels had dropped from his crown and in time the thirteen American colonies were lost to Britain.

At Westminster Hall, observing the Duchess of York and the other royal ladies who were darkly veiled, Mrs Simpson later facetiously informed 'Chips' Channon that it was the first time she had worn black stockings since she had forsaken the can-can. Mrs Simpson would regret her ill-natured remark.

From the outset, the King indicated his desire for change. Symbolic was the incident on the night of his father's death. Both Edward VII and George V, sticklers for punctuality, had kept the clocks at Sandringham half an hour fast. Mr Daniel Burlingham, the clockmaker responsible for maintaining the clocks, once explained: 'On the night when George V lay dying and it was announced by the BBC that "the King's life was drawing peacefully to its close", the Prince of Wales thereupon ordered that the clocks should be put back to Greenwich Time immediately.' On the surface it seems to have been a thoughtless, even

The Queen Mother poses with members of the Royal Family on the eve of her daughter's coronation.

With Princess Margaret in the coronation procession.

callous act, but it has been attributed to a mistake caused by the discrepancy between the two times. 'I'll fix those bloody clocks,' the Prince is said to have cried.

Cosmo Lang wondered what other customs would be put back as well. The Duchess of York also expressed her fears of what the future held, writing to Lord Dawson, physician and courtier, that 'everything is different – especially spiritually and mentally ... I mind things that I do not like, more than before.' She would have reason for greater resentment before 1936 had expired.

Maybe at this juncture it was not quite clear if Mrs Simpson exerted an overwhelming influence on the King. What perturbed the Royal Family – and certainly the Yorks – was the King's conceit and lack of consideration for others. Reforms, for instance, were doubtless long overdue at Sandringham and Balmoral. At King Edward's request, therefore, the Duke of York submitted his report of proposals in the case of the Norfolk estate, but the changes to personnel and establishment were effected at Balmoral by the monarch himself.

Sir John Wheeler-Bennett has explained: 'In this case, however, the decisions were taken by His Majesty in consultation with the Crown authorities alone, and without reference to his brother, although the latter was in residence at Birkhall. The Duke was pained at being thus ignored. He was also disturbed at the nature of King Edward's decisions regarding his Scottish home and its retainers.'

The Duke's annoyance was confirmed in a letter that he wrote from Glamis to Queen Mary. It ran: 'David only told me what he had done after it was over, which I might say made me rather sad. He arranged it all with the official people up there. I never saw him alone for an instant....'

Domestic tranquility had dominated the Yorks' life before the King had met Mrs Simpson in 1930. The relationship of Prince Albert and his brother had been affectionate and rather close, Bertie having tremendous admiration for the future sovereign. But now, to her dismay, the Duchess realized how her husband was being ousted from among the intimates with which the King surrounded himself. She detected the reason and must have resented it. Increasingly the King allowed into his circle only the people who met with Mrs Simpson's approval.

If Mrs Simpson had not sensed the Duchess's attitude before, she was keenly conscious of it when she and the King drove to the Royal Lodge in 1936. As Lady Longford has explained: 'Mrs Simpson noted that whereas the Duke of York admired the King's American station wagon, the Duchess did not take to his other American acquisition.'

The fact that the King was afflicted by an inner torment most probably accounted for his attitude towards his family. During March, at a dinner at Windsor Castle, the King was determined to safeguard his 'secret and private life with a kind of desperation' (according to Lady Hardinge), and dwelt considerably on the affair of George IV and Mrs Fitzherbert. The time was threatening, however, when he could conceal his private life no longer.

On 27 May a Court Circular issued to Fleet Street editors announced that Mr and Mrs Simpson were among the guests at a dinner party given by the King. Until then the Simpsons must outwardly have maintained a semblance of marital stability. Yet on 9 July, at a party at York House, to which the Duke and Duchess of York and government ministers were invited, Mr Simpson's name was absent although his wife's was included. Four days later, *Time* quoted that the insurance rate at Lloyd's was shortening from 11–1 to 5–1 against the King's marriage. The following week the same news magazine reproduced two pages of photographs of Mrs Simpson and her London home.

Newspaper men had long since discussed the King and Mrs Simpson in Fleet Street taverns, but although the American and Continental press was in full cry, so far there had been no disclosures in British newspapers. The truth was still concealed from the populace when the King committed his worst indiscretion to date. Placed in perspective, it was the beginning of the final events which ended in the Abdication and brought the Yorks to the throne.

On 30 July, the *Daily Mirror* reported that King Edward had chartered Lady Yule's yacht, *Nahlin*, with the Baltic as the purported destination. It was an absurd subterfuge. In reality the cruise was to be the Dalmatian coast. On 9 August the King, travelling incognito as the Duke of Lancaster, entered the Orient Express and reached the Yugoslav port of Sibernik the following morning. Even by then the fiction had failed, for he was recognized wherever he went. So too was Mrs Simpson. The two had been photographed together even before they had left Salzburg. When the photograph was duly published in the British press, the lady was conveniently deleted. On 11 August, however, the London *Evening Standard* revealed that Mrs Simpson was among the King's party, and five days afterwards the *Sunday Referee* reproduced a large photograph of the King and Mrs Simpson together.

In the same week, *World's Press News*, a periodical for journalists, explained that two official requests had asked for a minimum to be published of the King's holiday. The *Sunday Dispatch* told its readers: 'Photographs and stories of his [the King's] shore excursions on the Dalmatian coast are being sent to English newspapers in great numbers. Unless these contain matter of proper national interest – such as the whereabouts of the King – the *Sunday Dispatch* will not publish them, believing that its readers realize and respect the King's natural desire for occasional respite from the public attention. . . .' On the following day, the *Daily Express* showed a photograph of the King rowing a dinghy around the *Nahlin*. He appeared alone. The American newspapers, in the same photograph, depicted Mrs Simpson in the stern.

During this period some newspapers printed photographs of Princess Catherine of Greece, hinting at possible marriage with King Edward. William Hickey, the *Daily Express* columnist, wrote on 20 August: 'Girl whose name has been most often mentioned as queen-to-be denies truth of story indignantly. Well, maybe it is someone else. . . .' Actually the King was then in Athens with Mrs Simpson at his side, but no photographs were printed in Britain.

This conspiracy of silence sprang from the press lords' acquiscence to the King's own request. He had told Lord Beaverbrook 'frankly of his position'. His own desire, the King explained, 'was to protect Wallis from sensational publicity, at least in my own country'. The King was exceedingly naïve if he believed that this situation could be prolonged. To the foreign press, his visits to the heads of Greece, Turkey, Bulgaria, Yugoslavia and Austria were of little consequence compared with the presence of Mrs Simpson.

To the chagrin of the Royal Family, American publications published stories and photographs of the couple almost daily; rumour reached new heights of speculation and sensationalism. On 17 October, the *Washington Post* actually declared that the King, irrespective of the consequences, was bent on marrying his American friend. Moreover, he had approved her divorce suit and might 'indeed have suggested it'. The situation gave particular anxiety to the Duke and Duchess of York. Their disapproval intensified in September when the King travelled to Balmoral for his Scottish holiday, his guests including a leavening of 'less exalted but nonetheless stimulating people' – no other than Mrs Simpson and her intimates Mr and Mrs Hermann Rogers.

Some time earlier the King had been asked to open Aberdeen's new Royal Infirmary, but he had declined, claiming that he was still in mourning for King George v. In that case, so too was the Duke of York, yet the King never hesitated to depute him for the ceremony. To Scottish anger, the King then openly awaited his future wife and her friends at Ballater station. People observed that she had sat beside him in the car, the Hermann Rogers taking the seats at the rear. 'Chips' Channon wrote: 'Aberdeen will never forgive him.'

The Duke and Duchess of York stayed as usual at nearby Birkhall. True or not, it is recorded that, on visiting Balmoral, 'the Duchess of York openly showed her resentment at being received by Mrs Simpson'. It seems obvious that Mrs Simpson had been empowered with some authority, for there is evidence that she antagonized the servants by requiring American three-decker toasted sandwiches to be served late at night. If the alleged annoyance of the Duchess of York is true, it was a blatant manifestation of Mrs Simpson's mastery over the King.

For the Yorks it was a disconcerting and difficult pointer to the future, for the Duke – untrained for kingship – was next in line to the throne. As for the Duchess, like King George v, she possessed an imperishable sense of the duties entailed in kingship and strove at all times to safeguard the throne. The idea that the institution of monarchy should be the subject of scandal and idle gossip was anathema. Yet on the day that she and the Duke attended the ceremony in Aberdeen, the *New York Woman*, serving the latest royal tittle-tattle to avid readers, informed that should Mr Simpson divorce his wife King Edward could not be sued for adultery in Britain.

Widely travelled, the Queen Mother was the first queen to circumnavigate the world by air.
The photograph recalls the 1947 South African tour with the King and the Princesses.

The prospect of Mrs Simpson seeking divorce was obviously of some anxiety and embarrassment to the Royal House. While she remained technically married, there could be no possibility of her becoming the Queen. Yet on 27 October 1936 their fears were confirmed. In nineteen minutes at Ipswich Assizes, Mrs Wallis Simpson of Beech House, Felixstowe, and Cumberland Terrace, London, secured a decree nisi with costs against her husband.

Ernest Aldrich Simpson did not sue the King. Whether there was collusion or not, one cannot say. Mrs Simpson told Mr Justice Hawke of her accidental discovery of a letter from Mr Simpson to 'the other woman', and servants from the Hôtel de Paris in Bray testified to misconduct by her husband with someone whose name was never disclosed.

The hearing had nothing to distinguish it from similar cases but for the influx of police and newspaper men. The next day, the divorce suit received much space in the American press, yet in Britain only the scantiest details were divulged. The gentleman's agreement still held.

Even so, stories had trickled into Britain from across the Atlantic, resulting in mounting indignation against what was thought to be American scurrility. People protested against what was ostensibly – both in the press and on radio stations – an insinuation that King Edward would marry Mrs Simpson as soon as her *decree nisi* was made absolute. Typical was the headline in William Randolph Hearst's *New York Journal*: 'King Will Wed Wally.' Having interviewed the King at Fort Belvedere, Hearst wrote:

King Edward's most intimate friends state . . . that almost immediately after the coronation he will take her [Mrs Simpson] as his consort. He believes . . . that in this day and generation it is absurd to try to maintain the tradition of royal intermarriages, with all the physical as well as political disabilities likely to result from that outgrown custom.

His brother, the Duke of York, has been extremely happy and fortunate in his marriage to a lady of the people, a commoner, so-called. King Edward believes that the marriage he contemplates would be equally happy, and that it would help him to do what he wants to do – namely, reign in the interest of the people.

The Duchess of York's reaction to such disclosures is not recorded, but as an ardent stalwart of the Anglican Church she was bound to uphold its tenets. The monarch was the secular head of the Church which looked upon marriage as indissoluble. For the sovereign to arrogate a royal right to marry a divorcee whose two previous husbands were still alive was quite abhorrent.

This is strictly conjecture, yet one can only imagine that the Duchess endorsed the opinion of a British citizen who, living in the United States, wrote to *The Times* reproaching the King for the 'dizzy Balkan musical comedy' currently being enacted in London. Lord Beaverbrook submitted that the letter was actually written in the office of *The Times* but this has been denied. In any event, the writer, under the name of 'Britannicus in Partibus Infidelium', claimed

Foreign tours. By
drinking kava, the Queen
Mother endeared herself
to the people of Fiji.

In Africa. The Queen
Mother listens to an address
of welcome read by Sheikh
Mbarak Ali Hinaway
during a visit to Mombasa.

that the foundations of the British throne are undermined, its moral authority, its honour, and its dignity cast into the dustbin. To put the matter bluntly George v was an invaluable asset to British prestige abroad; Edward has proved himself an incalculable liability.

For several months now the American public has been intermittently titillated with unsavoury goblets of news about the King and Mrs Simpson; but in the course of the last three or four weeks there has come a perfect avalanche of muck and slime.... One journal ... gives the alleged details of a conversation in which the Prime Minister reproves the King for his carrying on, and the latter curtly tells him to mind his own business. Another asserts that Queen Mary is being ousted from Buckingham Palace in order to clear the way for Mrs Simpson's installation as the King's official hostess....

The sting came later, the writer asserting that

nothing would please me more than to hear that Edward VIII had abdicated his rights in favour of the Heir Presumptive, who I am confident would be prepared to carry on in the sterling tradition established by his father. In my view it would be well to have such a change take place while it is still a matter of individuals, and before the disquiet has progressed to the point of calling in question the institution of monarchy itself.

The wish for abdication would be fulfilled – to the pain of the Duke and Duchess of York.

Geoffrey Dawson, editor of *The Times*, who received the letter the day before the divorce suit in Ipswich, took it to Major Alexander Hardinge, asking him to show it to the King. Dawson was informed by the King's Private Secretary that Stanley Baldwin, the Prime Minister, had told Edward VIII of his concern. Thus the Abdication crisis was in progress.

Troubled, too, were the Yorks. It can be argued that from this period the Duchess of York began to emerge as a significant force in royal affairs. Her husband was now his brother's heir and the proximity of the throne could not be evaded. The Duke, however, had never served any apprenticeship to kingship and, so it seemed, lacked the personal qualities to bear the onus involved. Neither could one ignore the impediment of speech which intensified in moments of stress, the self-destructive nervousness and the ingrained sense of inferiority bred by his brother's overshadowing charm. From now onwards, the Duchess would have all this to contend with.

As George VI, the Duke of York would be remembered for his moral and physical courage, combined with a genuine humility inspired by religious belief. Yet one should not overlook or minimize the significance of the person who evoked and consolidated those latent qualities. Without her undisputed strength of character, without that unshakeable, sustaining element and the skill to make those attributes malleable, history might now have had a different story to relate. To his undying credit, he would never tire of publicly affirming his tremendous debt. From the time that he had walked behind his father's coffin, the Duke of York was probably stalked by fears: if the new King chose bachelorhood and died, the Duke would succeed him; if Edward VIII resolved to wed Mrs Simpson,

With Maori girls – during a tour of New Zealand – after they had performed their Poi dance.

abdication was the only avenue left open to him. In either case, the Duke would be left wearing the crown, a prospect which at first appalled.

The Duchess's steadying influence exerted itself on the Duke's emotions. As well as the threat of abdication, there was the King's obsession for change. A cardinal characteristic of the Bowes-Lyons was the concern they felt for the welfare of their retainers. The Duke possessed similar sentiments towards the servants on the royal estates. The King's apathy over the well-being of the Deeside estate had worried him. 'I know so much about this place and I feel I am part of it. I like the people and I believe they like me,' he wrote to Lord Wigram.

Throughout this period the Duchess witnessed in her husband a lowering gloom, which she strove to counter. Her forceful character doubtless also bolstered Queen Mary who, like herself and in contrast to the King's short-sighted intractability, believed in the unyielding obligations of the monarchy.

The need to attune the Duke's mind to the inevitability of kingship perhaps first came to the Duchess after their return from a visit to Scotland. Major Hardinge had informed the Duke that on 20 October, the Prime Minister had pleaded with the obdurate King to induce Mrs Simpson to withdraw her divorce suit. Baldwin had also handed the King some of the letters which, sent from abroad, in some cases scathingly condemned him for his liaison. The King's foolhardy determination to wed Mrs Simpson – selfishly ignoring the potential harm to the institution of monarchy – was conveyed to Baldwin on 16 November, repeated to his mother Queen Mary that evening, and to the Duke of York the next day.

An inkling of the Duke of York's state of mind (with which the Duchess doubtless had to cope) is reflected in a letter, still preserved in the Royal Archives at Windsor, that he wrote to Queen Mary early in November: 'I have been meaning to come and see you but I wanted to see David first. He is very difficult to see and when one does he wants to talk about other matters. It is all so worrying and I feel we all live a life of conjecture; never knowing what will happen tomorrow, and then the unexpected comes....'

Yet within a week of his brother's painful news, all conjecture seems to have vanished. 'If the worst happens and I have to take over,' the Duke wrote on 25 November to Sir Godfrey Thomas, one of the King's assistant private secretaries, 'you can be assured that I will do my best to clear up the inevitable mess, if the whole fabric does not crumble under the shock and strain of it all.' Four nights later he travelled with the Duchess to Scotland to be installed as Grand Master Mason of Scotland, an appointment which had been held by the King as Prince of Wales. In retrospect, it presaged more dramatic events within the next two weeks. The Yorks were loath to leave London, the Duke confiding in a letter to his Private Secretary, Sir Eric Miéville, that he hated going to Scotland 'to do what I have to do as I am so worried over the whole matter. I feel like the proverbial "sheep being led to the slaughter", which is not a comfortable feeling.'

During the days spent by the Duke and Duchess in Edinburgh, the heavy clouds of the Abdication storm gathered over Fleet Street. Executives were warned to prepare for the most momentous story since the war. Later, people recalled that Sunday newspapers had published photographs of the Duke and Duchess of York in their happy domesticity, with the little Princesses and their dogs. Others remembered the clamorous welcome accorded to the Yorks in Edinburgh. There had also been a waggish political remark: 'There is a Yorkist Party again. Where is the Popish plot?'

The first thunder-clap, however, sounded from an unexpected quarter. On 1 December, initiating a 'Recall to Religion' campaign in his diocese, Dr Walter Blunt, Bishop of Bradford, commended the King – 'a man like ourselves' – to God's grace, adding: 'We hope that he is aware of his need. Some of us wish that he gave more positive signs of his awareness.' The Bishop's speech was 'a blow with a Blunt instrument', for it had been written some weeks earlier, even before he was conscious of Mrs Simpson's existence, and was merely a criticism of King Edward's irregularity in attending divine service on Sunday. Unlike the Yorks, whose constant dedication to the Church was unquestioned, the King had been the subject of sharp comment in Church circles. As far back as 30 March, *Time* had disclosed how editors were receiving letters asking when the Court Circular would announce that the King had attended church. Queried the magazine: 'Who'll be the unknown clergyman to bring *that* up?' The answer had been supplied, but ironically Blunt's words were wildly misinterpreted; his remarks were intended to go no deeper than a reproach of the monarch's church-going.

Nevertheless, Fleet Street hesitated that night, but the provincial press, led by the *Yorkshire Post*, published the speech with disclosures which had appeared in the more reputable United States journals. By 3 December the national press had cast all reserve aside.

This was the critical situation when the Duke and Duchess of York returned from Scotland to London. At Euston station they were 'surprised and horrified' to see the glaring headline on newspaper posters: 'The King's Marriage'. The Duke and Duchess hastened to Queen Mary to explain their shock for 'the whole matter had been published'. Next the Duke saw his brother, 'who said he would leave the country as King after making a broadcast to his subjects and leave it to them to decide what should be done.'

The Duke heard his brother commit – with an almost callous disregard – himself and the Duchess of York to a fate from which both recoiled. The Duchess of York had hesitated before marrying the Duke, disliking the loss of private life which such a step would necessitate. Soon she would be subjected to the relentless glare of the publicity that beat down on the British throne.

Reflecting his distress, the Duke recorded in his diary:

The Prime Minister went to see him [the King] at 9.0 pm that evening and later (in Mary's and my presence) David said to Queen Mary that he could not live alone as King and must marry Mrs ——. When David left after making this dreadful announcement to his mother he told me to come and see him at the Fort the next morning (Friday, 4 Dec.). I rang him up but he would not see me and put me off till Saturday. I told him I would be at Royal Lodge on Saturday by 12.30 pm. I rang him up Saturday. 'Come and see me on Sunday,' was his answer. 'I will see you and tell you my decision when I have made up my mind.' Sunday evening I rang up. 'The King has a conference and will speak to you later' was the answer. But he did not ring up. Monday morning came. I rang up at 1.0 pm and my brother told me he might be able to see me that evening. I told him 'I must go to London but would come to the Fort when he wanted me.' I did not go to London but waited. I sent a telephone message to the Fort to say that if I was wanted I would be at Royal Lodge. My brother rang me up at ten minutes to 7.0 pm to say 'Come and see me after dinner'. I said 'No, I will come and see you at once'. I was with him at 7.0 pm. The awful and ghastly suspense of waiting was over. I found him pacing up and down the room, and he told me his decision that he would go.

The finale of the next day – Tuesday – was a dinner party at Fort Belvedere. Among the nine guests were the Dukes of York and Kent and the Prime Minister. In the oak-panelled room the King sat at the head of the table, his boyish face aglow with a smile; the rest 'were pale as sheets'. The Duke of York, turning to his neighbour, Walter Monckton (the King's legal adviser) remarked: 'Look at him. We simply cannot let him go.' Yet the following day, in a talk with the King, the Duke grimly realized that nothing would change his decision.

The Duke motored to London to visit Queen Mary. Engulfed by the awesome future that fate, it seemed, had brutally decided for himself and his consort, the highly nervous Duke, unable to suppress his emotions, broke down and wept. 'Bertie arrived very late from Fort Belvedere,' Queen Mary entered in her diary, 'and Mr Walter Monckton brought him and me the paper drawn up for David's abdication of the Throne of this Empire because he wants to marry Mrs Simpson!!!!!' She concluded: 'It is a terrible blow to us all and particularly to poor Bertie.'

Thursday, the day of the Instrument of Abdication, dawned. An oppressive fog which had spread its clammy gloom over Fort Belvedere now lifted; but not the depression of the Yorks. With his two younger brothers, the Duke witnessed the documents and later retired to the Royal Lodge 'for a rest as the tension was getting unbearable at the Fort. But I could not rest alone and returned to the Fort at 5.45.'

Unhappily for the Duke he faced his ordeal alone, lacking the consoling companionship of the Duchess of York who, having contracted pneumonia, lay ill at their Piccadilly home. That evening, returning to No. 145, he was amazed to discover that Londoners had converged like a human floodtide on Hyde Park Corner and their London house. Realizing that the crowd was expressing loyalty and affection, the Duchess calmly advised her sensitive husband to go and speak to the people. Humbly he asked: 'But what am I say to them?'

In a sense this would be the motif of the pattern for the future – the calm, smiling, resolute assurance of the diplomatic Queen infusing, certainly in the earlier part of the reign, confidence into a sometimes hesitant King.

From the outset, before the Accession Council King George VI, stressing the burdensome duties of monarchy that had been thrust so sensationally upon him, declared: 'With My wife and helpmeet by My side, I take up the heavy task which lies before Me.' Even Churchill, characteristically adorning the ex-King's historic broadcast, would sentimentalize on the harshness of Edward's bachelorhood in contrast to the Duke of York's connubial bliss: 'And he has one matchless blessing enjoyed by so many of you and not bestowed on him – a happy home life with his children.'

The degree to which the Queen would be taxed in her role of consort was graphically demonstrated in a passionate outburst on that memorable night. Witnessing his brother's final hours before life-long exile, the distressed King remarked impetuously to Lord Louis Mountbatten, his cousin: 'Dickie, this is absolutely terrible. I never wanted this to happen. I'm quite unprepared for it. David has been trained for this all his life. I've never even seen a State paper. I'm only a naval officer, it's the only thing I know about.'

Comforting the King, Lord Louis replied: 'This is a very curious coincidence. My father once told me that, when the Duke of Clarence died, your father came to him and said almost the same things that you have said to me now, and my father answered: "George, you're wrong. There is no more fitting preparation for a king than to have been trained in the Navy."'

Today, now that the dust has long since settled on the Abdication, one can see with crystal clarity the enormity of the difficulties that confronted George VI and Queen Elizabeth. Neither had sought personal aggrandisement; indeed, to stalk in the limelight of world publicity was alien to both their characters. The almost insuperable handicaps were glaring. Apart from the emotional disruption in the Royal House – which was immense – there was the dramatic suddenness and unpreparedness to contend with. Neither King nor Queen had ever been schooled in the skills of constitutional monarchy. Indeed, all too blatant was the folly of George V's insistence in refusing to initiate Prince Albert even in the simple rudiments of government. Only now was the new sovereign truly conscious of the exacting burden of official business arriving relentlessly each day in the leather dispatch boxes.

This never-ending flow, regardless of all other royal obligations, quickly made him aware of his physical incapacity. Coupled with this was his misguided belief that as a person he was inferior to his scintillating elder brother. The years would shatter this fallacy. King George VI would be seen as the ideal monarch for his time. Much of the credit, however, must be attributed to the temperament and attitude of his consort.

The urgent need early in the reign was to repair the damage to the centuries-old institution of monarchy. The foundations had been undermined. The crisis had left cracks in the throne. Within a year one sovereign had died and his successor had cast the crown aside. For most of the British people, the constitutional cataclysm had descended on them with shocking abruptness. In their perplexity, many people had sympathized with Edward VIII until he chose what he believed would be temporary exile. Then attitudes changed. That the monarchy was not more seriously imperilled and emerged more strongly than hitherto, reflects handsomely on King and Consort.

Yet in those early critical weeks, there was much to foment uneasiness at Buckingham Palace. The late Sir Arnold Wilson, a Conservative Member of Parliament, opined that if the House of Commons had voted on the issue, at least one hundred votes would have been cast favouring a republic.

In the Abdication debate, Mr James Maxton, the would-be revolutionary, ranted: 'We are doing a wrong and foolish thing if, as a House, we do not seize the opportunity with which circumstances have presented us of establishing in our land a completely democratic form of government which does away with old monarchical institutions and the hereditary principle.' Moving an amendment to the Abdication Bill, he stressed what he claimed to be the danger to Britain and the Commonwealth inherent in the monarchy; the peace and prosperity of the people required a more stable and dignified form of government of a republican kind. 'This crack-up of the monarchy', he went on, 'is not merely a matter of the failures of a man.... It is something deeper ... the whole break-up of past ideas of a Royal Family that was clear of the ordinary taints and weaknesses of ordinary men....'

But good sense came uppermost. By their integrity, humility and conscientious devotion to public service, the King and Queen won the nation's adulation. To the Archbishop of Canterbury the Queen had written: 'I can hardly now believe that we have been called to this tremendous task and (I am writing to you quite intimately) the curious thing is that we are not afraid. I feel that God has enabled us to face the situation calmly.' Here one senses the steadying influence and confidence engendered by the Queen.

Commendably the King publicly expressed his gratitude by bestowing the Order of the Garter upon the Queen. Writing to Queen Mary, the Queen explained that the King 'had discovered that Papa gave it to you on his, Papa's, birthday, June 3rd, and the coincidence was so charming that he has now followed suit.' It was an outward sign of the King's sense of indebtedness to his consort. In his first speech to Parliament George VI had spoke of his 'constant endeavour, with God's help, and supported as I shall be by my dear wife, to uphold the honour of the realm and promote the happiness of my peoples.'

For George VI the mental agitation and the physical strain taxed him severely, and it seemed that he wished all to know the anchorage which gave stability.

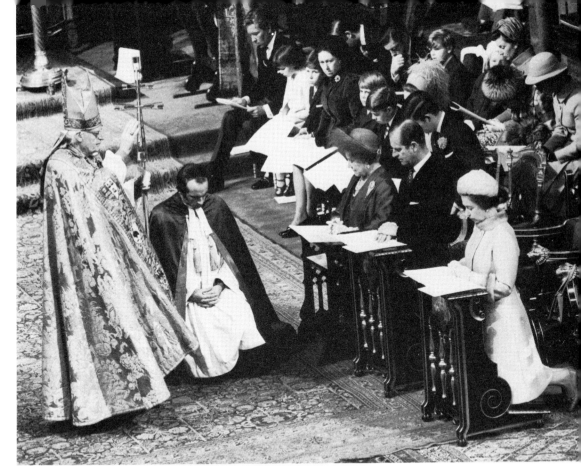

A Royal Silver Wedding. The Queen Mother kneels with the Queen and Prince Philip for the Archbishop of Canterbury's blessing in Westminster Abbey.

The Queen Mother enjoying a joke with the Pearly King and Queen of Peckham and their family.

In a New Year's broadcast to the Empire and Commonwealth, he spoke of the responsibilities of his noble heritage; he shouldered them, he said with 'all the more confidence in the knowledge that the Queen and my mother Queen Mary are at my side.... To repeat the words used by my dear father at the time of his Silver Jubilee, my wife and I dedicate ourselves for all time to your service....'

8

In the Critical War Years

The decision to retain the date – Wednesday, 12 May 1937 – arranged for the Coronation of Edward VIII left the new monarch and his consort a mere five months (as opposed to the normal year or more) in which to prepare themselves. To Queen Elizabeth's pleasure, Queen Mary broke with a longstanding tradition whereby a dowager consort never witnessed the crowning of her successor. But this necessitated the designing of a new crown for Queen Elizabeth. As a result, she was the first Queen to choose platinum as the mounting, and included in the jewels was the fabulous Kohinoor, or Mountain of Light.

The Queen's main concern at this period was for the King. Because George VI had merely postponed a durbar at Delhi for another year, malicious tongues spread the false news that the King, now claimed to be in frail health and a highly-nervous state, was losing the power to discharge his monarchical duties. Even the Coronation service, it was whispered, was in doubt because of his inability to speak in public.

These cruel, baseless calumnies of the King's 'physical and mental weakness' were indignantly refuted and condemned in public by the Rev. Robert Hyde. This spiteful campaign imputing that the King was destined to be a royal recluse was utterly groundless. True, his speech impediment gave the King certain anxiety, the more so because of the decision to broadcast the Coronation to his people. But with quiet determination and the services of Mr Lionel Logue, the Queen rehearsed the King in his Coronation responses. The consort's belief in her husband's latent qualities countered the dismay caused by the treacherous rumours.

On the Sunday evening that preceded the Coronation, the King and Queen knelt with humility before the Archbishop of Canterbury at Buckingham Palace for spiritual preparation. Later the Archbishop recalled: 'I met them in their room. . . . I prayed for them and for their realm and Empire, and I gave them my personal blessing. I was much moved, and so were they. Indeed, there were tears in their eyes when we rose from our knees.'

In spite of the precautions, the Coronation had its mishaps. A Presbyterian chaplain fainted in the Queen's procession in Westminster Abbey, delaying the King's progress for some while. This was not His Majesty's sole concern. After the Introduction, the Dean of Westminster insisted on trying to place the surplice on him inside out until the Groom of the Robes came to the King's rescue. Earlier the Bishops of Durham, Bath and Wells, holding the Form of Service for him, failed to find the words when he was due to deliver the Coronation Oath. The Archbishop opportunely held out his copy but to the King's alarm the words were hidden by the cleric's thumb. When the time arrived for the Lord Chamberlain to dress his sovereign, he fumbled with such shaking hands that the hilt of the sword almost struck His Majesty on the chin. Finally, George VI thought it more prudent to attach it to the belt himself.

That was not all. Before the ceremony a piece of red cotton had been attached to St Edward's Crown to denote the front. But, ignorant of its purpose, someone had removed it, and the King was in doubt as to how he was crowned. But the most harassing moment occurred when, on leaving the Coronation Chair, the King almost tripped over; a bishop was standing on his robe. 'I had to tell him to get off it pretty sharply,' George VI recorded, 'as I nearly fell down.' Nothing ruffled the dignity of his consort. 'The little Queen advanced with a real poetry of motion,' commented Dr Cosmo Lang later.

An incident in the Coronation month was of great importance to the Queen; it was then that the style and title of the Duke of Windsor was formally confirmed. In the *London Gazette* on 28 May, it was announced by Letters Patent that the Duke was accorded the title of 'Royal Highness' for himself alone; his future wife would be debarred from sharing that dignity.

On 3 June, HRH the Duke of Windsor and Mrs Wallis Simpson (the name she had assumed after her divorce) were married at the Chateau de Candé near Tours, the home of Charles Bedeaux, an affluent industrialist. No members of the Royal Family were present, and Queen Mary entered in her diary: 'Alas! the wedding day in France of David.'

After the honeymoon at Carinthia, the immediate aftermath – a visit to Nazi Germany – caused much embarrassment to the King and Queen. Like the British Government, they were anxious about its possible effect on the people. Already it was rumoured that the Duke and his newly acquired wife had Fascist sympathies. Whether the Windsors were aware of it or not, the Fascist tendencies of Bedeaux, whose home had been their nuptial setting, were beyond dispute; he would commit suicide after the Second World War rather than face the consequences of Nazi collaboration.

Lord Beaverbrook tried to dissuade the Duke from visiting the Reich but, obstinate as ever, the ex-king ignored the plea. The Windsors – welcomed by Dr Robert Ley, the liquor-addicted leader of the Labour Front – met Nazi leaders including Hitler himself. Photographs of this fraternization were published all over the world, to the ultimate dismay of King George and Queen Elizabeth.

Asking his mother to reveal her true feelings about his abdication, Queen Mary replied: 'You will remember how miserable I was.... You did not seem to take in any point of view but your own.... I do not think you have ever realized the

In early widowhood, the Queen Mother acquired the Castle of Mey with the object of living for long periods in Scotland. However, her multifarious duties compelled her to live mainly in London.

The Queen Mother amid the solitude of Caithness.

shock which the attitude you took up caused your family and the whole nation. It seemed inconceivable to those who had made such sacrifices during the war that you, as their King, refused a lesser sacrifice.... All my life I have put my country before everything else, and I simply cannot change now.'

There can be little doubt that Queen Elizabeth shared the same view. She is widely known as a charitable and warm-hearted person, but evidence implies one notable exception: her attitude towards the two people who, by their actions, caused her and her husband to sit on the throne. The Abdication in the eyes of the Queen was clearly a dereliction of duty and her contention would have a resounding impact.

The act of depriving the Duchess of Windsor of the title of Her Royal Highness became the Duke's bitterest grievance. The Duchess complained that the outcome 'was to debar me in defiance of all custom from taking my place alongside my royal husband'. The Duke went to his grave still wounded by what he correctly interpreted as 'an ultimate slur upon his wife, and, therefore upon himself'. The grievance scarred his life, turning his expatriation – originally envisaged by himself as a matter of years – into a lifelong exile; he declined to return to Britain officially unless his wife were treated as his equal. Ironically, he had discarded the crown to marry her truly, scorning suggestions that she might be his mistress or morganatic wife. Nevertheless, he now found himself palmed off with what was merely a morganatic duchess.

The legality of the contents of the Letters Patent have been questioned, but the outcome obviously represented the reaction of the Royal Family and, it has been claimed, of the Queen in particular. Yet in the earlier years of the Windsors' marriage there was a valid reason for this. The Duke of Windsor was the Duchess's third husband and there was no guarantee that he would be the last; indeed, there was no absolute certainty in 1937 that the union would endure. Who could completely discount fresh scandals, the remarriage of one or both partners, and the proliferation of Royal Highnesses after the marriage had failed? The thought was decidedly alarming when viewed from the throne, especially when the situation had become sour due to an entrenched dislike of the American divorcee.

Desirous of returning provided his wife received the same status as the royal duchesses, the Duke asked Walter Monckton to serve as intermediary. Monckton subsequently disclosed that the Prime Minister, Neville Chamberlain, who had succeeded Baldwin as the Conservative leader, thought that the Duke of Windsor should be treated as a younger brother of the King 'who would take some of the royal functions off his brother's hands'. King George VI was not fundamentally opposed to this but was not anxious for the Duke to return as early as November 1938.

A third person, however, was less cooperative. The Queen, Monckton revealed, 'felt quite plainly that it was undesirable to give the Duke any effective sphere of work. I felt then, as always, that she naturally thought that she must be on

Angling for the salmon in the River Dee while on holiday at Birkhall. With the royal angler is her head gillie.

Patron of both the National Hunt Committee and the Injured National Hunt Jockeys Fund, the Queen Mother is concerned for the safety of the men who ride the horses.

her guard because the Duke of Windsor, to whom the other brothers had always looked up, was an attractive, vital creature who might be the rallying point for any who might be critical of the new King, who was less superficially endowed with the arts and graces that please.'

There appears to be little doubt that the Queen's vision and practicality coldly came to the fore in good measure at this time. Figuratively, since childhood her husband had been virtually mesmerized by David's vitality, leaving him with an inferiority that had become deeply ingrained by young manhood. The Queen however suffered from no such complex. If it was a question of confident, scintillating charm she knew she possessed it to a striking degree, and to an extent that would match, or even surpass, that of her brother-in-law. If the challenge were to be a test of shrewdness and forceful character, then the Duke was easily outmatched. Those qualities – with simple piety as their mainstay – would be commented upon in Nazi documents captured after the war.

In the meantime, the darkening Nazi shadow grew larger over Europe. In March 1938, the Germans shocked Europe by annexing Austria, then directed their discordant propaganda against the Czechs. The latter had signed a mutual defence pact with France and now needed to be assured that the treaty was not worthless. France, in turn, sought assurance from Britain of moral and military support.

It so happened that a State visit to France, agreed to in the previous year, now coincided with this need to restore mutual confidence. The Queen's subtlety in such matters was eloquent in her choice of dress. Reviving the gowns of the Empress Eugenie, she commissioned Norman Hartnell to prepare some thirty dresses. Unfortunately an unexpected incident threw both Court and couturier into confusion. For the London season, Lord and Lady Strathmore occupied a flat in Cumberland Mansions, Portman Square, where the Queen invariably visited them at least twice weekly. On 22 June, merely a week before the departure to France, the Queen received the news that her mother, stricken by a heart attack, was dangerously ill. At 2 am the next morning, the Countess died in the presence of the King and Queen and other members of her family.

In her grief it seemed that the Queen must inevitably withdraw from the visit to France. But the journey was postponed for three weeks, leaving Mr Hartnell but a fortnight to design a new wardrobe in keeping with mourning. The colours were restricted to one of three: black, purple or white, and the latter was chosen. Hartnell wrought his magic with satins and silks, taffetas and lace, and Parisians gathered in vast crowds to glimpse Britain's White Queen. A leading newspaper, summarizing public acclaim, stated: 'Today France is a monarchy again. We have taken the Queen to our hearts. She rules over two nations.' As Lady Diana Cooper commented: 'Each night's flourish outdid the last.'

It was history repeating itself once more. In 1907 the beauty of Queen Alexandra, consort of Edward VII, had contributed appreciably to the success of the

Entente Cordiale. And now, three decades later, Queen Elizabeth had helped, merely by her presence, to cement Anglo-French solidarity, whose aim, as the King expressed at the Elysée banquet, was to find a 'solution of those political problems which threaten the peace of the world'. The cynics might have recalled that, after King George v and Queen Mary visited Paris in April 1914, the British and the French were at war with Germany within four months. Two months after the State visit in 1938, Chamberlain and Deladier for Britain and France, and Hitler and Mussolini for Germany and Italy gave their signatures to the Munich Agreement. An Anglo-German naval agreement was signed 'as symbolic of the desire of our two nations not to go to war with one another again'. Despite the eventual treachery of the Axis powers, both the King and Queen, having subscribed towards Anglo-French harmony, could derive satisfaction from having helped to secure temporary peace before the advancing storm.

The Queen would not include herself among Chamberlain's critics when, humiliated and sick, he was displaced by Churchill from the premiership. With typical kindliness, she wrote: '. . . during these last desperate and unhappy years you have been a great support and comfort to us both.'

More far-reaching in its ultimate effects would be Their Majesties' North American tour. When Mackenzie King, the Canadian Prime Minister, attended the Coronation festivities in 1937, he tried to get preliminary assurance of a royal visit to his country. He conveyed this information to his friend, Franklin D. Roosevelt, the us President, who had suggested a call in Washington as part of the itinerary should King's suggestion be accepted.

When 1939 dawned, the war looked depressingly inevitable. In March, the jackboots overran Czechoslovakia and in the following month Mussolini invaded Albania. 'Peace in our time' was now seen as a hollow sham. The time had arrived when Britain must strengthen alliances.

The prospect of journeying to the United States intrigued the Queen, for in her ancestry she could trace an American link. Not only is she connected through her family with General Robert E. Lee, the Confederate leader, but she is the second cousin six times removed to George Washington.

This transatlantic connection began through her paternal grandmother, Frances Dora, daughter of Oswald Smith, of Blendon Hall, Kent, who in 1853 married the future thirteenth Earl of Strathmore. Frances Dora provided the American offshoot which originated in 1650 when Augustine Warner, an English gentleman, crossed to the New World to avoid the severities of the Cromwellian régime. Acquiring wealth in Virginia, he enhanced his family's status through the marriages of his daughter, Sarah, and Augustine, his son. Sarah and Lawrence Townley, whom she married, were the ancestors of General Lee, but it was through Augustine that a descendant would one day marry a Bowes-Lyon. He himself married Mildred Reade, of Virginia, and though he died in 1681, he was survived by two daughters. The union of Mildred, the eldest, with Lawrence Washington, would result in a grandson named George, better known as the first President of the United States. Augustine's daughter, Mary, took as husband John Smith of Purton, and in 1700 their daughter, Mildred, wed Robert Porteous, a Virginian planter. Mildred and Robert Porteous returned to England in 1720 and their son, Robert, entered the Church. As a rector in Bedfordshire, he married Judith Cockayne. Their great-great-granddaughter would reside at Glamis as the Countess of Strathmore.

The journey to the New World was unique and at times exciting. Never before had a reigning monarch set foot in Canada; at no time had a British king or queen stood on American soil. But at first there were fears that Their Majesties would never get there. According to Lord Halifax, when they boarded the *Empress of Australia* on 5 May 1939, it was rumoured that a Nazi warship might intercept the unarmed liner and take them captive.

However the hazards came not from Germany but from the dangers of fog and ice. On writing to Queen Mary, the Queen revealed that for three and a half days the liner merely progressed a few miles. So dense was the fog 'that it was like a white cloud round the ship, and the foghorn blew incessantly. Its melancholy blasts were echoed back by the icebergs like the twang of a piece of wire. Incredibly eerie, and really very alarming, knowing that we were surrounded by ice, and unable to see a foot either way. We very nearly hit a berg the day before yesterday, and the poor Captain was nearly demented because some kind cheerful people kept on reminding him that it was about here that the *Titanic* was struck, and *just* about the same date....'

There were those who arrived to scoff. In the past there had been hints of Canada's eventual secession from the Commonwealth and of neutrality in the event of war. But all this was swept away in a tide of ecstasy after Their Majesties stepped ashore at Quebec on 17 May. The Queen's smile matched the brilliant sunshine. 'The Queen Who Smiles Like an Angel', 'Forever May She Smile' the headlines enthused. Her fluency in their language won the hearts of the French-speaking people in Quebec, and in Montreal there were rapturous cries as the King and Queen drove through twenty-three miles of flag-hung streets. In Ottawa the noisy reception was echoed again.

As the Governor-General, Lord Tweedsmuir (John Buchan, the Scottish novelist), wrote later, the Queen 'has a perfect genius for the right kind of publicity'. While laying the foundation stone of the new Judicative Building in Ottawa, on learning that some of the masons were Scots she insisted on seeing them, 'and they spent at least ten minutes in Scottish reminiscences, in full view of 70,000 people, who went mad!' She asked to get closer to 10,000 war veterans 'and we were simply swallowed up. But the veterans made a perfect bodyguard. It was wonderful to see old fellows weeping, and crying, "Ay, man, if Hitler could just see this...."'

Pupils of the Royal School for Deaf Children at Margate, Kent, meet the Queen Mother.

Queen Elizabeth had conquered Canada. A second conquest awaited her in the United States. A Senator loudly told the King: 'My, you sure are a great Queen picker!' A newspaper headline extolled: 'The British Re-Take Washington'. In New York almost four million people lined the route to the World's Fair where a gigantic crowd sang 'Land of Hope and Glory'. The *New York Times* conveyed its willingness to give the keys of the city 'back to George and Elizabeth', and an American column, syndicated to four hundred newspapers and magazines, nominated the Queen as 'Woman of the Year', 'because arriving in an aloof and critical country, she completely conquered it and accomplished this conquest by being her natural self.'

A much needed interlude from protocol was a weekend's relaxation with President Roosevelt, his mother Sarah Delano and wife Eleanor, at Hyde Park, their home on the Hudson River. Long after Their Majesties left there would be a memento of their visit. In advance of the royal guests, Mrs Sarah Delano Roosevelt had arranged to effect sanitary improvements to the visitors' bathroom. This included a new lavatory seat. When the plumber rendered his account the old lady, arguing that the price was excessive, declined to pay. Retrieving the lavatory seat from Hyde Park, he displayed it in solitary state in his shop window, with the notice: 'The King and Queen Sat Here.'

The success that accrued from the North American tour was tremendous. Now, there was no doubt as to the action Canada would take in the event of war. But maybe the crowning achievement was the impression imprinted on the President's mind. He expected to find 'two nice young people', but also found much more to admire. No one could underestimate this rapport which would help lubricate the machine that would deliver American aid to Britain at a vital time.

For Their Majesties the North American experience had instrinsic value. 'That tour made us,' confided the Queen to Mr Mackenzie King.

After the North American tour George VI reviewed the Reserve Fleet during the summer of 1939. If it was intended as a gesture to defuse the Nazi time-bomb, it was a naïve hope. Contemptuously, in August Hitler announced the non-aggression pact between the German Reich and the Soviet Union, and on the first day of September unleased his fury on Warsaw, arrogantly challenging Britain's guarantee against aggression in Poland. The flames in the burning Polish capital spread into the greatest conflagration in history.

At 11.15 am on Sunday, 3 September, Neville Chamberlain, then seventy years old, speaking from the Cabinet Room at 10 Downing Street, declared Britain to be at war with Germany. In the evening King George, broadcasting to his people, declared: 'For the sake of all that we ourselves hold dear, and for the world's peace and order, it is unthinkable that we should refuse to meet this challenge.'

There would be much heartbreak and tragedy in those critical wartime years,

Ballet has won the Queen Mother's patronage. She is seen with Dame Margot Fonteyn (back to camera) at a gala matinée presented by the Royal Academy of Dancing.

but it would be a period which mirrored the qualities of Queen Elizabeth at their most magnificent. As Herbert Morrison, the Home Secretary, explained, by personal example Their Majesties inspired an unconquerable morale which buoyed up the nation, particularly in the crucial year when Britain alone confronted Nazi might. The knowledge that the Royal Standard still flew over Buckingham Palace kindled a fighting spirit amongst the blazing rubble of the blitz.

But first Their Majesties met with a personal dilemma. Within a fortnight of the outbreak of hostilities, the Duke and Duchess of Windsor had returned to London. The former king wished to serve his country.

After the Abdication the Windsors had lived in Austria and France. Until the early part of 1937, the Duke had frequently telephoned his brother the King, pestering him with worries and trivial matters as well as proferring opinions and advice. Moreover, he still smarted over his wife's exclusion from using the title of 'Royal Highness'. Then all direct communications ceased, and one questions if the cause was due to the Queen. At least the King informed his brother: 'I'm afraid it is not going to be possible to continue these talks. It is too difficult to explain over the telephone. I will tell you about it in my next letter.' Apparently this letter was never received, and the Duke commented later: 'The Iron Curtain had gone clanging down.'

On 14 September, after Their Majesties toured the London docks, the King received his brother with 'no recriminations on either side'. The King informed the Duke that his services could best be applied as a member of the Military Mission in Paris. Acceptance, however, would mean relinquishing the rank of field-marshal which he had received as sovereign.

The next day, in a secret discussion with Leslie Hoare-Belisha, the War Minister, the Duke indicated that he had changed neither in temperament nor attitude. He insisted that the Duchess should accompany him not only to Paris, but in Britain on a tour of the commands. Hoare-Belisha, who had heard that the Duchess wished to take charge of a hospital on the south coast of England, was, as his diary reveals, caught unawares. The King was similarly perturbed, for when the Minister was summoned to the Palace the next morning, the King 'seemed very disturbed and walked up and down the room .... in a distressed state.... He said the Duke had never had any discipline in his life.... He thought that if the Duchess went to the commands, she might have a hostile reception, particularly in Scotland.'

The King made it abundantly clear that at no time did he want the Duke to visit the commands. When the Minister departed that morning and returned with Ironside, the Chief of the Imperial General Staff, in the afternoon, George VI agitatedly observed that his predecessors had worn the crown only after the people they succeeded were dead. 'Mine,' he rightly protested, 'is not only alive, but very much so.' He was extremely anxious to prevent the Duke and Duchess from travelling about the country.

It says much for the tact and diplomacy of politician and soldier that the Duke accepted his appointment forthwith (the day that the Queen became Commander-in-Chief of the three women's defence services). Less than a year later, after the Nazi invasion of France, the Windsors were fugitives in Madrid, then a hot-bed of intrigue and espionage. After the British retreated from Dunkirk, the rumours that German agents were discussing with the Duke the possibility of his becoming an English Pétain in the event of Britain being invaded, date from this time. Were King George and Queen Elizabeth informed of these Nazi overtures?

Whatever the answer, the Nazi leaders received the mistaken idea that the Windsors were inclined towards the ideals of National Socialism. Contrary to the attitude of Edward VII and George V, the Duke was attracted by the German people and, to the annoyance of some of his intimates, in the pre-war years had made no attempt to conceal his affinity.

In June 1934, 'Chips' Channon had entered in his diary: 'Much gossip about the Prince of Wales's alleged Nazi leanings. He is alleged to have been influenced by Emerald [the American Lady Cunard] (who is rather *éprise* with Herr Ribbentrop) through Mrs Simpson. The Coopers [Duff and Lady Diana] are furious, being fanatically pro-French and anti-German. He has just made an extraordinary speech to the British Legion advocating friendship with Germany; it is only a gesture, but a gesture that may be taken seriously in Germany and elsewhere.'

Ribbentrop certainly had unusual friends in Britain and Mrs Simpson's name has been included among them. Now in charge of the German Foreign Office, Ribbentrop really thought that he had willing pawns in the Windsors in 1940. If captured German Foreign Office documents are to be believed, Ribbentrop heard from the German ambassador in Madrid that the Duke had 'expressed himself against Churchill and against the war'. The ex-king, it was claimed, was 'convinced that if he had remained on the throne war could have been avoided, and he characterized himself as a firm supporter of a peaceful arrangement with Germany.'

The Duke had already offered his services to the British Government and had accepted the Governorship of the Bahamas. If no re-employment had been forthcoming, the Windsors, it is claimed, had planned to remain in Spain in a castle provided by Franco's government. But now they were in Lisbon and the Nazis tried hard to induce them to return to Spain.

In a secret telegram Ribbentrop informed the German ambassador:

At a suitable occasion the Duke must be informed that ... Germany is determined to force England to peace by every means of power and upon this happening would be prepared to accommodate any desire expressed by the Duke, especially with a view to the assumption of the English throne by the Duke and Duchess. If the Duke should have other plans, but be prepared to co-operate in the establishment of good relations between Germany and England, we would likewise be prepared to assure him and his wife of a subsistence which would permit him ... to lead a life suitable for a king.

An ss Officer, Walter Schellenberg, was deputed to bring the Windsors back to Spain, Ribbentrop offering the Duke as an inducement fifty million Swiss francs. The Führer was 'quite ready to go to a higher figure'.

The captured documents claim that the Spanish government was conversant with the plan. Miguel Primo de Rivera, a friend of the Duke, journeyed to Lisbon to invite the Duke to participate in a conference about Anglo-Spanish relations and for a hunting party. The German ambassador reported to Ribbentrop:

He had two long conversations with the Duke, at the second one the Duchess was present also. The Duke expressed himself very freely.... Politically he was more and more distant from the King and the present British government. The Duke and Duchess have less fear of the King, who is quite foolish, than of the shrewd Queen who is intriguing skilfully against the Duke and particularly against the Duchess.... When Rivera gave the Duke the advice not to go to the Bahamas but to return to Spain, since the Duke was likely to be called upon to play an important role in English policy and possibly to ascend the English throne, both the Duke and Duchess gave evidence of astonishment. Both replied that according to the English constitution this would not be possible after the abdication. When Rivera then expressed his expectation that the course of the war might bring about changes even in the English constitution, the Duchess especially became very pensive....'

Within days of the despatch of this report to the Nazi hierarchy, Sir Walter Monckton appeared in Lisbon, advising the Windsors to hasten their departure to Bermuda. When the contents of these documents were eventually disclosed, the Duke agreed that there had been Nazi overtures to keep him in Spain but he had spurned all thoughts of 'complying with such a suggestion'.

If Ribbentrop's ruse had failed, so too had the Duke's ultimatum. In September 1939, when the Windsors came to England, the Duchess had never been received at Court. This in itself was indicative of the Royal Family's attitude towards her. While the Windsors were in Spain Winston Churchill suggested that they should return to England. The Duke was agreeable but stipulated two conditions: he desired to be acquainted in advance of the duties intended for him, but paramount was the future status of his wife. 'It must be the two of us together – man and wife with the same position,' he contended, and demanded that his wife should be elevated to the same status as other royal duchesses. However, his efforts to coerce both family and government proved futile. As Lady Longford has written: 'The Battle of Britain, with its multiple risks and rumours, would have been no place for a couple who still attracted, willy nilly, the lurid attentions of the enemy propaganda machine.'

Unlike other parents who debated whether or not to send their children to the safety of the New World, for the King and Queen the query never arose. The Queen was adamant, explaining: 'The children cannot go without me, and I cannot possibly leave the King.' To Sir Harold Nicolson, she remarked: 'I should die if I had to leave.' Sir Harold told his wife: 'I cannot tell you how superb she was. I anticipated her charm. What astonished me is how the King is changed. . . . He was so gay and she so calm.'

Windsor Castle would be the Princesses' wartime home, but in the event of a Nazi landing a refuge had been devised in strictest secrecy for the Royal Family. A select bodyguard chosen from the Brigade of Guards and the Household Cavalry, known as the Coats' Mission (from its commander, Col J. S. Coats), was charged with their care. Four houses in different areas were stocked with all the requirements for an emergency, and armoured cars specially marked to ensure priority stood by to whisk them away.

Picked military professionals protected Buckingham Palace from possible para-troopers, but the King, Queen and royal household also equipped themselves for defence. Frequently they practised with rifle and revolver in the Palace gardens, the Queen explaining that she would fight to the end. 'I shall not go down like the others,' she said, meaning other royalty in Europe.

At first Their Majesties remained in the normal way at Buckingham Palace, staying at the Royal Lodge merely at weekends. But as the bombing of London grew more intense, they secretly left for Windsor at night in an armoured car. Disliking its claustrophobic interior, Queen Elizabeth often contrived to clutter up the car with personal items, thus leaving no space for herself so that she could travel in one of the royal Daimlers.

Altogether Buckingham Palace would be bombed nine times, the missiles in-cluding a flying bomb which crashed into the gardens. An unexploded bomb fell through the Queen's apartments and a large time-bomb detonated while Their Majesties were at Windsor. The first bomb fell on the garden side of the Palace, beneath the King's study, exploding the next day and smashing much glass. But three days later the King and Queen came close to death. As they discussed the day's work with a household official, the sirens suddenly wailed and down through the heavy rain roared a Nazi bomber, flying precariously over the Mall towards the Palace. In those terrifying moments, through their open window Their Majesties glimpsed two bombs come crashing down. Amid the noise and confusion they dashed out into the neighbouring corridor, relieved that they had both sur-vived. Altogether two bombs had fallen in the quadrangle, leaving gaping craters, and two more had wrought havoc in the forecourt. Another had left the chapel a total wreck, and a sixth had ended in the garden. 'What had been the Chapel,' wrote Princess Marie Louise (Cousin Louie), 'was nothing but a huge aching void, and the only thing saved from it was the old family Bible in which the births, marriages and deaths of the Royal Family over many generations were recorded.' Into the sitting-room overlooking the quadrangle, which Their Majesties had occupied only minutes earlier, gushed a stream of water from a broken main. As they inspected the shambles, it was suspected that one of the bombs in the forecourt was of the delayed action type. They therefore repaired to a shelter which in fact was a maid's sitting-room. To their relief four workmen had lived through the destruction of the plumbers' shop.

It is curious how the gravity of this raid was hidden even from the Prime Minister. In *Their Finest Hour*, the second volume of his history of the Second World War, Winston Churchill revealed that neither he nor his colleagues were aware of the peril of that incident. 'Had the windows been closed instead of open,' he wrote, 'the whole of the glass would have splintered into the faces of the King and Queen, causing terrible injuries. So little did they make of it that even I . . . never realized long afterwards . . . what had actually happened.'

This act of Nazi daring would rebound on Germany, for the dominions and the United States were shocked and angered. To Americans generally, it destroyed any doubts about the wisdom of the destroyer-bases exchange and the gargantuan aid programme to besieged Britain – called Lend-Lease – in January 1941. Added to this, one cannot exclude the excellent relationship established by Their Majesties, especially with President Roosevelt, during their North American tour.

Harry Hopkins, the President's personal representative who finalized the Lend-Lease negotiations, also fell under the Queen's spell on being received at Buckingham Palace. 'The Queen', he wrote, 'told me that she found it extremely difficult to find words to express her feelings towards the people of Britain in those days. She thought their actions were magnificent and that victory in the long run was sure, but that the one thing that counted was the morale and determination of the great mass of the British people.'

She herself stoutly maintained that morale, especially so among the victims of the blitz. 'Many an aching heart found some solace in her gracious smile,' commented Churchill. In the hospitals she heightened the morale of the doctors and nurses, and also of the workers in industry. Indeed, it was revealing that after her visits to factories, production would invariably rise. And as the King and Queen picked their way over the smoking bomb sites, an unbreakable bond was forged between them and the people. As a bystander observed: 'For him we had admiration, for her adoration.'

There was nothing spurious in the spontaneous gesture; it was merely an outward expression of the Queen's true nature. She asked, for instance, why an elderly woman was weeping and was told that her pet terrier, hiding in rubble, was too terrified to come out. The Queen, actually a dog-lover herself, then kept eight dogs at the Royal Lodge. 'I'm rather good with dogs,' she assured the woman, kneeling in the dirt and calling to the frightened animal, which responded to her coaxing. Another instance was when the Queen assisted a woman with a disabled arm to dress her baby among the ruins of her home.

Prince Charles, the heir apparent, is reputed to be the Queen Mother's favourite grandchild.
Photographed together at the Royal Lodge, in character they have much in common.

When Lord Woolton, the Minister of Food, founded a fleet of vans to take hot meals to the blitzed areas of Britain, she allowed him to christen them Queen's Messengers, as well as insisting on financing a convoy herself.

It was a scheme which endeared itself to the Queen's cousin, Miss Lilian Bowes-Lyon who, as an organizer for the Women's Voluntary Services in Bow and Stepney, worked selflessly for the poor. The sacrifices of this remarkable woman – justly described as a true 'Florence Nightingale of the Slums' – never received the accolade that her altruism justified. This unsung heroine of the East End blitz was the daughter of Francis Bowes-Lyon, of Ridley Hall, Northumberland, brother of the fourteenth Earl of Strathmore. Like Queen Elizabeth she had nursed the wounded in the First World War, and when Hitler's megalomania brought destruction and death to London's East End she left her cosy West End home and rented a flat in a Victorian house in Bow Road, Poplar. It was to this modest dwelling that she invited her cousin the Queen, Sir Anthony Eden, then Foreign Secretary, and other notables to let them witness realistically the suffering and heroism resulting from nocturnal – and even daytime – horror.

Lilian Bowes-Lyon helped to extract the dead and the wounded from the smouldering ruins, and treated the wounded. She took many children to the greater security of country homes, then returned to work in the crowded shelters and among the bomb-torn homes. At times she herself could only walk with pain, for arthritis had by now begun to cripple her legs. In a sense, there was a close parallel between herself and her cousin's husband, the King, for her life would also be shortened by the stress of war.

Returning one day from dockland, where she had been serving cups of tea, a bomb dropped near the bus in which she was travelling. Cut by flying glass, in the ensuing panic she was kicked violently in the leg. Although she could scarcely hobble she somehow reached her flat. But from now onwards, to walk imposed a strain. She refused, however, to abandon the slums. Hiring a Cockney greengrocer's pony and van, she told her housekeeper: 'We can get about with this. I will be the driver and you will be the van boy.' With the van laden with food and hot drinks, medicines and blankets, at the sound of a bomb blast Lilian Bowes-Lyon would send her pony trotting into the blackout.

Tragically, the terrible pain in her leg grew worse, and towards the end of the war the limb was amputated when it turned gangrenous. And by the time Britain celebrated the Allied victory, she was living again in the more congenial West End of London. On that day of jubilation she heard that East End evacuees were swarming back to their former homes, but food was scarce, a situation which to Lilian Bowes-Lyon was intolerable, especially at a time of national rejoicing. Telephoning Buckingham Palace, she asked to speak to Queen Elizabeth, but was informed that Her Majesty was preparing to accompany the King on a State drive round London. A lady-in-waiting, however, conveyed her message. Soon

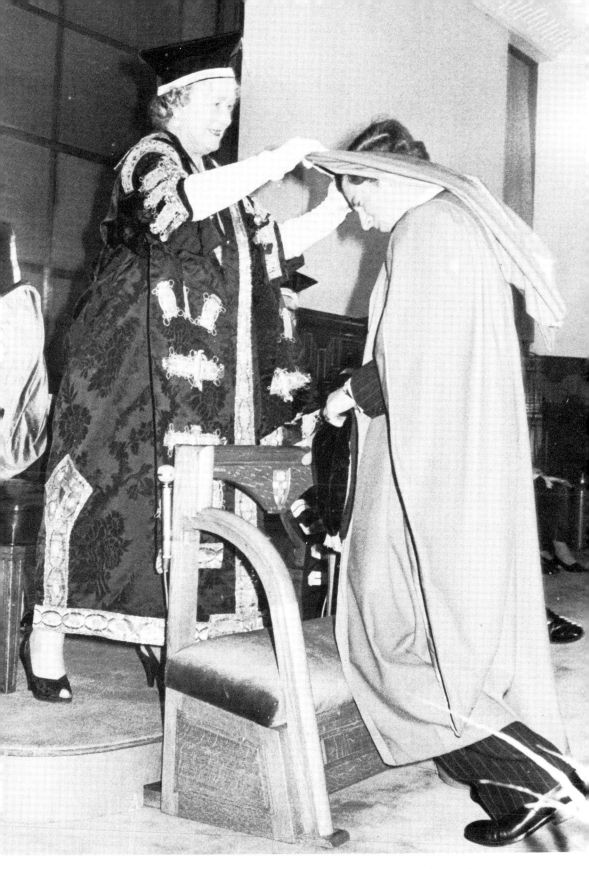

As Chancellor of the University of London, the Queen Mother conveys an honorary degree of Doctor of Law to the Prince of Wales.

a fleet of new American mobile canteens, standing unattended in Hyde Park, were moving eastwards filled to capacity with free food.

On occasions fate seems to be inexcusably callous to those who devote their lives to others. Lilian Bowes-Lyon was one such case. As well as suffering for years from diabetes, gangrene now deprived her of her other leg. Then the pain suddenly ceased; on a morning in 1949, when her maid entered her room to waken her, she found her mistress dead. It was the end not only of a woman of great courage and devotion to others, but one of artistic refinement. Lilian Bowes-Lyon was a poetess of distinction whose poems – some of which reflected her experiences in wartime London – received the plaudits of fellow poets. As Cecil Day Lewis would write, the dreadful pain that she suffered 'could be felt in her writing'.

To serve others was a Bowes-Lyon trait. Usually with the King, Queen Elizabeth spent much of the war years among the people, travelling many thousands of miles in their ten-coach train and using it as a mobile headquarters. Each night it stopped at some quiet branch line or siding, where Their Majesties could take an undisturbed stroll and the King could telephone his aides at Buckingham Palace, and the Cabinet, by a special hook-up.

To Queen Elizabeth, unstinted loyalty to one's country should be unyielding, an attitude that she firmly imprinted on an Army deserter one evening at Windsor. Preparing to take a bath, she noticed an intruder behind the door. Believing that he would enlist her support and sympathy, he had deliberately secured employment at the castle to waylay the Queen. He related to Her Majesty a maudlin story of persecution, but the Queen concluded that it amounted to nothing more than self-pity. She had witnessed too much misery to be deceived by a malingerer. Sternly admonishing the man, she rang a bell and turned him over to the castle guard, adding: 'I advise you to take your punishment like a man, and to serve your country like one.'

How different was her reaction to the Polish refugee family who travelled through Belgium to Calais, desperately anxious to board one of the last steamers leaving for England. The wife and her child had managed to embark, but the husband had been left behind while searching for food. Believing that he had escaped south to unoccupied France, the wife presented the British authorities with what was ostensibly an impossible task. Could they locate her husband? And was he alive or dead? Her plea was brought to Queen Elizabeth's attention. At her request coded messages were despatched to the French resistance who, tracing the man, planned his reunion with his family in England.

Their Majesties were at Sandringham when news reached them of the imminence of Germany's unconditional surrender. On Monday, 7 May came the public declaration, a fitting climax to Hitler's suicide in a Berlin bunker six days earlier. The people thronged the streets, thousands in London gravitating to Buckingham Palace, the focal point of national emotions. To the clamorous crowd the King and Queen appeared eight times on the traditional balcony, and were still waving there at midnight.

'The Queen and I have been overcome by everyone's kindness,' wrote the King to the Archbishop of Canterbury. 'We have tried to do our duty in these five long exacting years.' He could also write with justification: 'I feel burned out.' Anxieties and over-conscientiousness had left their mark, facts which had not escaped the Queen's notice. Her husband's reign was already drawing to a close, but there would be no respite in the seven years left to him.

The immediate peace bred a new order with its crop of social demands. George VI was more liberal in outlook than his father, but both possessed a latent fear of what Socialism might do to both monarchy and the state. 'Everything is going nowadays. Before long, I shall also have to go,' is the despairing remark attributed to him when learning that Knole, the ancestral home of the Sackville-Wests, had been taken over by the National Trust. The King and Queen were shocked when Clement Attlee ousted Winston Churchill as Prime Minister at the first post-war General Election; to Their Majesties public rejection of their wartime colleague was arrant ingratitude.

The weary King, writing to his brother, the Duke of Gloucester, then Governor-General of Australia, confided that he was suffering from 'an awful reaction from the strain of war' and felt very tired. 'Medicine, even Weir's, is not of any use as I really want a rest, away from people and papers but that of course is impossible. . . . My new Government is not too easy and the people are rather difficult to talk to.'

At such times, if the Queen were present, her sprightly conversation would break the tension of uneasy silences. This resilient personality did not share the King's gloom and doubts for the future. To the Queen an unshakeable religious faith was the antidote to most ills. 'I can truly say,' she told a meeting of the World's Evangelical Alliance, 'that the King and I long to see the Bible back where it ought to be, as a guide and comfort in the homes and lives of our people. From our own experience we know what the Bible can mean for personal life.' But in that restless, unstable post-war world the people were disinclined to listen.

In the case of the King, nothing seemed to alleviate his obvious exhaustion. As Attlee commented on George VI after his death: 'He was rather the worrying type, you know.' But the Attlee Government did not lighten the strain. The King and Queen (accompanied by the two Princesses) were asked to tour South Africa in 1947, a political manoeuvre intended to cleanse the country of Republicanism. That it failed was no reflection on Their Majesties. The Queen was as adroit as ever. When a Boer War veteran regretted that he could not wholly forgive Britain's conquest, the Queen is said to have countered sweetly: 'I understand that perfectly. We feel very much the same in Scotland.' But gradually the Empire was disintegrating, and Elizabeth would be the last Queen-Empress.

As for the King, to the Queen's alarm his health was also breaking up. He

would witness the wedding of Princess Elizabeth and Prince Philip, Duke of Edinburgh, and would welcome his grandchildren, Prince Charles and Princess Anne.
There would be the Silver Wedding celebrations when, after the traditional
thanksgiving service in St Paul's Cathedral, the King and his consort traversed
a twenty-mile route along London streets packed with cheering crowds.

Of his reign, the King confessed: 'I make no secret of the fact that there have
been times when it would have been almost *too* heavy but for the strength and
comfort which I have always found in my home.' Of married life, the Queen
remarked: 'There must be many who feel as I do that the sanctities of married
life are in every way the highest form of human fellowship, affording a rocklike
foundation on which all the best in the life of a nation is built.' The time would
come when the sanctity of marriage and her own family would cause her acute
distress. Before that happened her courage concerning the monarch would be
tested to the hilt.

First the King experienced cramps in the legs and pains in the chest, then in
March 1949 His Majesty underwent a right lumbar sympathectomy. With heartfelt relief the Queen noticed some regeneration in health and spirit, then life dar-
kened again. In 1951 the Queen learnt in confidence that the King was ill with
cancer, and in September the doctors removed his left lung. Her husband's health
again showed some sign of improvement but in that fateful year the King
recorded: 'The incessant worries and crises through which we have to live got
me down properly.'

On 31 January 1952, the monarch stood bareheaded at London Airport, waving to Princess Elizabeth and Prince Philip, who, deputizing for Their Majesties,
flew off on the Australian tour which the King's illness had caused to be postponed
twice. Behind the Queen's infectious smile there was the fear that death might
creep up on the King. Yet his health seemed to improve and when death finally
struck it caught everyone unawares.

At Sandringham on 5 February, the wintry sun coaxed him out of doors with
his dogs for his favourite pastime – shooting. After dinner that night he amused
himself with a jigsaw puzzle and Princess Margaret played to him on the piano
for a while before he retired to his bed. The King was reading a magazine when
a footman, Daniel Long, took him a cup of cocoa at eleven o'clock. At seven-
thirty the next morning he lay as if in a tranquil sleep from which James Macdonald, his assistant valet, could not wake him. His heart had failed him.
Coronary thrombosis had ended his life. For King George VI kingship had moved
in unexpectedly. So, too, had death. As someone has rightly pointed out: 'His
marriage was the great exception.'

His consort's earlier anxieties that the burden of his duties as sovereign might
gradually threaten her husband's life had proved to be starkly true. Perhaps this
thought nagged the mind of the Duke of Windsor as he walked behind his brother's
bier on the day of the burial. At least he would have the integrity to write years

later: '. . . I am not insensible of the fact that through a decision of mine he was projected into sovereign duties that may at first have weighed heavily against him. . . .'

On the evening of 8 February, a wagon bore the coffin of King George VI, crossing Sandringham Park to the church of St Mary Magdalen. There, draped with the Royal Standard, it was placed on trestles before the splendour of the silver altar. It was the dramatic finale to three years of devoted nursing by his consort. A week later, at St George's Chapel, Windsor, the King's body passed through a cavity in the choir floor to the vaults below. As his consort watched her daughter, Queen Elizabeth II, sprinkle Windsor soil from a silver bowl, it was a poignant, even harsh, reminder that a phase in her life had concluded. The monarch and husband who had bestowed so much affection was dead. In that sense she was alone and at that moment the future seemed cold and bleak.

9

Royal Pillar of Strength

While the sovereign lives, his consort plays the second major part on the royal stage. The moment he dies she is at once relegated to a minor and rather undefined role. The Queen Dowager cannot claim to have any specific precedence and is indeed somewhat dependent on the incoming monarch. She must quit Buckingham Palace, and it is only by the sovereign's permission that she can use any possessions of the Crown. Queen Victoria, for instance, was thought to be highly compassionate by allowing Queen Adelaide, widow of William IV, to take her bedstead away from Windsor.

Elizabeth was still allowed the royal title of Her Majesty and could sign herself Elizabeth Regina, but in a legal sense it had ceased to be high treason to plan her death. She would, moreover, still require the monarch's consent should she marry again, but would not sacrifice her royal status by marrying a commoner. After the accession of Queen Elizabeth II, it was announced that her mother would be known as Queen Elizabeth the Queen Mother to avoid confusion with her own name. Her grandmother would be formally styled Queen Mary the Queen Dowager (a title she never cared for).

Over the years the Queen Mother had conscientiously served the nation and in return the people now sustained her in her grief. This was best symbolized in the person of Winston Churchill, who assured her ('that valiant lady') that the future must be full, not arid: her influence and mature experience, he explained, must still be available to Britain and the Commonwealth, and, above all, must be used to reinforce the new reign.

For the latter, wise counsel would certainly be needed in the later fifties. After the euphoria surrounding the accession of an attractive young Queen, the Court came under attack although the criticisms were not as scathing as those levelled at Queen Victoria at a comparable period during her reign. Even so, they were unprecedented in modern times.

The Queen, for example, then at Goodwood Races, had been censured for not returning to London to sign the Forces call-up at the time of Suez. It does appear, on reflection, that she was wrongly advised. And when Sir Anthony Eden, the Prime Minister, later resigned, she had chosen Harold Macmillan and not R. A. Butler, who had deputized for Eden and was regarded by many as his obvious

A portrait by Norman Parkinson. In the story of the British monarchy in the twentieth century, the Queen Mother will emerge as one of its pillars of strength.

successor. Regrettably no one had made it clear that the Queen's choice was the outcome of a majority vote in the Tory Cabinet itself. Yet it was enough to untap left-wing cynicism. The Queen, who had been hailed by the New Elizabethans at the outset of her reign as symbolizing national regeneration, was now wrongly condemned as being the pawn of a right-wing caucus responsible for the country's current malaise.

Snide falsehoods even crept into the Queen's own personal life. Her young consort, they implied, finding it difficult to adjust himself to the rigidities of palace life, had sought escapism at dubious parties; hence his despatch by an irate Queen on a long Commonwealth tour.

A shy and reserved person by nature, and more so in the earlier years of her reign, the Queen doubtless found in the Queen Mother a bastion of strength against captious comment.

But what perhaps left the Queen and the Queen Mother with the greatest unease was the insinuation that standards were deteriorating even in the Royal Family itself. As Princess Elizabeth, the Queen, addressing a London rally of the Mothers' Union, had drawn attention to the misery caused by the break-up of homes ('... we can have no doubt that divorce and separation are responsible for some of the darkest evils in our society today'). The Queen Mother echoed these sentiments, yet for some while, definitely since her daughter's Coronation in June 1953, it had been known to her that Princess Margaret wished to be betrothed to a divorcé.

The Queen Mother had appointed Group Captain Peter Townsend as Comptroller of her Household, an appointment for which she has perhaps since reproached herself. As a Battle of Britain pilot, Townsend was decorated for 'outstanding leadership ... in aerial combat'. King George VI had appointed him an Equerry of Honour, an imaginative wartime appointment, and due to industry and skill his promotion had been meteoric – to Deputy Master of the Household.

But royal duties had imposed a strain on his marriage and in the autumn of 1952 Townsend divorced his wife. In the following spring, when Mrs Townsend had remarried, Princess Margaret concluded that according to law she was now at liberty to wed.

The royal machine would cease to hum but for the members of the Household, the descendants of those courtiers who centuries ago formed the royal government. They are men and women of proven calibre and no aspect of their behaviour must in any way blemish the Crown. The nature of the duties involved breed a certain intimacy between royalty and household, but underlying all is the acceptance of trust. Whatever the emotions, this unwritten code had been infringed. It is said that some two months before the Coronation in 1953, Townsend visited Sir Alan Lascelles, the Queen's Secretary, explaining that he and Princess Margaret wished to be betrothed. The same source claimed that simultaneously with this interview, Princess Margaret warned her mother of her intent. For the Queen Mother, still suffering the pain and loneliness of early widowhood, it was a re-awakening of the fears and anxieties created by the Windsors' romance.

As in the thirties, when the rumours leaked out the British press again exercised the same remarkable reticence. Not so their American counterparts. Commenting on the Princess's 'emotional experience', one New York newspaper reported that the 'two who are being mentioned in her life ... are Group Captain Townsend and Mark Bonham Carter ... behind the scenes the group captain is considered the favourite.' The *New York Daily News* surmised that the Queen and the Arch-bishop of Canterbury were secretly discussing the problems raised. In Britain, the Sunday newspaper *The People* heatedly submitted that the British public should be acquainted with the 'scandalous rumours.... The story is, of course, quite untrue.' Unfortunately for the Queen and the Queen Mother it was undeni-ably correct. Moreover, both knew that, regardless of their hostility to divorce, the Queen was the secular head of the Anglican Church which declined to con-done it.

In June 1953 – a few weeks after the Queen's Coronation – the Queen Mother, accompanied by Princess Margaret, visited Southern Rhodesia to open the Rhodes Centenary Exhibition at Bulawayo. Townsend, who organized the visit, had expected to accompany them, but instead he was replaced by Captain Lord Plunket. He himself travelled with the Queen and the Duke of Edinburgh to Northern Ireland, and by the time of Princess Margaret's return he had been installed as air attaché at the British Embassy in Brussels. Not for two more years would they meet.

Meanwhile the Queen Mother, ardently hoping that absence might cool emo-tions, visited the United States and Canada. At Southampton, then partly para-lyzed by a dockers' strike, workers – running the risk of being called blacklegs by fellow trade unionists – had exhibited their affection. Defying their unions, they had carried the Queen Mother's luggage aboard the liner *Queen Elizabeth* 'for the nicest lady in the world'.

In New York the Queen Mother recaptured her zest for life. Temporarily rid of the austerities in Britain, she indulged herself in a spending spree in Fifth Avenue stores. 'I am buying too much,' she chuckled, her face radiant with delight. In Times Square she drank champagne with the cast of *The Pyjama Game*; at a Pilgrims' lunch she unveiled Frank Salisbury's painting of George VI opening the Festival of Britain; and she received the honorary degree of Doctor of Laws at Columbia University. But it was not just the élite but also the humble with whom she mixed, talking, for instance, to children in the slums of Harlem. 'Hey, ain't you the Queen Mum?' asked one Negro boy.

One gossip writer reported that the royal lady 'not only drew a record crowd of 2,800 smart-setters to the Waldorf-Astoria ballroom: she sent them away hum-ming "God Save the Queen" like a first night audience whistling the top tunes of the hit show.' Wherever the Queen Mother went, the traffic stopped and the crowds soon gathered. The *New York Daily News*, concluding that the 'Queen Mum is strictly OK', also congratulated 'Mama Liz' for having, on a visit to the United Nations, deflated 'the stiffed shirts.... The UN turned out more than a hundred cops to keep the Press and public away from Britain's Queen Mother Elizabeth, who only wanted to be friends with everybody.'

In Washington, where she renewed her friendship with Mrs Eleanor Roosevelt, she was the guest of President and Mrs Eisenhower at the White House.

Assessing the value of the Queen Mother's visit to the United States, the *Daily Mail* claimed that she had 'done more to promote Anglo-American friendship and understanding than all the diplomatic activities of the entire year'. Her bonhomie captivated Canada as well, to the point that it was hinted that she should assume the duties of the next Governor-General. Doubtless the appointment would have been an immeasurable success, for as *The Times* commented on her tour: 'She is able to speak for the Commonwealth straight to the hearts of friendly peoples, at a level of feeling the politicians cannot reach.'

One heart to which the Queen Mother had to address herself was that of Princess Margaret. On Sunday, 21 August 1955, the Princess attained the age of twenty-five and no longer needed to seek the Queen's approval to marry. When the Princess celebrated her birthday at Balmoral some ten thousand people gathered at the grey stone Craithie church. No doubt there were well-wishers among them, but it was undoubtedly a microcosm of the world-wide audience curiously awaiting the curtain to rise on another royal drama.

Princess Margaret reiterated her resolve to become betrothed to the one-time royal servant, and when Group Captain Townsend strode on to the stage by arriving in London in October, the cast was complete for the constitutional crisis. To the Queen Mother, service to the people took precedence over self. It was manifest at the Abdication; it was apparent now. She knew the possible thorny implications and so far as she was concerned, nothing must be allowed to weaken the throne. As one newspaper expressed it, for the Princess to wed Townsend 'could lead to a controversy capable of splitting Church and State more profoundly than anything for three hundred years'.

When, also in October, Sir Anthony Eden, the Prime Minister, journeyed to Balmoral to advise the Queen, the Queen Mother doubtless knew the gist of what he would say. Princess Margaret must write to the Privy Council explaining her desire to become betrothed to Group Captain Townsend. If Parliament did not object within one year, she would be free to marry. But there lurked a snag: marriage, he explained, would no doubt mean renouncing her royal status, an action which would be confirmed by the Commonwealth governments. Thus she would be deprived not only of her rights of succession, but also her portion of the Civil List would be withdrawn. Furthermore, to avoid a possible cleavage of public

On her seventieth birthdy, the Queen Mother was visited at Clarence House, her London home, by some of her grandchildren – Prince Edward, Viscount Linley and Lady Sarah Armstrong-Jones.

opinion (with obvious unpleasant repercussions on the throne) it might be imperative to live in exile, at least for a while.

Princess Margaret and Group Captain Townsend spent a weekend together at Allanbury Park in Berkshire, the home of the Hon. Jean Wills, a married niece of the Queen Mother. Whether the personal sacrifice was too immense for the man she professed to love, or whether loyalty to the Crown was the decisive factor, one cannot say. Yet the Princess's determination to be betrothed to Townsend would wilt.

On 14 October the Queen Mother returned to Clarence House, just before Townsend's arrival at the invitation of Princess Margaret. For the next two weeks the Queen Mother's London home would be the focal point of the world's press. Whether this easily-accessible address, rather than the remoteness of Balmoral, was deliberately staged is not known. Four days later the Queen Mother and Townsend met alone. What transpired between them has never been publicly revealed. Yet on 26 October, in an interview with Dr Geoffrey Fisher, Archbishop of Canterbury, the Princess told him 'to put away his books'; the matter had been resolved. There is no published proof, one way or the other, that the Queen Mother attempted to dissuade her daughter from issuing a statement. Princess Margaret announced that 'mindful of the Church's teaching that Christian marriage is indissoluble, and conscious of my duty to the Commonwealth, I have resolved to put these considerations before others. I have reached this decision entirely alone.'

Townsend withdrew to Brussels. Three years later, in 1958, the tattlers were active again when Townsend, invited to tea at Clarence House, again met the Queen Mother and Princess Margaret. No one knows what was then discussed. Later, in the United States, John Payne, the Princess's ex-footman, who published his recollections of life at Clarence House, could only attribute to the Queen Mother the rather banal remark: 'Good afternoon, Peter, it has been a long time. It's so very lovely to have you here again.' (It was a measure of the Queen Mother's commendable will-power that in 1960 she gained an injunction restraining Payne from disclosing his reminiscences of the time he spent in her service.)

For Princess Margaret a new romance would ripen, this time with the new Court photographer, Mr Antony Armstrong-Jones, son of Mr R. O. L. Armstrong-Jones, QC, and the Countess of Rosse. On 26 February 1960, the Queen Mother announced their betrothal. The inherent weaknesses in such a marriage must have been strikingly apparent to Her Majesty. The cynics and the facetious would dangle a camera from the throne. They would perhaps sarcastically remind Princess Margaret that her first child would present the nation with a Jones fifth in line to the throne. But the Queen Mother's primary aim was the happiness of her daughter. One could not dismiss the fears of what might result from a second emotional upset.

In disposition there appeared to be a remarkable parallel between Princess Margaret and her husband, each sharing an alertness of mind and ready wit. Ostensibly, with its similarity of temperaments, the match seemed to be supremely ideal. It was therefore yet another distressing episode in the eventful life of the Queen Mother when, sixteen years later, her son-in-law, who had been created the Earl of Snowdon, announced that he and Princess Margaret were to lead separate lives. The Queen Mother's attitude towards marriage – 'the highest form of human fellowship' – was already known.

When Eden discussed the Townsend affair with the Queen at Balmoral, the Queen Mother had withdrawn to the seclusion of the Castle of Mey in Caithness. This historic pile, empty and rather derelict for some years, would have been demolished if the Queen Mother had not purchased it. Using her skill for home-making, she injected new life into it, beautifying it with such items as Queen Anne furniture and Regency and Empire lamps, clocks and candelabra.

Acquiring it during the sadness of early widowhood, the Queen Mother entertained thoughts of living in Scotland for substantial periods. At that time the other homes in which she had resided were too crowded with painful memories. Remote Mey was her own acquisition, something entirely new, where she could shake off the past and live for the present. But the foreign tours and the multi-farious duties were resumed, compelling her to reside in the main in London.

10

Eighty Years Young

To widespread acclaim, the Queen Mother has attained her eightieth birthday. It is neither hyperbole nor sycophancy to assert that no octogenarian in Britain today is the object of such profound and genuine affection. Since her début years ago as the 'smiling Duchess', that famous smile has cast its captivating gleam on both troublesome and happy times, penetrating national gloom or spreading its ambience in rosier moments. As one newspaper once commented, the 'very thought of her, unaffected, good-humoured, beloved by her family and by the nation, is as good as a pick-me-up'.

Endowed with an irrepressible sense of humour, she wholeheartedly relishes the impish – even irreverent – drollery of others. Such a situation occurred at a Sandringham flower show, when a nine-year-old talking mynah bird, contemplating her feathered hat with a cold, calculating eye, asked Her Majesty: 'Can your mother skin a rabbit?' When the amused Queen Mother explained that she had no idea, he snapped abruptly: 'Well, clear off!'

The immutable sparkle of her character is perhaps seen at its liveliest at race meetings. Although she herself has not ridden since childhood, the Queen Mother's love of horses and the turf has never diminished. She personifies the tradition set by Queen Anne, founder of Royal Ascot, who died the day after her horse, Star, won a £14 Plate over a sixteen-mile course on 31 July 1714. From that time no racehorse carried a queen's colours until 1950.

The Queen Mother's zeal for racing was fired by Lord Mildmay of Flete, an immensely enthusiastic and knowledgeable rider who was on four occasions the Champion Jump Jockey. In 1949 he was invited to Windsor Castle as one of the Royal Ascot guests and at his instigation the Queen Consort, together with Princess Elizabeth, bought Monaveen (which had fetched a humble £35 at an Irish auction two years earlier) for £1,000. Lord Mildmay and Major Peter Cazalet, the royal trainer, had recommended the purchase of this spirited gelding. Ridden by Cazalet's jockey, Tony Grantham, and wearing Princess Elizabeth's colours, Monaveen ran to victory at Fontwell Park on 10 October 1949. Having won some £3,000 in prize money, Monaveen was predicted as a likely winner of the 1951 Grand National when, tragically, in December 1950, he had to be destroyed after falling and breaking a leg in the Queen Elizabeth Handicap Chase at Hurst Park.

His grave is not far from the course, and his name is perpetuated by the Monaveen Chase.

After the death of Monaveen, the Queen Mother's interest in the turf might have ceased, but two factors kept it alive. Sir Winston Churchill, himself an owner, encouraged her to create her own string of thoroughbreds; and, more significant perhaps, was the disaster that befell Lord Mildmay. In May 1950, then forty-one years old, he was drowned while swimming off his private beach at Mothecombe in Devon. To some people Mildmay's daredevil antics – as exemplified when he endured agonies riding in a Grand National with a slipped disc – smacked of crass foolishness. But the Queen Mother had admired Mildmay's courage. She bought his horse, Manicou, and embarked on a serious racing career.

Whereas the involvement of her husband (and that of her daughter, the Queen) centred on flat racing, the Queen Mother has rigidly channelled her enthusiasm towards steeplechasing. But as bloodstock breeders all three have contributed substantially to British exports as well as invigorating the sport by their participation. Their interest was particularly welcome during the stagnant post-war period when breeding was at low ebb. Since the death of Lord Mildmay it is generally accepted that no one in Britain has done more than the Queen Mother to give National Hunt racing both prestige and stability. Her efforts in that sphere have been described as a memorial to Mildmay who, more than anyone, typified the bold spirit with which he infused steeplechasing.

To convey her earnestness for, and true patronage of, the sport, she revived and registered the Strathmore colours – blue jacket with buff stripes, blue sleeves and gold-tasselled black cap. It was an evocation of the days when the Bowes-Lyons, although rarely in the forefront as prize-winning racehorse owners, had been well-known members of the racing fraternity. One ancestor, however – John Bowes of Streatlam Castle, son of the 10th Earl of Strathmore – held a distinguished place in the record book, being four times winner of the Derby between 1835 and 1853.

As David Duff points out in his *Elizabeth of Glamis*,

... love of racing is on both sides of the Queen Mother's blood. She brought back to the paddock, after half a century, the famous colours of her grandfather ... Through her mother she is related to Lord George Bentinck, the startling son of the Duke of Portland who dominated English racing in the early years of the reign of Queen Victoria. Lord George could not resist a wager. He lost £26,000 on the St Leger of 1826. Going into racing on a big scale, he decided to get his own back on the bookmakers. He had a horse, Elis, which he thought could win the St Leger of 1836. In those days runners were walked to meetings, and a clear fortnight was needed to get Elis to Doncaster. A week before the race the scouts reported to the bookmakers that the horse was still in Hampshire. Out went the odds.

In deep secret Lord George had arranged to be constructed a horse-box, which, drawn by post horses, could cover eighty miles in a day. It took three days to reach the Town

Moor. Elis stepped out fresh and in the peak of condition. He won easily, to the great financial advantage of his owner. But Lord George came near to losing his life in another betting venture, which ended in a duel with Squire Osbaldeston. The squabble was over the running of an Irish four-year-old named Rush. Lord George fired into the air, but the Squire put his round through the Bentinck hat.

Not long before Monaveen was killed, Manicou bore the Queen Mother's colours to victory for the first time at Kempton Park in November 1950. Since that day she has experienced many thrilling triumphs. Doubtless the most dramatic concerned Devon Loch during the memorable Grand National in March 1956. Although his collarbone, broken a fortnight previously, was heavily strapped, her jockey, Dick Francis (then the champion steeplechase jockey, today a bestselling author of thrillers) had supreme confidence in the speed and stamina of the Irish-bred horse; he had come to that conclusion after first riding Devon Loch in 1952.

Well-placed in a field of twenty-nine, the horse dashed ahead with only three fences to negotiate. Devon Loch surmounted all three perfectly. The Queen Mother, the Queen and Princess Margaret watched excitedly as the crowd roared itself hoarse in anticipation of a royal win. The Queen Mother was recording the final stages of the race with her ciné camera when the inexplicable occurred: some fifty yards from the winning post Devon Loch, with legs outstretched, collapsed and skidded along the ground. E.S.B., closely pursued by Ontray and Gentle Moya, galloped past to take the coveted prize. Had a slight heart attack or a muscular spasm or simply cramp deprived the horse of a spectacular victory? No one could say.

Devon Loch, now riderless, struggled to his feet to be led away by a stable-boy. Francis walked off disconsolately. It was indicative of the Queen Mother's solicitude that she immediately placed the feeling of people before the loss of personal gain in prize money. Describing the incident in a letter to his wife, Vita Sackville-West, some days later, Harold Nicolson explained:

The Queen Mother never turned a hair. 'I must go down,' she said, 'and comfort those people.' So down she went, dried the jockey's tears, patted Peter Cazalet (the trainer) on the shoulder, and insisted on seeing the stable lads, who were also in tears.

Her concern was also directed to Devon Loch who, fortunately, was unhurt. To Francis's insistence that the Queen Mother should have won the race, she philosophically replied, 'There will come another time. After all, that's racing.'

Devon Loch appeared in another memorable event at Nottingham some months later. When midway along the course, he lagged so far behind that victory seemed impossible, yet with an incredible burst of energy he rushed past Northern King to win by two lengths. His racing days, however, were dwindling; in the following New Year he lamed himself in the Mildmay Memorial Chase at Sandown Park.

In the grounds of the Royal Lodge, the Queen Mother's Windsor home, where she loves to indulge her passion for gardening.

The Queen Mother never bets. Here she pats Sunyboy after his victory – her 300th National Hunt win – in the Fernbank Hurdle Race at Ascot.

To maintain and enter horses at meetings up and down the country is a costly and highly competitive business, affording scant scope for sentiment if one wishes to stay solvent. Yet unlike some owners, the Queen Mother does not discard her horses indifferently once they begin to flag. Returned to stables in Berkshire for treatment, Devon Loch, who had seemed certain of being the first royal triumph in the Grand National since the Prince of Wales's Ambush II won in 1900, was retired from racing and became Mr Noel Murless's hack before passing the rest of his days at Sandringham.

Another instance of the Queen Mother's genuine regard for her mounts involved Rodney. This horse, trained by Major Eldred Wilson, a Sandringham tenant, could not attain the right speed for racing. Rather than sell the horse indiscriminately, she gave him to the daughter of a friend of some years – Crown Equerry Brigadier W.M. Sale.

This attitude reflects her approach to racing in general. She never places bets and relies solely on the precarious possibility of winning prize money to maintain her horses. Such items as training bills, veterinary charges, insurance and stud fees, dealt with by the manager of the thoroughbred stud at Hampton Court, are very costly. Nowadays Fulke Walwyn is her chief trainer, with whom she often communicates. Her judgment on the choice of horses chosen to run under specific conditions is admired – a knowledge which, based on long experience, is neither casual nor capricious.

Even today the Queen Mother is quite likely to rise early to watch her horses at their early morning training. After their workout she invariably rewards them with lumps of sugar or chopped carrots. The Queen Mother is acknowledged not only as an enthusiast and patron (since 1954 she has served in this capacity to the National Hunt Committee) but also as an authority on steeplechasing. Perhaps she regrets that there are no stables to wander round at Clarence House, though by coincidence her London home occupies the site of the one-time stable-yard of neighbouring St James's Palace. On her book-shelves the detailed form books have been augmented over the years and are consulted whenever she considers buying a new thoroughbred. To complement these records, she files data relating to her own particular horses, past and present, and their photographs.

For a long time now the Queen Mother has been a familiar figure at race meetings. Sometimes she travels there by car, sometimes in a maroon coach bearing the royal coat of arms which is linked to a train at one of the London railway termini. She insists that the occasion should be stripped of formality. The routine is simple: her Private Secretary merely warns the Senior Steward and the Clerk of the Course in advance, thus enabling police patrols to be informed. Other than this, the Queen Mother is accompanied by her Private Secretary and detective (who may be seen carrying umbrellas, raincoats and rugs) and possibly a lady-in-waiting.

The Queen Mother, colonel-in-chief of the Light Infantry Regiment, chatting with a veteran at an assembly of old comrades.

Her father having been a former officer, the Army has been familiar to the Queen Mother since childhood. Talking here to 'scarecrow soldiers' of the King's Regiment.

Clearly her public duties take precedence over her personal interests. Whenever, therefore, official engagements prevent her from watching her horses run, she can resort to 'the blower', a device which the Exchange Telegraph Company installed in the dining-room of Clarence House. Thus at mealtimes she receives the detailed commentary relayed to subscribers and the betting shops: starting prices, weights, jockey and other changes, the weather and so on. She also watches racing programmes on television.

If, in the early stages, anyone was inclined to look upon the Queen Mother as a mere dabbler in the sport, they were disillusioned in the winter of 1961–2. One London newspaper, noticing the impetus with which her keenness for the turf was gaining, commented that she was at Sandown Park again for the second successive day that week, making it her third day's racing. 'Surely the sport of kings should be renamed the sport of queens,' the report added. At that time Peter Cazalet was training eight of her thoroughbreds; there were two each with Jack O'Donoghue and Tom Masson, and one with Boyd-Rochfort. Her successes for the season totalled twenty-four. The Queen Mother's colours, moreover, had been borne to victory three times at one meeting – at Lingfield early in December – the winning horses comprising Laffy, Double Star and The Rip.

The latter horse stood high in his royal owner's affections, not only because of his capacity to stay the course but because he symbolized more than any other her flair to detect potential talent. While returning from a race meeting to Sandringham, the Queen Mother had first seen the Rip (as she subsequently christened him) browsing in a field behind an inn called The Red Cat at North Wootton. Bred by Mr J.A. Irwin, The Rip was out of Easy Virtue by her own stallion, Manicou. Examining him in the hotel yard, she agreed to buy him.

In 1965 The Rip, then ten years old, was hopefully entered for the Grand National. Sir Martin Gilliatt, the Queen Mother's Private Secretary, observed that it seemed almost too good to be true that a horse chosen entirely on the Queen Mother's own judgment and bred by her own stallion should now be in that position. But again, the Queen Mother failed to attain the apogee of National Hunt racing; The Rip ran seventh.

But her judgment has not always been wrong. Records reveal that there have been spectacular victories. Twice her horses have achieved 'hat tricks' at respective meetings. No current figures are available but at the outset of her nineteenth season, in 1967–8, her horses had secured for her some £75,000 in prize money in 160 races. Financial rewards, however, are not the dominant attraction. She revels in the excitement and the element of chance in racing, the conviviality of the paddock, and chatting with other owners and their trainers.

She also likes to meet fellow racing brethren on her visits abroad; for instance, while in Rome accompanied by Princess Margaret, she called at the stud farm – some ten miles from the city – owned by the Marchese Incisadella Rochetta at Olgientte. She was fulfilling a promise to call at the Italian stables and see

King Carl Gustav of Sweden (left) chatting with the Queen Mother and the late Earl Mountbatten of Burma at a London banquet at which he was the host.

once more Ribot, a remarkable stallion which had beaten the Queen's High Veldt by five lengths at Ascot.

The Queen Mother's consideration for horses is equalled by her concern for the safety of the men who ride them. As its patron since 1974, she greatly increased the finances of the Injured National Hunt Jockeys Fund to assist such victims as Paddy Farrell, whose spine was broken at Aintree, and the paralysed Tim Brookshaw. One programme which has supplemented funds to a great degree has been the sale of scarves, ties and handkerchiefs printed with a jockey wearing the Queen Mother's racing colours.

Her philosophical acceptance of victory or failure on the racecourse somehow reflects her sensible view of life. Indeed, at a National Hunt Committee dinner in London, she was described as the greatest example of those who can meet triumph and disaster and 'treat those two imposters just the same'. This cardinal characteristic has been self-evident during the three main stages of her eighty years as Duchess of York, Queen Consort and Queen Mother. Time has failed to quench that youthful spirit which has enabled her to accept with equanimity and fortitude whatever life has set before her. It has been invaluable, too, in preserving and strengthening the monarchy at a time of revolutionary change.

In 1900 (the year of the Queen Mother's birth) only one major European state was a republic. Then warnings of future revolutionary change were sounded with clarion clearness. In 1906 an anarchist's bomb burst beneath the carriage of Alfonso XIII of Spain; the death toll was high but the King survived, a fate not granted to Carlos of Portugal who succumbed to an assassin's bullet two years later. At Sarajevo in 1914 the Archduke Franz Ferdinand, heir apparent to the throne of the Austro-Hungarian Empire, was destroyed by the bomb which crudely detonated the First World War. Four years earlier the Braganza throne of Portugal had collapsed to the furious onslaught of rebellion. The Hohenzollerns in Germany, the Habsburgs in Austria, the Romanovs in Russia and the Montenegrin throne were ruthlessly swept away in the deluge of war. In 1937 the Spanish Bourbons collapsed under the brutal bludgeoning of revolution; the monarchies in Bulgaria, Romania and Yugoslavia foundered beyond rescue in the cataclysm of the Second World War; and in its aftermath Italy's House of Savoy receded ingloriously before a republic.

Though Europe was strewn with the wreckage of royal dynasties, the House of Windsor not only survived but endeared itself even beyond the coasts of Britain. Yet at the critical period of the Abdication history might have taken a different course. At Windsor on the night of 11 December 1936, as the former Edward VIII bade his brothers farewell, the new King – no longer able to conceal his emotions – protested: 'It isn't possible! It isn't happening!'

Had it been common knowledge, George VI's outburst would surely have deflated even further the nation's faith in an untried sovereign whose destiny was to regain the dignity and purpose of the monarchy, then so sullied by scandal. The situation could scarcely have been less inspiring. Untrained for monarchy, George VI had barely three weeks to prepare for office. Absolutely denuded of exhibitionism, like his father George V, the King never hankered after the role of sovereign in that critical period.

Enough time has now elapsed to place the events of those days in their true perspective. It is now clear that without doubt the greatest asset to King George VI was his wife. By the time of his accession, he had the reputation of being sharp-tempered, and his consort – doubtless under great strain herself – had to apply all the attractiveness and affability of her personality in the unstable early years of the reign. The extent of her skill can be gauged by the fact that her husband was to render the throne a symbol of stability and continuity in increasingly revolutionary times.

In the year of the Queen Mother's birth the significance of the United States on the international scene was negligible. The world which really mattered comprised those European powers with colonial empires connected with them. It was Britain's proud boast that the sun never set on the British Empire. The notion that the most gargantuan empire that the world had experienced was indestructible – either by physical or peaceful means – would have seemed wild conjecture then. The small, dumpy figure of Queen Victoria, represented in stone in many lands, gazed with stern benignity on the peoples of varied colour and creed sharing her protection.

George VI was the last king-emperor, but the Queen Mother and her husband were never to witness the pomp and panoply of an Indian durbah. For although Victoria's Empire seemed durable for ever, some sixty years after her Golden Jubilee the Union Jack was lowered for the last time over the Vice-Regal Palace in New Delhi. India had been the glittering jewel of the Empire, a source of British wealth and power since 1600 when Elizabeth I granted a charter to the East India Company. The Indian sub-continent was divided into self-governing republics.

It is recorded that King George VI advised the Labour Government of the day that he did not entirely favour the granting of independence to British India, claiming that India must be governed, and that to release Ghandi from gaol would be absurd. Many, indeed, hailed independence as a sign of British weakness; in fact, it was the result of a natural course of events combined with British exhaustion in the turmoil of war.

From that time the Empire started to shrink. Other British possessions agitated for autonomy, and received it, and from the British Empire was born the Commonwealth of Nations.

One somehow suspects that the Queen Mother was sad to see the decline of the Empire just as much as she deplored the withdrawal of South Africa – where she had many friends – from the Commonwealth. But her good sense has made her realize that change was inevitable. Her husband, too, was conservative in outlook, but in contrast to the reactionary George v he appreciated the inevitability of yielding to the prevailing currents of the time.

Whether or not he was influenced by his wife, one cannot confirm. In any event her desire to support and see the Commonwealth thrive is unquestioned. As Queen Consort she was probably as well acquainted with world affairs as the politicians; much knowledge was amassed for her tours abroad. With typical thoroughness she has always prepared herself for those visits by studying the social, historical and other aspects of a country's background. To all the people she meets she gives equal attention, leaving each with the roseate feeling that he or she was the one who really mattered.

Crowds seem to endow her with strength. At a function in South Africa in 1947 the Queen Mother was told that everyone had felt a warmth radiating from her, and was asked: 'Do you feel that you are giving something out?' 'I must admit', she explained, 'that at times I feel something flow out of me. It makes me feel very tired for a moment. Then I seem to get something back from the people – sympathy, goodwill – I do not know exactly: and I feel strength again – in fact, recharged. It is an exchange, I expect.'

In her tours overseas, she is still one of the nation's finest ambassadors, engendering goodwill, and her appearances in the Commonwealth have yielded political profit. In advancing age, her journeyings have grown less frequent. Yet when seventy-five years old she could still cope with a strenuous official visit to Iran. To her regret, she was unable to experience travelling faster than sound in Concorde and had to be content with flying in a Royal Air Force Comet.

On arrival in Tehran she was the guest of the now exiled Shah at the Sad-Abad Palace. Next morning she was shown archaeological treasures at the Iran Bastan Museum and in the afternoon held a garden party at the British Embassy for the British community in Tehran. Within the next twenty-four hours she was standing outside the tomb of the medieval poet Saadi'z in the south of Iran, then proceeded to the ruins of Persepolis some twenty-five miles away which, sacked by Alexander the Great, was deemed the richest city in Asia. The Queen Mother also visited a museum that afternoon, and stayed at Bagh-e-Eram.

The itinerary included Isfahan, the one-time capital, some two hundred miles south of Tehran, on the third day. Here she was received at a school for the blind and a hospital administered by the Church Missionary Society, and was welcomed at several mosques before attending a reception as the guest of honour.

Two days before she left Iran, she returned to Tehran to visit yet another museum, hold an investiture on behalf of the Queen at a reception at the British Embassy, and inspect the War Graves Commission Cemetery and the new site for the British Institute of Persian Studies. Finally, she dined in state with the Shah and his wife, the Shahbanou.

On her return to Britain, strenuous hours during five days of travel in Middle

Receiving a posy from a soldier's child after the Queen Mother presented the colours of the
6th Battalion of the Light Infantry Regiment.

Eastern heat did not deter her from stopping at Akrotiri, the R A F station in Cyprus, which she toured, prior to having lunch with the officers.

In the same year, while the Queen was travelling in Mexico, the Queen Mother deputized for her daughter as a Counsellor of State, before departing on a tour of the Channel Islands.

When the Queen's official duties take her abroad the Queen Mother, under the Regency Act of 1953, serves as one of the Counsellors of State. These consist, as a rule, of the four senior members of the Royal Family in succession to the throne, provided they are eligible by age. The Queen Mother and Prince Philip are also Counsellors. In practice, the duties are usually undertaken by the Queen Mother and Princess Margaret. Never before has a dowager queen been so closely engaged with the duties of the Head of State. Two Counsellors are permitted to discharge some of the Queen's powers such as holding Privy Councils, signing state papers, receiving ambassadors and, if it is the monarch's desire, dissolving Parliament should the situation arise.

If the Queen is residing in London, Privy Councils normally take place at Buckingham Palace in the white and gold 1844 Room, so called because the Emperor Nicholas of Russia occupied it that year. Meetings over which the Queen Mother presides are convened at Clarence House, the Privy Counsellors assembling in the morning-room (which is approached through double doors in the library) at the ringing of a bell. Business is conducted standing. On her right the Lord President reads the various items of business, then she gives her verbal assent and the Clerk signs on her behalf.

In the Queen's absence, the Queen Mother may also conduct investitures and certainly receives the red despatch boxes containing Government documents, which arrive by horse-drawn carriage at Clarence House. To impress upon her that her services were still needed in national affairs, at the beginning of the Queen Mother's widowhood the Queen supplied her with new boxes.

Apart from the ill-founded and fatuous criticism of Mr Willie Hamilton MP throughout her unmatched record of public service, it is significant that the Queen Mother has never been publicly censured, even in the Fifties when the monarchy was temporarily the target for captious comment. Mr Hamilton, however, who has singled out the Queen Mother for his barbed comment, claims that Britain cannot afford the Royal Family: 'I believe the monarchy and its privileges to be immoral.'

Much of the Civil List is defrayed in the form of salaries, wages and pensions for retired staff, the maintenance of the royal homes (excluding Sandringham and Balmoral), and the running costs of the Queen's Flight and the yacht *Britannia*. At one period the Civil List failed to cope with all the financial demands and the deficit was balanced from the Privy Purse and the Queen's own private resources. Not even royalty have divine protection from the ravages of inflation. As for the charge that the Royal Family does not justify its income, royalty is

Seen together at the Royal Opera House, Covent Garden, the now ex-Empress Farah was the
Queen Mother's guest in 1976 following the latter's visit to Iran.

an integral part of British society, fulfilling – as demonstrated by the Queen Mother – many functions annually. When abroad, members of the Royal Family serve as the nation's ambassadors. The pageantry and tradition (to which the Queen Mother has subscribed for so long) is an essential part of the British way of life – and cheap at the price. Moreover, by having a non-political Head of State, Britain is preserved from much of the corruption which is prevalent in some republican countries. That safeguard alone is invaluable and cannot be assessed in pounds and pence.

Bagehot, the Victorian constitutionalist, contended: 'There are arguments for not having a Court, and there are arguments for having a splendid Court; but there are no arguments for having a mean Court.' It is not a question of splendour or meanness but one of reality. Some Members of Parliament keenly resented the decision to extend the Civil List in 1975. No doubt most people would agree that 'such controversy shadows the aura that should surround the monarchy. It involves the symbol of national unity in national dispute. It is distasteful and unnecessary.'

The total expenditure by the taxpayers on the monarchy is akin to the cost of a general election. To the individual, the cost is paltry. Again, one should not forget that the Civil List was first arranged in the reign of George III in return for all the revenues from the Crown Estates – a sum which today exceeds the Civil List several times over. What is more, when overseas, members of the Royal Family are often in the van of British business achievements.

But it is a matter of the heart, and not what can be categorized as cold commercial transactions, in which the true value lies. Throughout the year, simply from their attendance at charity functions, immense sums of money accrue for needs which might otherwise be a burden on the state. After almost six decades of public service it would be enlightening to learn how much can be attributed in this respect to the Queen Mother. The fortunes of some three hundred organizations, of which she is still patron, have profited from her seemingly tireless energy.

No queen consort ever accomplished her duties more conscientiously than Queen Elizabeth (as she is referred to by her household) and neither has a widowed queen been so enshrined in the people's hearts. As the daughter-in-law, sister-in-law, wife and mother of four successive sovereigns, her record is unique.

She shatters the cynical and inaccurate generalization that the Royal Family is, without exception, composed of philistines. Music is her overwhelming passion. In the sphere of paintings – she and Sir Winston Churchill shared a common interest – she accumulated a collection which mirrors her catholic taste. The nucleus of the collection (which includes prints and paintings of famous racehorses) was begun when she first resided at the Royal Lodge. Works by Wilson Steer, Walter Sickert and Augustus John were early purchases, but she is also drawn to the Impressionists, and her choice of modern pictures is somewhat contrary to traditional royal standards. At her request, John Piper was commissioned during her husband's lifetime to complete a set of watercolours and drawings of Windsor Castle.

Since entering the Royal Family, she herself has been the subject of portraits. After sitting to Pietro Annigoni, the artist spoke of her 'inner beauty', his assessment crystallizing the Queen Mother's basic quality. Merely to look glamorous was superficial, he explained, and without 'that personal quality your subject is nothing but a dummy. The Queen Mother is one of the loveliest people I have ever met. It is hard to imagine a kinder, warmer, more appealing human being.'

In her easy-going, relaxed yet courteous mode of living, the Queen Mother might have felt herself to be a misfit in our brash and unsettled times. In the last few decades many aspects of life have altered drastically. Man's achievements – and stupidities – have exceeded the imagination of people born early this century. A great chasm divides the young from their grandparents. It would be understandable, therefore, if Her Majesty, born in more stable and less frenetic days, found modern trends irksome. The constant warmth of her personality, buttressed by the Christian faith which has always been at the core of her thinking, implies that interest in, and caring for, people should be the paramount theme of any age.

She is not unmindful of the fact that some developments, as this century advanced, have functioned in the Royal Family's favour. At the time of her birth no successful flight had been made in an aircraft. Radio had still to be invented. The evolution of air travel has facilitated tours to distant peoples who would otherwise have been deprived of royal visits. On her first flight – to Brussels for a 'British Week' in 1935 – the Queen Mother suffered the torment of air sickness, but later became a seasoned traveller and the first queen to circumnavigate the globe by air. The speed with which she recovers after exhausting tours is astonishing.

Television, the most intrusive medium yet devised, might easily have been an embarrassment, undermining what had long been the mystique of royalty. Instead it has forged a stronger intimacy between the Royal Family and the people, a bond which foreign TV networks have extended abroad.

One might speculate that one offshoot of the social revolution which the Queen Mother deplores is the erosion of the great landed estates through exorbitant taxation. Even her own family, the Bowes-Lyons, have not escaped its exacting demands. Many acres of land have fallen under the auctioneer's hammer and, while she was Queen Consort, part of the family silver – together with other ancient treasures – was sold to pay death duties.

Her elevation from the status of commoner to that of royalty spared her the worries that confront many members of the nobility whose fortunes are in decline. But it was not a social attainment that lacked sacrifice. A countrywoman at heart, years ago she at first opposed all thoughts of entering the Royal Family, opting to retain precious privacy and freedom. That she yielded eventually to royal blandishments, and devoted herself to public service, has been to the gain of the United Kingdom and the Commonwealth.

Nowadays, when at Clarence House, the Queen Mother's official programme begins with a light breakfast. By 9.30 she is seated at her desk. There is a non-stop daily flow of mail to deal with (most of which she attends to herself), followed by the normal discussions with the comptroller of her household (the largest after that of the Queen), her secretary and occasionally her treasurer. Perhaps she will speak to the lady-in-waiting on duty that day, and to her chef about the menus (she favours French cuisine, fine sauces and has a particular liking for shellfish). There are often dignitaries to meet.

On most days when in London, the Queen Mother lunches with her household officials and about twice a week, during the summer, she forsakes the dining-room for the garden. To counter the effects of sunburn, to which she is prone, she invariably wears a hat. Drinks are first served in the morning-room, but when lunch is announced the Queen Mother leads her staff through connecting doors into the library.

Afternoons are confined more often than not to engagements, usually within a radius of some twenty miles, entailing a couple of hours spent opening events, laying foundation stones and so on. No matter how tedious the engagement, the buoyant, irresistible twinkle in the royal eye is there for everyone.

So far the Queen Mother, now eighty years of age, has conveyed no desire to retire from public life. When Queen Mary heard that Queen Wilhelmina of the Netherlands was abdicating at the age of sixty-eight, she remarked a trifle scornfully that it was *no* age at which to give up one's job. Her successor as Queen Dowager has the same resilient attitude of mind.

But by the same token the Queen Mother quite commendably permits nothing to deflect her from her own established pattern of life. She still upholds the old-fashioned principles and standards. For that reason her design for living (so it is claimed) has a bias towards regality rather than frugality. And if Prince Philip may strive to streamline the monarchy and effect economies in the royal homes, she cheerfully continues a life-style described as beneficent, gracious and discreetly reactionary. No one would wish to deprive Her Majesty of this gentle flirting with the past, and for a cardinal reason.

As *The Times* observed at the time of her seventy-fifth birthday, the Queen Mother was born just before the close of Queen Victoria's reign. Her life, therefore, spans the whole development of the modern British monarchy to which she herself has added so much. The most striking contrast is afforded by the vanishing of most European monarchies during her lifetime and the new vitality and burgeoning of the British Royal Family. The institution which has emerged this century is the creation of three generations and of both the sovereign and the consort of each generation.

The present framework of monarchy was originally moulded by King George

Installed at Dover Castle in 1979 as the 160th Warden and Admiral of the Cinque Ports, the Queen Mother became the first woman to hold this ancient office in its nine centuries' existence.

v and Queen Mary. Its unaffected modesty endears itself to the nation and although it has not been divested of its grand ceremonial, the new monarchy is straightforward in its personal attitudes.

For almost sixty years the Queen Mother has loomed prominently in the grand ceremonial – a function which is imperative to provide a symbolic focus for the profound and emotional feelings of loyalty, unity and continuity which preserves and animates the nation. To represent Britain, or the other Commonwealth nations, has immense importance, but it is a task which is expected to be undertaken in a spirit of humility and not in a sense of self-aggrandizement. Within this delicate pattern the Queen Mother has constantly revealed the virtues of ordinary life in an extraordinary life, and enriched it with her own valuable influence, under which the British monarchy has gradually rid itself of its unnecessary cocoon, becoming more approachable than in earlier years. As history has demonstrated, royalty in revolutionary times needs both tact and skill to remain untrammelled. To that extent the Queen Mother's contributions have been immeasurable. Indeed, when the day arrives to write the comprehensive story of the British monarchy in the twentieth century, Queen Elizabeth the Queen Mother will qualify as one of its towering pillars of strength.